DATE DUE

APR 07 2011	

America's Second Revolution

America's Second Revolution

How George Washington Defeated Patrick Henry and Saved the Nation

Harlow Giles Unger

John Wiley & Sons, Inc.

Copyright © 2007 by Harlow Giles Unger. All rights reserved

Published by John Wiley & Sons, Inc., Hoboken, New Jersey
Published simultaneously in Canada

Credits appear on page 259 and constitute an extension of this copyright page.

Wiley Bicentennial Logo: Richard J. Pacifico

For general information about our other products and services, please contact our Customer Care Department within the United States at (800) 762-2974, outside the United States at (317) 572-3993 or fax (317) 572-4002.

Wiley also publishes its books in a variety of electronic formats. Some content that appears in print may not be available in electronic books. For more information about Wiley products, visit our web site at www.wiley.com.

Library of Congress Cataloging-in-Publication Data:

Unger, Harlow G., date.
    America's second revolution : how George Washington defeated
Patrick Henry and saved the nation / Harlow Giles Unger.
      p. cm.
    Includes bibliographical references and index.
    ISBN 978-0-470-10751-5 (cloth)
    1. United States—History—Confederation, 1783–1789. 2. United States.
Constitutional Convention (1787). 3. United States—Politics and government—
1783–1789. 4. Constitutional history—United States. 5. United States.
Constitution. 6. Federal government—United States—History—18th century.
7. Washington, George, 1732–1799. 8. Henry, Patrick, 1736–1799. I. Title.

    E303.U555 2007
    973.3'18—dc22

                                 2007006193

Printed in the United States of America
10 9 8 7 6 5 4 3 2 1

To Pete and Manie
and Jacques and Françoise

We the People

of the United States, in Order to form a more perfect Union, establish Justice, insure domestic Tranquility, provide for the common defence, promote the general Welfare, and secure the Blessings of Liberty to ourselves and our Posterity, do ordain and establish this Constitution for the United States of America.

Article. I

Section 1. All legislative Powers herein granted shall be vested in a Congress of the United States, which shall consist of a Senate and House of Representatives.

Section 2. The House of Representatives shall be composed of Members chosen every second Year by the People of the several States, and the Electors in each State shall have the Qualifications requisite for Electors of the most numerous Branch of the State Legislature.

Overleaf:

The Constitution of the United States. Page one of an original copy of the U.S. Constitution after ratification by the Constitutional Congress in Philadelphia in September 1787.

Contents

Illustrations

Acknowledgments

John P. Kaminski, the longtime editor in chief of the massive *Documentary History of the Ratification of the Constitution*, was incredibly kind and generous in his support for this project. Not only did he encourage me when I suggested writing a new book on the ratification, he also went beyond the bounds of generosity by reviewing, correcting, and editing the finished manuscript. I shall always be grateful for his professional help and honored by his friendship.

Others to whom I owe thanks for their help in producing this book include Mrs. Louise Jones, librarian at the Yale Club of New York City; the reference specialists in the Prints and Photographs Division of the Library of Congress; and the many behind-the-scenes specialists at my publisher, John Wiley & Sons, Inc., including Senior Production Editor John Simko, copy editor William D. Drennan, and indexer Alexa Selph.

The appearance of this, my sixth book for John Wiley & Sons and fifteenth book overall, marks the tenth year of a wonderfully happy association with Hana Umlauf Lane, senior editor at Wiley, and my literary agent Edward Knappman, of New England Publishing Associates. Together, they have been brilliant mentors and inspiring friends who brought new life and great joy to my writing career. I shall always be deeply grateful.

Chronology

1785

March 28   Mount Vernon conference on Chesapeake Bay
                      navigation rights.

1786

September   Annapolis convention on interstate commerce.
  11–14   Five states call for general convention
                        "to render the constitution . . . adequate
                        to the exigencies of the Union."

August–
  December   Shays's Rebellion.

1787

February 4   Shaysites routed.
February 21   Congress calls Constitutional Convention.
May 25   Constitutional Convention begins. Rhode Island
                        refuses to participate.
September 17   Constitution signed; Convention adjourns.
September 28   Congress transmits Constitution to states.
November 3   Rhode Island legislature refuses to consider
                        Constitution.
December 7   Delaware is first to ratify Constitution.
December 12   Pennsylvania ratifies.
December 18   New Jersey ratifies.
December 31   Georgia ratifies.

1788

January 9   Connecticut ratifies.
February 6   Massachusetts ratifies.

February 22	New Hampshire convention adjourns without ratifying.
February 29	Rhode Island legislature rejects Constitution again; opts for referendum.
March 24	Rhode Island voters reject Constitution in statewide referendum.
April 26	Maryland ratifies.
May 23	South Carolina ratifies.
June 21	New Hampshire ratifies.
June 25	Virginia ratifies.
July 26	New York ratifies.
August 2	North Carolina refuses to ratify.

1789

January 7	First presidential election.
March 4	First U.S. Congress convenes in New York.
April 30	George Washington inaugurated as first president of the United States.
November 21	Second North Carolina convention ratifies Constitution.

1790

May 29	Rhode Island ratifies.

1791

December 15	First ten amendments to Constitution— Bill of Rights—adopted.

Introduction

CONTRARY TO POPULAR POLITICAL MYTHS, independence from Britain did not send America and her people gliding gently into peaceful self-government under constitutional rule. Indeed, within a short time after independence the nation was ablaze in anarchy and civil strife, with farmers in rebellion across the countryside in three states, separatists threatening to seize power in five states, and six states warring with one another over conflicting territorial claims. Virginia troops battled Pennsylvania in the West and Connecticut *and* Pennsylvania in the East, and after New York and New Hampshire militias had fought to a standstill over southern Vermont, Ethan and Ira Allen's ferocious Green Mountain Boys threw them and all their settlers out. Vermont had declared independence in 1777, and separatist movements in Maine, Pennsylvania, Kentucky, and Tennessee were threatening to split parts or all of those states from the rest of the country.

As civil war threatened, Congress asked the states to send delegates to Philadelphia in the spring of 1787 to amend the existing constitution—the Articles of Confederation—and strengthen the government of the Confederation of American States. Under Washington's leadership, however, the Convention ignored congressional instructions and staged what can only be called a coup d'état. With Washington warning of "anarchy and confusion" and demanding "a Supreme Power to regulate and govern," the majority of delegates at the Convention ignored the congressional mandate and the instructions from their state legislatures and wrote a new Constitution that replaced the American government with a powerful new federal government and stripped the states of their sovereignty. Like the earlier British government, the new national government would have powers to tax citizens and, if necessary, use troops to enforce collection and punish states that challenged the supremacy of the federal government.

Virginia's Patrick Henry and New York governor George Clinton exploded with rage, threatening to secede and form a "middle confederacy" with North Carolina. Clinton railed that Washington and his followers had "exceeded the authority given to them" and that any government formed under the Constitution would be "founded in usurpation." Patrick Henry cried out against centralized authority as he had in 1775, saying it would stifle local self-rule: "Liberty will be lost," he thundered, "and tyranny will result."

Over the next nine months, America warred with itself. State after state joined the seesaw "ratification revolution" and threatened to rip the nation apart and plunge Americans into the same sort of bloodbath that would soon engulf the French after their revolution. Mobs ran riot in big cities—Philadelphia, New York, Providence— and in small ones such as Carlisle, Pennsylvania, and Albany, New York. Across the nation, the wealthy, propertied elite—merchant-bankers, shippers, and plantation owners—rallied behind Washington and the promise of a strong central government that would defend the nation against Indian raiders and foreign enemies and crush internal rebellions. But a majority of ordinary people—owners of small farms in the East and the West—were opposed, and populist leaders threatened to lead them in secession.

Ratification by nine states was required for the Constitution to take effect, and by mid-May 1788, eight had ratified. But political leaders in two key states stood firmly against union—New York and Virginia, with the latter not only the largest in land and population, but also the strongest economically. Because of their strategic locations, both states were essential to geographic unity of the new nation; without them the union of the other states would be as fragile as the parchment on which the Constitution had been written. With the fate of the country in the balance, Washington and his supporters could only hope for a miracle to save the nation from civil war. *America's Second Revolution* tells the story of that miracle, the turmoil that led up to it, and the men who made it possible. Rich and powerful, they displayed humor, sarcasm, fire, brilliance, ignorance, hypocrisy, warmth, anger, bigotry, and hatred. Their struggle turned friend against friend, brother against brother, father against son—with sometimes bloody results. Each embodied some good, some evil, some banality, but in the end, each helped create a new government, a new nation, and ultimately a new civilization. The Declaration of Independence had liberated one continent from domination by another, but the Constitution revolutionized the world by entrusting the citizenry with rights never before in history granted to ordinary men—and eventually women.

I

Victory's Bitter Fruits

THE CROWD OF OFFICERS FELL SILENT as he entered the hall and walked to the lectern. His powerful frame still towered over them, but he had aged visibly. Deep furrows crossed his brow; his head and shoulders slumped just a bit; despair masked his usually stony face. Past fifty, exhausted physically and emotionally after eight years in wartime encampments, George Washington had seldom had a day's respite, let alone a visit to his home and family. Now, with his glorious victory at Yorktown but a distant memory, his officers were threatening to mutiny; his dream of a free and independent people living in Utopian brotherhood was turning into a nightmare. The road to independence had led straight to the edges of hell.

Americans everywhere were turning against one another: separatist factions in five states were in rebellion and threatening to secede; a British blockade was decimating American commerce; two massive fires had left half of New York City in ashes; and, with British troops still in New York, Washington's own officers were threatening to lead the Continental Army to the western frontier and set up their own independent state. Meanwhile, the American government, such as it was, sat helplessly in Philadelphia—bankrupt, with no money to pay its army, no power to tax, virtually no power to do anything.

Eighteen months had elapsed since the bulk of the Continental Army had marched northward in triumph from Yorktown, its pennants flying high, but its troops in tatters—barefoot, hungry, and broke. Many had not been paid for years. "Our Men are almost naked," Washington pleaded to Congress, state leaders, and anyone else who would listen. Few did. "We are without money," he moaned, "totally unprepared for Winter. . . . There is not a farthing in the military chest."[1]

Only a year before Yorktown, troops in Pennsylvania and New Jersey had mutinied, but after winning promises of redress, they had followed Washington to Virginia to fight in what would prove the decisive, last battle of the American Revolution—though not the end of the war. Washington left Major General Nathanael Greene to command southern operations and led his ragtag northern forces to defend the Hudson River Valley, where, as they had throughout the Revolution, they languished loyally for months without pay or adequate food or clothing, pillaging local farms for scraps to eat, fearing that at any moment they would have to engage the immaculately equipped British enemy. Realizing that requests to Congress for supplies were futile, Washington appealed to the states.

"Officers and Men have been almost perishing for want," he complained to "The Magistrates" of New Jersey. "They have been alternating without Bread or Meat . . . and frequently destitute of both. . . . Their distress has in some instances prompted the Men to commit depredation on the property of the Inhabitants."[2] But the states were as bankrupt as Congress. Although state governments had powers to tax property and levy duties on imports, farmers operated on a barter system that produced virtually no cash to pay taxes, and the British blockade all but ended the flow of duties from foreign trade.

After two years, however, Britain signed the articles of peace, and in the spring of 1783, American soldiers and officers expected to go home with back pay in their pockets. But Congress still had no money, and the army resumed its mutiny—this time with the support of outraged officers, including General Horatio Gates, the hero at the Battle of Saratoga. In Newburgh, New York, an anonymously written leaflet appealed to Washington's officers to take up arms and march against Congress once peace with Britain became a certainty. If, however, Britain resumed the fighting, the letter urged officers to abandon their posts and "set up a new state in the wilderness," thus leaving Congress and the coastal states defenseless.

"My God!" Washington thundered. "What can this writer have in view by recommending such measures? Can he be a friend to the Army? Can he be a friend to the Country? Rather, is he not an insidious foe?"

Appalled by what he saw as a call to treason, Washington had called his officers to assembly in an effort to recapture their loyalties and restore their patriotism and love of country, and now he stood at the lectern before them. He began cautiously, all but mumbling that "an anonymous summons . . . was sent into circulation . . . and is designed to answer the most insidious purposes." He went on to read and condemn the letter, his voice gradually gaining strength as he described and acknowledged the hardships his officers and troops had faced. He then pledged his name and honor "that, in the attainment of compleat justice for all your toils and dangers . . . you may freely command my services." He assured them Congress was working "to discover and establish funds . . . but like all other large Bodies, where there is a variety of different Interests to reconcile, their deliberations are slow.

"While I give you these assurances," he pleaded, "and pledge myself . . . to exert whatever ability I am possessed of in your favor, let me entreat you, Gentlemen . . . not to take any measures, which . . . will lessen the dignity, and sully the glory you have hitherto maintained."[3]

After reminding his officers that he was "among the first who embarked in the cause of our common Country" and that "I have never left your side one moment," he called the idea of "deserting our Country in the extremest hour of her distress or turning our Arms against it . . . something so shocking in it that humanity revolts at the idea. . . . Let me conjure you, in the name of our common Country, as you value your own sacred honor, as you respect the rights of humanity, and as you regard the Military and National character of America, to express your utmost horror and detestation of the Man who wishes, under any specious pretences, to overturn the liberties of our County, who wickedly attempts to open the flood Gates of Civil discord, and deluge our rising Empire in Blood."[4]

Washington paused; his eyes seemed to falter. He laid his papers on the rostrum, fumbled in his pocket, and pulled out a pair of new glasses that evoked murmurs of surprise from his skeptical young audience.

"Gentlemen," Washington's voice quavered, "you must pardon me. I have grown gray in your service and now find myself growing blind."[5] The evident sadness in his voice, according to those present, recaptured the hearts of his officers. Washington had served without pay throughout the war, had won near-universal reverence by remaining with his troops through the most severe winters, when most officers in every army in the world routinely left their troops in winter quarters and returned to the comfort of their homes. "He spoke," according to one officer at the Newburgh meeting, "[and] every doubt was dispelled—and the tide of patriotism rolled again in its wonted course. Illustrious man!"[6] The mutiny ended with a unanimous resolution of confidence in Congress and a request that Washington represent the interests of all army officers.

In fact, there was little that Washington—or Congress, for that matter—could do to ease the army's plight. A vestige of the Continental Congress that had declared independence in 1776, it had sought reforms, but split into bitter factions that fought incessantly about how much power to assume over the states. The Nationalists—later renamed Federalists—demanded supreme powers for the central government over international and interstate commerce, interstate disputes, national finances, and military affairs—in effect, an American replacement for the ousted British government. Antifederalists insisted that the states remain sovereign and independent, retain all political powers, and only occasionally dole out temporary powers to Congress to deal with a problem or crisis common to all the states, such as national defense.

After eighteen months of debate, Congress sent the Articles of Confederation and Perpetual Union to the states, which took four years to ratify them, completing the job late in 1781. The Articles of Confederation created a new central government of sorts, with executive and legislative authority combined in a unicameral, or one-chamber legislature, in which each state would have one vote. To pass any important law dealing with war, treaties, or borrowing money, nine of the thirteen state delegations in Congress had to approve—and even with their approval, the Confederation had no powers to enforce any of the legislation Congress passed.

Still worse, the Articles denied Congress the single most important legislative and executive power for governing any nation: the power to raise money. Congress could not levy taxes or collect duties on imports and exports. In the end, the only "power" the Articles gave the national government was the right to borrow money—a difficult process for a bankrupt government with no means of repaying its debts. In effect, the Confederation left the thirteen states sovereign, independent, and free, and the Confederation Congress as impotent in peace as the Continental Congress had been in war—a mere forum for state representatives to meet, argue, and do nothing.

When formal confirmation of American independence arrived, Washington fulfilled his promise to his officers by issuing a blistering condemnation of the way Congress and the states had managed the nation and the war. Immediately dubbed "Washington's Legacy," his four-thousand-word "Circular to the States" announced his imminent retirement as commander in chief, demanded full payment of all debts to soldiers and officers, the award of pensions equal to five years' pay for all soldiers, and annual life pensions for those "who have shed their blood or lost their limbs in the service of their country. . . . Nothing but a punctual payment of their annual allowance can rescue them from the most complicated misery . . . without a shelter, without a friend, and without the means of obtaining any of the necessaries or comforts of Life; compelled to beg their daily bread from door to door!"

Warning that "the eyes of the whole World" focused on the United States, he called on Congress to repay its foreign creditors and declared,

> this is the moment to establish or ruin [our] national Character forever, this is the favorable moment to give such a tone to our Federal Government, as will enable it to answer the ends of its institution, or this may be the ill-fated moment for relaxing the powers of the Union, annihilating the cement of the Confederation, and exposing us to become the sport of European politics, which may play one State against another to prevent their growing

importance, and to serve their own interested purposes. With this conviction of the importance of the present Crisis, silence in me would be a crime.

Washington went on to cite what he considered essential to the survival of the United States as an "Independent Power," including "An indissoluble Union of the States under one Federal Head." In calling for reform of the Articles of Confederation, he demanded nothing less than a revolution in which the states would "delegate a larger proportion of Power to Congress." Failure to do so, he predicted, would "very rapidly tend to Anarchy and confusion. . . .

> It is indispensable . . . that there should be lodged somewhere a Supreme Power to regulate and govern the general concerns of the Confederated Republic, without which the Union cannot be of long duration. . . . There must be a faithful and pointed compliance on the part of every state with the demands of Congress, or the most fatal consequences will ensue, That whatever measures have a tendency to dissolve the Union, or contribute to violate or lessen the Sovereign Authority, ought to be considered as hostile to the Liberty and Independency of America, and the Authors of them treated accordingly.[7]

Washington's prediction of "anarchy and confusion" came to pass sooner than even he could have anticipated. About ten days after issuing his "Circular to the States," nearly one hundred soldiers marched from Lancaster, Pennsylvania, to Philadelphia on June 17, 1783, to extract justice from Congress and the state government. Streams of men from other regiments swelled their numbers to more than five hundred when they reached the Philadelphia State House (now Independence Hall), where both the Confederation Congress and Pennsylvania's Supreme Executive Council were in session. As rifle barrels shattered and poked through the windows, legislators fled the hall and reassembled in New Jersey, across the river. Congress reconvened in Princeton on June 24, and met there on and off until the end of October, when it moved to more spacious quarters in Annapolis, Maryland, and ultimately New York City. Over and again, Washington reiterated his demands to reform the Articles of Confederation,

> for certain I am, that unless adequate Powers are given to Congress for the general purposes of the Federal Union that we shall soon

George Washington. As presiding officer of the Constitutional Convention, Washington did not participate in debates, but he had spent almost four years writing leaders in every state of the need "to revise, and amend the Articles of Confederation." In the end, it was his constitution that they ratified.

moulder into dust and become contemptible in the Eyes of Europe, if we are not made the sport of their Politicks; to suppose that the general concern of this Country can be directed by thirteen heads, or one head without competent powers, is a solecism, the bad effects of which every Man who has had the practical knowledge to judge from, that I have, is fully convinced of; tho' none perhaps has felt them in so forcible, and distressing a degree.[8]

In the fall of 1783, Britain closed the British West Indies to American vessels and blocked entry of American lumber and food-stuffs into what had been a huge, lucrative market. For a short time, increased trade with northern Europe and China compensated for the decline in British trade—until overseas merchants discovered that a trade agreement with Congress was meaningless without trade agreements from individual states, each of which was sovereign, independent, and able to impose tariffs or embargoes on goods that crossed its borders. Rather than trying to negotiate separate agreements with thirteen states, therefore, many foreign traders simply stopped doing business with America.

After an unsuccessful attempt to negotiate a reversal of the British trade decision, John Adams, the American minister to Britain, wrote to Congress and echoed Washington's words. The British, Adams declared, had acted "in full confidence that the United States . . . cannot agree to act in a body as one nation; that they cannot agree upon any navigation act which may be common to the thirteen states." A strong proponent and signer of the Declaration of Independence, Adams issued a stark warning:

> if there is not an authority sufficiently decisive to draw together the minds, affections, and forces of the States, in their common, foreign concerns, it appears to me, we shall be the sport of transatlantic politicians of all denominations, who hate liberty in every shape, and every man who loves it, and every country that enjoys it.[9]

Adams's warning combined with the British trade embargo to convince some defenders of state supremacy of the need for shoring congressional powers. Indeed, even the patron saint of local rule, former governor Patrick Henry, then a member of Virginia's House of Delegates (state assembly), stunned his colleagues by predicting "Ruin inevitable unless something is done to give Congress a compulsory Process on delinquent States & c." Henry's close friend and political ally Richard Henry Lee agreed and urged calling a convention "for the sole purpose of revising the Confederation" to permit Congress to act "with more energy, effect, & vigor."[10]

Learning of Henry's declaration, Washington grew optimistic: "Notwithstanding the jealous and contracted temper which seems to prevail in some of the states, I cannot but hope and believe that the good sense of the people will ultimately get the better of their prejudices," he wrote to one of his wartime aides, Jonathan Trumbull Jr.,

John Adams. Named the first American minister to Britain after helping to negotiate the peace treaty that established American independence, Adams warned Congress that the United States would be "the sport of transatlantic politicians of all denominations" unless it established a strong central government.

the son of Connecticut's governor. "Every thing, My Dear Trumbull will come right at last."[11]

But nothing came right. In fact, the "nation" hardly deserved to be called a nation. Rather than heed Washington's call to convention, to give "energy" to the Articles of Confederation, state political leaders emasculated the Confederation, using their powers and wealth to transform the former colonies into independent fiefdoms. Some states set property qualifications for holding high office at £10,000 (about $750,000 today[12]). Others limited voting eligibility to owners of at least five hundred acres. In the end, the reins of state government fell into the grip of powerful merchant-bankers in the North and owners of the largest plantations in the South. In addition to control over trade, market pricing, and lending rates, merchant-bankers and plantation owners gained control of state taxing powers and the courts, which gave them an economic stranglehold over shopkeepers, craftsmen, and farmers.

As popular dissatisfaction swelled, Congress continued its disingenuous debates over national unity, even as the states warred with one another over conflicting territorial claims: New York and New Hampshire over claims to Vermont, Virginia and Pennsylvania over territory in the West, and Pennsylvania and Connecticut over the Wyoming Valley in northeastern Pennsylvania. In addition to territorial disputes, six states were involved in fierce economic disputes over international trade. States with deepwater ports such as Philadelphia, New York, and Boston were bleeding the economies of neighboring states with heavy duties on imports. "New Jersey, placed between Phila & N. York, was likened to a cask tapped at both ends," complained James Madison, one of Virginia's delegates in Congress, "and N. Carolina, between Virga & S. Carolina [seemed] a patient bleeding at both arms."[13]

Other factors, such as geography and language, also worked against national unity. Philadelphia lay more than three days' travel from New York, about ten days from Boston, and all but inaccessible from far-off cities such as Richmond or Charleston during various times of year. Foul winter weather and spring rains isolated parts of the country for many months each year and made establishment of close cultural ties difficult at best and often impossible. In many significant respects, the South—and southerners—were as foreign to most New Hampshire men as China and the Chinese. Indeed, only 60 percent of Americans had English origins. The rest were Dutch, French, German, Scottish, Scotch Irish, Irish, even Swedish. Although English remained the common tongue after independence, German prevailed in much of eastern Pennsylvania, Dutch along the Hudson River Valley, French in Vermont and parts of New Hampshire and what would later become Maine. As early as 1750, Benjamin Franklin was already complaining that Germantown was engulfing Philadelphia and that Pennsylvania "will in a few years become a

German colony. Instead of learning our language, we must learn theirs, or live as in a foreign country."[14]

With Congress impotent and New York City so distant, delegates from far-off states appeared only intermittently, and a few states stopped appointing delegates. When they did meet, they had little in common and barely fathomed each other's thinking. Without money or means to raise any, Congress stopped repaying principal and interest on foreign debts, disbanded its navy, and reduced its army to a mere eighty privates.[15]

Secretary at War Henry Knox, who had been a major general and Washington's chief of artillery from their early days in Cambridge in 1775, warned his old friend that "different states have . . . views that sooner or later must involve the Country in all the horrors of civil war. . . .

> A Neglect, in every State, of those principles which lead to Union and National greatness—An adoption of local, in preference to general measures, appear to actuate the greater part of the State politicians—We are entirely destitute of those traits which should stamp us *one Nation*, and the Constitution of Congress does not promise any alteration. . . . Every State considers its representative in Congress not so much the Legislator of the whole Union, as its own immediate Agent or Ambassador to negociate, & to endeavour to create in Congress as great an influence as possible to favor particular views &c.[16]

In 1784, Spanish authorities added to America's miseries by closing the Mississippi River to American shipping. The shutdown isolated farmers in those parts of Virginia, Georgia, and the Carolinas that lay west of the Appalachian Mountains. Not only could they no longer ship to New Orleans, primitive dirt roads left the Appalachians all but impenetrable and made it impossible to haul grain eastward. Settlers took up arms and threatened to march on New Orleans. Intent on blocking American access to its lucrative Mexican colonies, the Spanish government sent an envoy, Don Diego de Gardoqui, to the United States in the spring of 1785 to open ports in Spain to American trade if the United States would waive their rights to navigate the Mississippi. Gardoqui met with Secretary for Foreign Affairs John Jay, the wealthy New York attorney who had written his state's constitution and had been a primary negotiator of the peace treaty with Britain.

Suspicious that the easterner Jay would give away what western-ers called their "natural rights" to the Mississippi, North Carolina's western territory seceded, renaming itself the State of Franklin and electing Revolutionary War hero and Indian-fighter John Sevier as governor. A wily land speculator, he joined the so-called "Spanish Conspiracy" led by Kentucky's James Wilkinson, who was leading the agitation for Kentucky independence. The unscrupulous Wilkin-son, however, was also negotiating secretly with Spanish authorities, who promised Wilkinson and his inner circle a trade monopoly if he succeeded in provoking the American settlements west of the Appalachians to secede and establish a new nation friendly to Spain.

A year later, Jay confirmed westerner fears and agreed to relin-quish American navigation rights on the Mississippi River for twenty-five years in exchange for Gardoqui's agreement to open ports in Spain to American trade—an agreement that would prima-rily benefit the Northeast. Congress voted seven (northern states) to five (southern states) in favor—short of the nine states needed to ratify treaties, but more than enough to outrage the South and expose the willingness of northern states to sacrifice the interests of other states and regions for the right price. Virginia and other south-ern states whose boundaries extended to the Mississippi River threatened to secede.

"To sell us and make us vassals to the merciless Spaniards, is a griev-ance not to be borne," protested a Kentuckian in the *Maryland Jour-nal*. He went on to warn that "Preparations are now making here . . . to drive the Spaniards from the settlements at the mouth of the Mississippi.

> In case we are not countenanced and succored by the United
> States . . . our allegiance will be thrown off, and some other power
> applied to. Great-Britain stands ready, with open arms to receive
> and support us.—They have already offered to open their resources
> for our supplies.—When once reunited to them, 'farewell—a long
> farewell to all your boasted greatness'—The province of Canada
> and the inhabitants of these waters, of themselves, in time, will be
> able to conquer.—You are as ignorant of this country as Great-
> Britain was of America.[17]

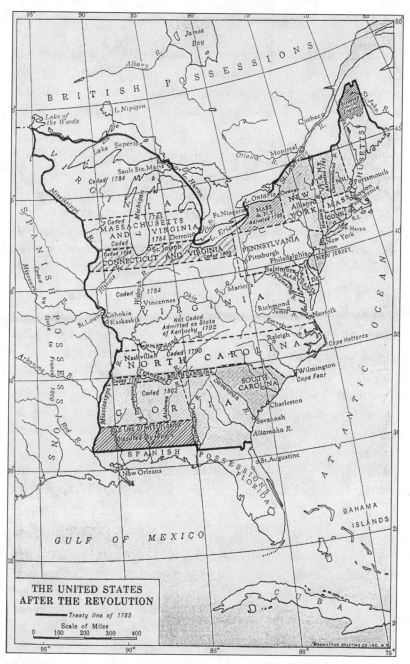

Map of the United States in 1783. The original state boundaries after independence conformed to those of the former British colonies, with many reaching to the east bank of the Mississippi River. After warring over conflicting claims, most of the states eventually ceded their western territories to the U.S. government to establish new states.

Southern threats of secession emboldened New Englanders to call for establishment of a northern confederacy. "How long," asked a correspondent in the *Boston Independent Chronicle*, "are we to continue in our present acquiescence . . . ?

> The five States of New-England, closely confederated can have nothing to fear. Let then our General Assembly immediately recall their Delegates from . . . Congress, as being a useless and expensive establishment. Send proposals for instituting a new . . . nation of New-England, and leave the rest of the Continent to pursue their own imbecile and disjointed plans, until they have . . . acquired magnanimity and wisdom sufficient to join a confederation that may rescue them from destruction.[18]

By 1786, the states began abandoning the Confederation of American States, and the nation all but collapsed politically and economically. Civil war seemed imminent. Pennsylvania's Charles Petit called the political situation "wretched—Our Funds exhausted, our Credit lost, our Confidence, in each other and in the federal Government destroyed."[19]

Discouraged by the nation's deterioration, Henry Knox again turned to George Washington: "We have arrived at that point of time," Knox warned, "in which we are forced to see our national humiliation . . . something must be done or we shall be involved in all the horror of faction and civil war without a prospect of its termination. . . .

> We imagined that the mildness of our government and *the virtue* of our people were so correspondent, that we were not as other nations requiring brutal force to support the laws—But we find that we are men, actual men, possessing all the turbulent passions belonging to that animal and that we must have a government proper and adequate to him. . . . Unless this is done we shall be liable to be ruled by an Arbitrary and Capricious armed tyranny, whose word and will must be law.[20]

In fact, Washington was already responding to the crisis, hoping to use common commercial interests to unite the nation. In the spring before the Jay-Gardoqui negotiations, Washington had hosted a conference at his palatial Mount Vernon mansion in northern Virginia, for representatives of Maryland and Virginia to establish joint jurisdiction over the commercial shipping channel in Chesapeake Bay and the lower Potomac River and apportion expenses appropriately. Virginia's delegates included Washington's neighbor the wealthy planter George Mason, and James Madison, who had served in Congress for three years and was now an influential young member of the Virginia House of Delegates.

The Mount Vernon conference saw the two states go beyond expectations by adopting uniform commercial regulations and a uniform currency—in effect, establishing a commercial union. At Washington's suggestion, they agreed to support one of his longtime pet projects—a system of canals and portage roads to link the Ohio, Monongahela, and Allegheny rivers and the Great Lakes to the Atlantic Ocean via the Potomac River and Chesapeake Bay. The gigantic waterway would ultimately solve the conflict with Spain over Mississippi River navigation rights by allowing the wealth of the continent beyond the Appalachian Mountains—furs, ore, timber, and grain—to flow swiftly, easily, and inexpensively to Atlantic ports for transport to Europe and the West Indies. Owner of more than thirty thousand acres of rich western farmlands, Washington stood to enhance his personal fortune from the project, but he had other, grander motives for engaging state governments in the waterway. As he explained to his friend Virginia governor Benjamin Harrison,

> I need not remark to you Sir, that the flanks & rear of the United States are possessed by other powers . . . nor, how necessary it is to apply the cement of interest, to bind all parts of the Union together by indissoluble bonds—especially that part of it, which lies immediately west of us. . . . The Western settlers, (I speak now from my own observation) stand as it were upon a pivot—the touch of a feather, would turn them any way—They have look'd down the Mississippi, until the Spaniards (very impoliticly I think, for themselves) threw difficulties in their way; & they looked that way for no other reason, than because they could glide gently down the stream . . . & because they have no other means of coming to us but by a long Land transportation & unimproved roads. These causes have hitherto checked the industry of the present settlers. . . . But smooth the road once, & make easy the way for

them, & then see what an influx of articles will be poured in upon us—how amazingly our exports will be encreased by them, & how amply we shall be compensated for any trouble & expence we may encounter to effect it.[21]

In the months following the Mount Vernon conference, the Virginia and Maryland legislatures appropriated funds to develop Potomac and James river navigation and build portage roads to Ohio River tributaries. Leaders in both states hailed Washington's success and named him president of the Potomac Company. In just four months, he had succeeded in organizing the greatest public works project in North American history and unified two states that had hitherto been in continuing conflict over rights to the waterways they shared. In ratifying the waterway agreement, Virginia and Maryland agreed to review interstate commercial relations annually and to invite neighboring Delaware and Pennsylvania to participate because of their proximity to the waterway.

But Washington's vision was wider still, and he began a letter-writing campaign to enlist supporters from almost every state, including Massachusetts merchant and political activist James Warren; New York's John Jay; the brilliant North Carolina scholar, scientist, and political leader Hugh Williamson; and, of course, the leading figures in Virginia—Thomas Jefferson, James Madison, and Richard Henry Lee, Virginia's elder statesman, who had been president of Congress the previous year and remained a member of that body.

"We are either a United people, or we are not," Washington wrote to Madison. "If the former, let us, in all matters of general concern act as a nation, which have national objects to promote, and a National character to support—If we are not, let us no longer act a farce by pretending to it, for whilst we are playing a dble game, or playing a game between the two we never shall be consistent or respectable—but *may* be the dupes of some powers, and most assuredly, the contempt of all."[22]

In an effort to respond to Washington's concerns, Madison suggested that Virginia expand the scope of the proposed four-state commercial convention by inviting all states to participate in a convention at Annapolis, Maryland, the following September, to consider unifying interstate and foreign commerce regulations, eliminating interstate trade restrictions, and facilitating trade agreements with foreign nations. A member of Congress since 1780, Madison had been too frail and sickly to serve in the army and had waged his own personal war for America by leading the struggle in Congress to promote interstate unity—a goal he believed could be reached by expanding the powers of Congress to include the right to levy taxes to support a standing army and navy for national defense.

Congress responded favorably, with the renowned South Carolina attorney Charles Pinckney proposing a reorganization of government. A "grand committee" then worked out seven amendments to the Articles of Confederation to strengthen congressional powers. But the bitter sectionalism generated by the Jay-Gardoqui Treaty proved too strong, and the amendments were tabled when a brash Virginia delegate, Revolutionary War hero James Monroe, set congressional tempers ablaze by accusing New England and New York leaders of plotting secession from the Confederation. The furor he incited not only forced Congress to table the reform amendments, it almost demolished hopes for the success of the interstate convention scheduled at Annapolis in September.

Although nine states had agreed to participate, the delegates of only five states showed up on time—New York, New Jersey, Delaware, Pennsylvania, and Virginia—too few to take any action, but nonetheless fervently committed to government reform. They issued a dramatic call for all states to attend a second, more substantial convention in Philadelphia the following May "to take into consideration the situation of the United States, to devise further provisions as shall appear to them necessary to render the constitution of the Fœderal Government adequate to the exigencies of the Union."[23]

As the year progressed, the nation plunged into economic depression and near anarchy. More than 30 percent of the nation's farmers were unable to pay their debts to merchants and shopkeepers, let alone taxes. Foreign trade dropped nearly 25 percent, farm income 20 percent. Adding momentum to the economic decline, Spain's ban on American shipping on the Mississippi had bankrupted untold numbers of farmers and merchants west of the Appalachians. As creditor suits multiplied, thousands of farmers saw their lands and homes confiscated, and their livestock and personal possessions—including tools of their trade—auctioned at prices too low to clear their debts. Hysterical wives and terrified children watched helplessly as sheriff's deputies dragged farmers off to debtors' prisons, where they languished indefinitely—unable to earn money to pay their debts and without the tools to do so. Publisher Isaiah Thomas, who had fought as a Minuteman at Lexington and Concord before starting the *Massachusetts Spy*, reported prisoners dying in small, damp, moldy cells—"a place which disgraces humanity." Samuel Ely, a Massachusetts farmer, testified of his suffering "boils and putrefied sores all over my body and they make me stink alive, besides having some of my feet froze which makes it difficult to walk."[24]

Enraged farmers across the nation, almost all of them Revolutionary War veterans, took up rifles and pitchforks to protect their properties, firing at sheriffs and others who ventured too near. Reassembling their wartime companies, they attacked and set fire to prisons, courthouses, and county clerk offices. Virginia mobs burned down the King William and the New Kent county courthouses. A mob in Maryland burned down the Charles County courthouse. In New Hampshire farmers marched to the state capital at Exeter, surrounded the legislature, and demanded forgiveness of all debts, return of all seized properties to former owners, and equitable distribution of property. In western Massachusetts, the farmer uprising grew into outright rebellion when former captain Daniel Shays, a farmer struggling to hold on to his property, convinced a rally of neighbors that local lawyers and judges were colluding with eastern merchants in the Boston legislature to raise taxes and seize farms for nonpayment. While the legislature plunged farmers deeper into debt, he said, judges appointed by the Boston establishment were sending debtor farmers to jail. With that he shouted the words that became the watch cry of farmers across the state: "Close down the courts!"

Echoing his call, farmers marched to courthouses in Cambridge, Concord, Worcester, Northampton, Taunton, and Great Barrington—and shut them all down. Hailed by farmers across the nation as the Second American Revolution, the court shutdowns brought an abrupt end to foreclosures in Massachusetts. Determined to expand his successes, Shays led a force of five hundred men to Springfield, intent on seizing the federal arsenal and marching to Boston to overthrow the state government.

"The commotions . . . have risen in Massachusetts to an alarming height," wrote Henry ("Light-Horse Harry") Lee to Washington from Congress. "After various insults to government, by stopping the courts of justice &c., the insurgents have in a very formidable shape taken possession of the town of Springfield. . . . This event produces much suggestion as to its causes—Some attribute it to the weight of taxes and the decay of commerce. . . . Others, to British councils."[25]

As rumors spread that British spies and provocateurs were behind the spreading riots, Lee grew alarmed and warned,

> A majority of the people of Massachusetts are in opposition to the government, some of their leaders *avow* the *subversion* of it to be their object together with the abolition of debts, the division of property and re-union with G. Britain—In all the eastern states the same temper prevails more or less, and will certainly break forth whenever the opportune moment may arrive—the mal-contents are in close connexion with Vermont—& that district it is believed is in negotiation with the Governor of Canada—In one word my dear Genl we are all in dire apprehension that a beginning of anarchy with all its calamities has approached & have no means to stop the dreadful work.[26]

Lee's letter shocked Washington, who replied that the Shaysites had exhibited "a melancholy proof . . . that mankind left to themselves are unfit for their own government. I am mortified beyond expression whenever I view the clouds which have spread over the brightest morn that ever dawned upon any country. In a word, I am lost in amazement when I behold what intriguing . . . desperate characters; Jealousy; & ignorance of the Minor part, are capable of effecting as a scourge on the major part of our fellow citizens of the Union."[27]

After forcing the state Supreme Court in Springfield to adjourn, Shays and his men encamped near Worcester, where one thousand more farmers armed with muskets and pitchforks rallied to his side. Some went off to recruit other farmers—and turned viciously on those who refused to join. "Farmyard wars" erupted, with Shaysites and anti-Shaysites pillaging each other's properties and, too often, slaughtering each other, as well as innocent farmers and their families who sought to remain neutral. In Boston, wealthy merchants helped the government organize forty-four hundred militiamen under former wartime general Benjamin Lincoln to march to Springfield and support the four-hundred-man force guarding the arsenal. Before Lincoln arrived, however, Shays's men attacked, but found their pitchforks no match for the arsenal's artillery, which unloosed a devastating barrage that sent the farmers fleeing in panic. Lincoln's army arrived on the scene soon after, capturing most of the rebel "army."

Shays and his officers fled to safety in Vermont, but in defeat they scored a resounding victory for Massachusetts farmers, who flocked to the polls as never before and turned Governor James Bowdoin and three-quarters of the state's legislators out of office. Although a member of the wealthy merchant class, Governor-elect John Hancock pledged amnesty for Shaysites, and the new, profarmer legislature acceded to almost all Shaysite demands. It passed a law exempting clothing, household possessions, and tools of trade from seizure in debt proceedings and allowed imprisoned debtors to win release and go back to work by taking a pauper's oath that they had no income. In a symbolic gesture to win farmer support, Governor Hancock cut his own salary, and, to quell civil strife and promote economic recovery, he convinced legislators to declare a tax holiday for a year and reduce property taxes substantially thereafter.

As farmer rebellions spread from state to state, fears increased that Shaysites had asked British emissaries in Canada to send troops back into the United States to help establish a new independent state covering Vermont and western Massachusetts. "British influence is operating in this mischievous affair," a Virginia delegate warned Governor Patrick Henry. "It is an undoubted truth that communications are held by Lord Dorchester with both the Vermonters, and the insurgents of Massachusetts, and that a direct offer has been made to the latter, of the protection and Government of Great Britain."[28]

James Madison was equally fearful: "It was known that there were individuals who had betrayed a bias towards Monarchy, and there had always been some not unfavorable to a partition of the Union into several confederacies. . . . The idea of a dismemberment had recently made its appearance in the Newspapers."[29]

Just as the shots fired at Lexington had echoed in London's Parliament, so the shots fired in Springfield reverberated loudly in Congress and in the nation's state capitals and jolted even the most
ardent state supremacists into realizing that their only hope of
retaining their wealth, power, and sovereignty lay in sharing enough
of each with a central government strong enough to ensure national
integrity. As popular demand grew for a stronger central government
to quell spreading violence and disorder, state legislatures responded.
In November 1786, Virginia authorized the election of delegates to
attend the Philadelphia convention, which it called "preferable to a
discussion of the subject in Congress . . . the crisis is arrived at which
the good people of America are to decide the solemn question."[30]
New Jersey's legislature followed suit a day later; Pennsylvania did
the same in December, North Carolina and New Hampshire in January 1787, and Delaware and Georgia in February. On February 21,
Congress itself approved the call to convention and recommended
that all states send delegates "for the sole and express purpose of
revising the articles of confederation . . . [and] render the federal
constitution, adequate to the exigencies of government and the
preservation of the union."[31]

In the months that followed, five more states—Massachusetts,
New York, South Carolina, Connecticut, and Maryland—agreed to
participate. Only Rhode Island refused—three times. James Madison
ascribed Rhode Island's response to "an obdurate adherence to an
advantage which her position gave her of taxing her neighbors
through their consumption of imported supplies." Rhode Island ports
eliminated the need to sail around Cape Cod to Boston to deliver
goods bound for most of New England. The heavy flow of duties that
resulted gave Rhode Island every incentive to remain independent
and sovereign.

Virginia's Assembly elected seven delegates, with the most votes
going to George Washington, who had retired from public life at the
end of 1783 with a theatrical surrender of his Revolutionary War
commission in Congress. "Having now finished the work assigned
me," he had proclaimed to Congress, "I retire from the great theatre
of action; and bidding an Affectionate farewell to this August
body . . . I here offer my commission, and take leave of all employments of public life."[32]

After retiring to Mount Vernon, he had written to his close friend the marquis de Lafayette, who was back in France:

> I am become a private citizen on the banks of the Potomac & under the shadow of my own Vine & my own Fig tree, free from the bustle of camp & the busy scenes of public life, I am solacing myself with those tranquil enjoyments, of which the Soldier who is ever in pursuit of fame . . . can have very little conception. . . . Envious of none . . . I will move gently down the stream of life, until I sleep with my Fathers.[33]

As violence and disorder threatened to plunge the nation into anarchy, however, the eyes—and voices—of state leaders turned to the man who had saved the Revolution. Even before Shays's Rebellion, John Jay had written to Washington, pleading, "Altho' you have wisely retired from public Employments, I am persuaded you cannot view . . . your country . . . with the Eye of an unconcerned Spectator. . . .

> Experience has pointed out Errors in our national Government, which call for Correction. It is in Contemplation to take measures for forming a general convention. . . . I am fervent in my Wishes, that it may comport with the Line of Life you have marked out for yourself, to favor your country with your counsels on such an important & single occasion. I suggest this merely as a Hint for your consideration.[34]

Despite his pledge to retire under his proverbial vine and fig tree, Washington had fought too long and hard in the Revolutionary War to relinquish his unique status as a national hero who could influence, if not dictate, national affairs. "I coincide perfectly in sentiment with you," Washington replied to Jay, "that there are errors in our National Government which call for correction. . . . That it is necessary to revise, and amend the Articles of Confederation, I entertain no doubt . . . something must be done. I do not conceive we can exist long as a nation, without having lodged somewhere a power which will pervade the whole Union."[35] And in a second letter to Jay he admitted, "I frankly acknowledge I cannot feel myself an unconcerned spectator."[36]

Washington grew more concerned as rioting spread across the nation's farmlands. "What a triumph for the advocates of despotism to find we are incapable of governing ourselves," he railed in another letter to Jay. "Would to God that wise measures may be taken in time to avert the consequences we have but too much to apprehend."[37]

As he organized the great waterway to bind East and West commercially, Washington used his correspondence on the project to express his views for governmental reform that would bind the country politically. Washington told leaders in every state that rather than simply amending the Articles of Confederation, he favored replacing the unicameral Congress of the Confederation with a new, stronger federal government with three separate branches—an executive, a judiciary, and a legislature—with collective, coercive powers over the states and their citizens. In effect, he favored scrapping the old American government and creating a more authoritarian regime that would strip the states of political and economic sovereignty in such areas as national defense, international and interstate trade, and interstate disputes. Far from adhering to the mandate of Congress and instructions from the various state legislatures, Washington favored nothing less than the overthrow of the American government—in effect, a revolution, albeit a bloodless one, to substitute one form of government with another.

Named to lead the Virginia delegation, Washington expressed some reluctance, fearing that if he reneged on his pledge to retire from public life, state supremacists might charge him with tyrannical ambitions and block efforts to establish a new central government.

"It is the general wish that you should attend," Secretary at War Henry Knox reassured his former commander a month before the Convention was to begin. "It is conceived to be highly important to the success of the propositions of the convention."[38]

Although he feigned disinterest, Washington acceded "to the wishes of many of my friends who seemed extremely anxious for my attending the Convention . . . tho' so much afflicted with a rheumatic complaint (of which I have not been entirely free for Six months) as to be under the necessity of carrying my arm in a sling for the last ten days." He said he made his decision to attend and "depart from the resolution I had taken of never more stepping out of the walks of private life . . . with a good deal of reluctance . . . from a conviction that our affairs were verging fast to ruin."[39]

Patrick Henry, who had completed his fifth one-year term as Virginia governor and had also retired from public life, received the second most votes among the delegates to the Constitutional Convention. He refused to go, despite pleas from Edmund Randolph, his successor in the governor's chair: "I most sincerely wish your presence at the federal convention at Philadelphia," Randolph pleaded.

> From your experience of your late administration, you must be persuaded that every day dawns with perils to the United States. To whom, then, can they [people of Virginia] resort for assistance with firmer expectation, than to those who first kindled the Revolution? In this respectable character you are now called upon by your country. You will therefore pardon me for expressing a fear that the neglect of the present moment may terminate in the destruction of Confederate America.[40]

Henry waited two months before replying, "I feel myself constrained to decline acting under this appointment." He gave no reasons, but James Madison saw Henry's refusal as an ominous sign that Henry was preparing to lead the fight to retain the Articles of Confederation:

"I hear from Richmond, with much concern," Madison wrote to Washington, "that Mr. Henry has positively declined his mission to Philada. Besides the loss of his services on that theatre, there is danger I fear that this step has proceeded from a wish to leave his conduct unfettered on another theatre, where the result of the convention will receive its destiny from his omnipotence."[41] Madison reiterated his suspicions to Thomas Jefferson, then serving as American minister to Paris: "Mr. Henry's disgust exceeds all measure, and I am not singular in ascribing his refusal to attend the convention to the policy of keeping himself free to combat or espouse the result of it."[42]

Besides Washington and Henry, the Virginia Assembly had elected Governor Randolph, John Blair, James Madison, George Mason, and George Wythe. They tried replacing Henry with Richard Henry Lee, but Lee declined the post, saying it would be in conflict with his position as a member of the Confederation Congress, which was the very government the Convention would be duty-bound to change. With Jefferson in Paris, Madison turned to a lesser-known political ally, Dr. James McClurg, a world-renowned physician who had served as surgeon to the American Navy and had been physician-general and director of hospitals for Virginia's military forces. An ardent advocate of a strong central government, he happily accepted election to the Convention.

Although Washington was pleased by the nationalist tinge of his home state's delegation, he realized that Patrick Henry and Henry's political allies were already plotting to undermine the work of the Convention. Instead of national unity under a strong central government, Henry seemed determined to effect "a dismemberment of the Union."[43]

2

The Great Debate

CANNONS FIRED CONTINUOUSLY and church bells pealed their
welcome as Washington rode into Philadelphia on May 13, 1787, a
Sunday afternoon. A committee of three generals, two colonels, and
two majors who had served under him in the Revolutionary War had
met him at Chester, Pennsylvania, that morning and, after a festive
luncheon and appropriate toasts, they escorted him to a hero's welcome at the Philadelphia city line. With a chorus of huzzas, hundreds
of mounted citizens awaited with the City Light Horse to greet the
general and lead him through cheering throngs to the Pennsylvania
State House (now Independence Hall), where the great Convention
was to assemble the following morning:

"The joy of the people on the coming of this great and good
man," the *Pennsylvania Packet* reported, "was shewn by their accla-
mations and the ringing of bells."

Washington stayed at the palatial home of Robert Morris, the
great merchant-banker who had acquired fame as "financier of the
Revolution" and primary source of supplies for Washington's army.
Two years younger than Washington, Morris had been born in Liv-
erpool, England, and came to America at age fourteen. He was
apprenticed to Philadelphia merchant Charles Willing, and Morris's
talents, hard work, and charm earned him a full partnership in the
firm by the time he was twenty. A member of the Continental Congress, he signed the Declaration of Independence, then contracted
with Congress to provide war supplies. He established a national

bank and pledged his own personal credit to buy supplies for the Continental Army and, like other merchant-bankers, he ensured himself handsome profits and appropriate commissions on every deal—with the full assent of Congress. He emerged from the war one of the wealthiest men in America—perhaps the wealthiest. The embodiment of a successful merchant-banker, his roseate face glowed with laughter; his hand reached out to those of friends and foes alike to guide them to the nearest tavern for a cup, or to one of his homes for a lavish meal. Morris openly mixed business with pleasure and always "found them useful to each other." He loaned funds freely, gave investment advice to members of Congress, and obliged other men of influence in any way he could, willingly creating jobs in his countinghouse for the offspring of important friends, including one of Washington's nephews. Besides his mansion in the city, Morris owned a country home above the Schuylkill River, staffed each with a score of liveried servants, and kept both residences stocked with an endless supply of fine foods and wines. Tired from his long trip, Washington eagerly accepted the invitation of Morris and his wife to install himself in a luxurious guest room in their home, about a block from the State House.

After settling in, Washington went to pay a courtesy call on eighty-one-year-old Benjamin Franklin, then president of the Pennsylvania Supreme Executive Council, and perhaps the most beloved and influential man in America after Washington himself. Normally the ancient Philadelphian greeted and expounded to visitors while sitting under the umbrella-shaped mulberry tree in his courtyard, but the threat of rain forced him to receive Washington indoors. They had not seen each other in more than ten years, since the early days of the Revolutionary War. Gout, arthritis, and kidney stones had wreaked havoc on the old man's body, leaving him slumped over, double-chinned, and with only a few unruly white hairs on either side to adorn his otherwise bald head. A crowd of admirers surrounded them and stood breathlessly, in expectation of words for the ages from the two demigods. Discomfited by the artificiality of the situation, they limited their meeting to expressions of deep—and sincere—admiration for each other and pledges to work closely together at the Convention. Franklin ordered glasses filled, and they celebrated their reunion with appropriate toasts to success at the Convention.

On May 14, when the Convention was to begin, it seemed as if Patrick Henry and the state supremacists had succeeded in undermining the event. Torrential rains drenched Philadelphia and forced Washington to ride the long block to the Pennsylvania State House in his carriage. Only the Pennsylvania delegates and a few Virginians were there. The rest of the great room where John Hancock had signed the Declaration of Independence was empty. There was no choice but to postpone the opening of the Convention. Annoyed, but unable to rectify the situation, Washington returned to the comforts of the Morris mansion and dinner with the Morris family.

When delegates reassembled at eleven the next morning, "no more states being represented than were yesterday . . . we agreed to meet again tomorrow," Washington noted in his diary. His annoyance increased on Wednesday, when there were still too few delegates to form a quorum. He salvaged the day by dining at Benjamin Franklin's house with what Franklin called *"une assemblée des notables,"* including Virginia's governor Randolph and other prominent delegates, and such noted Pennsylvanians as John Penn, a grandson of William Penn. Like members of the Congress of the Confederation and every state legislature, delegates to the Convention were indeed America's *notables*—its wealthiest, most powerful attorneys, merchants, and landowners—all of them elected by propertied men of their states and districts. It seemed natural to most Americans for those who "owned" the country and who stood to gain the most from its prosperity to determine its destiny. Small and "middling" freeholders, therefore, almost always voted for men of great wealth who dominated the economy in their districts. Ultimately, every farm in America, every merchant house, and every craftsman depended on trade with larger entities that depended on the great merchant-banking firms such as House of Hancock in Boston or Willing, Morris & Company in Philadelphia. And as election day approached, John Hancock, Robert Morris, and the others reminded voters that the state's prosperity—and their livelihoods—depended on letting those with power and wealth control their government. As an added incentive, candidates plied voters with a bounty of food and drink at

State House Row [Philadelphia], 1778, by Rembrandt Peale. Many of the delegates who came to Philadelphia for the Constitutional Convention had come eleven years earlier to sign the Declaration of Independence.

rallies. George Washington had drenched voters with forty gallons of rum, twenty-six gallons of rum punch, thirty-four gallons of wine, and forty-three gallons of beer to win his first seat in the Virginia House of Burgesses—about half a gallon of spirits per vote.

On Thursday, May 17, 1787, Washington awoke in an ugly mood, still suffering arthritis in his shoulder and agonizing pains in his mouth and jaw from ill-fitting false teeth. Although South Carolina and New York delegates had arrived, the Convention still lacked a quorum, and Washington lost all patience, saying the absence of other delegates was "highly vexatious to those who are idly, & expensively spending their time here."[1]

Over the next week, enough delegates arrived from Massachusetts, New Jersey, and Delaware to produce a quorum of seven states. Washington made a point of collaring most of them at various dinners in his honor or theirs and drumming into their minds that he favored a new constitution creating a strong central government with "Legislative, Executive & Judiciary departments concentered."[2]

Although gentle of voice, he was nonetheless an intimidating figure—a near-giant at six feet, three inches tall and two hundred
pounds, who towered over most people of his era. Adding to his stat-
ure were his legendary horsemanship and courage in battle, which
combined with his genius as a military commander, scientist, in-
ventor, architect, scholar, and entrepreneur to place him in the
pantheon of heroes. He was not only the most revered figure in
America, he was one of the wealthiest, with control of more than
sixty-five thousand acres of lands in eastern and western Virginia,
more than three hundred slaves, and a vast agro-industrial enterprise
in and about Mount Vernon that included a fishery, a meat process-
ing plant, a textile mill, a gristmill, a smithy, and a distillery. "I fancy,"
said an onlooker who had visited Mount Vernon, "he is worth
£100,000 sterling [$6 million today], and lives at the rate of three or
four thousand a year [between $200,000 and $250,000 today]."[3]

By the time the Convention got under way, Washington was prepared to ignore the instructions of Congress, and he convinced many
others to follow suit. Instead of revising the Articles of Confederation, they would write a new constitution and lay plans for a new
national government consisting of three "supreme" branches: a legislature, an executive, and a judiciary.

With six states still absent, only twenty-nine men made their
way through the driving rain to the State House on May 25, and
Washington's commanding presence notwithstanding, the absence—
and apparent disinterest—of so many delegates left those who entered the hall pessimistic that they would succeed in revising the
Articles of Confederation as directed by Congress. The charming
Robert Morris changed everyone's mood, greeting each with the
practiced smile, hearty handshake, and warm words of the consummate merchant-banker. When they were seated, Morris called the
Convention to order and immediately nominated Washington to
preside—a particularly gracious move, according to James Madison:

> Doc[r] [Benjamin] Franklin alone could have been thought of as a
> competitor. The Doc[r] was himself to have made the nomination of
> General Washington, but the state of the weather and of his
> health confined him to his house. . . . General Washington was ac-
> cordingly unanimously elected . . . president of the Convention . . .

and conducted to the Chair . . . from which in a very emphatic manner he thanked the Convention for the honor they had conferred on him, reminded them of the novelty of the scene of business in which he was to act, lamented his want of better qualifications, and claimed the indulgence of the House towards the involuntary errors which his inexperience might occasion.[4]

It was vintage Washington—the towering hero, coloring his omnipotence with enough humility to evoke empathy as well as awe. Although he was president of the Convention, he and all the delegates knew that customary procedural rules would forbid his commenting on or entering debates; his role would be to preside, not participate. But at least three dozen delegates seated before him had served under him in the Revolutionary War and knew all too well how to discern Washington's pleasure or displeasure from his all-but-imperceptible nods, frowns, scowls, or smiles. He knew them, and they knew him—some, intimately. Four of them—Pennsylvania Speaker of the Assembly Thomas Mifflin, Virginia governor Edmund Randolph, Maryland congressman James McHenry, and New York attorney Alexander Hamilton—had served as close personal aides on his staff during the Revolutionary War. Thirteen had been officers in the Continental Army; thirteen others, officers in the militia. Seven delegates had served with Washington in the Continental Congress of 1774 or 1775 or both. The few delegates who were unfamiliar with his expressions would quickly learn to recognize their meaning—and more often than not act accordingly.

After an abbreviated session, the Convention adjourned for the weekend, and Washington spent the rest of the day and the following morning visiting almost every delegate in town. Everywhere he looked, he saw new houses and buildings rising amid a din of hammering and sawing. Philadelphia's fathers planned to make their city the center of the New World—and perhaps the entire world. On Saturday afternoon, Washington walked to the City Tavern, about four blocks away from the State House, to host a group of delegates at a private table in the Long Room, on the second floor—away from the crowded public bar on the ground floor. As delegates joined him for drinks, he again made clear his views on the type of government he expected the Convention to create. Although they expected him to sit at the head of the table, Washington was an inveterate listener and insisted on sitting in the middle, to hear the talk across from him and on his right and left. Unlike his appearance at the end of the war, Washington had recaptured most of the robust look of the outdoors man. Four years of private life on his beloved Mount Vernon had worked wonders: riding across the fields each morning; immersing himself in farm life; basking in the love of his wife, adoring family, and friends; delighting in fine foods and wines at his own table; and sharing the delights of song, dance, and theater with his wife—all combined to produce a glow about him that exuded enormous strength and confidence and all but symbolized the new nation of which he was unquestioned leader. After the sessions at the Constitutional Convention in Philadelphia, Washington's ever jolly friend Gouverneur Morris kept tavern talk from remaining serious too long. After a few cups, even the usually morose Madison often displayed an uncharacteristic smirk to relate a slightly bawdy tale that produced howls of laughter and won the warm approval of Washington and the others.

On Sunday, Washington went to the "Romish Church"—probably St. Mary's Roman Catholic Church, about four streets away from the Morris House. He returned to dine with the Morrises and spent the evening immersing himself in studies of ancient republics, including several installments of *The History of the Decline and Fall of the Roman Empire*, which Edward Gibbon had started publishing in 1776 and was still completing.

Although many of the seventy-four delegates who had won election to the Convention did not attend, those who did included the nation's most illustrious men—in effect, America's "aristocracy": Connecticut's Roger Sherman and Oliver Ellsworth; Delaware's John Dickinson; Georgia's Abraham Baldwin; Maryland's James McHenry and Daniel Carroll; Massachusetts's Elbridge Gerry and Rufus King; New Jersey's governor, William Livingston, and William Paterson; New York's Alexander Hamilton; North Carolina's Richard Caswell; Pennsylvania's Benjamin Franklin, Robert Morris, Gouverneur Morris, and James Wilson; South Carolina's John Rutledge, Charles Pinckney, and Charles Cotesworth Pinckney; and, of course, the charismatic Virginians with Washington, Madison, Mason, and Gov-

ernor Randolph. Apart from wealth and power, they boasted the best
education: twenty-one held college degrees—nine from Princeton,
four from Yale, and three from Harvard. Twenty-nine were or had
been lawyers or judges, and nearly all held political offices or had
served on Revolutionary War committees. Their average age was
forty-four, but four were under thirty and five were over sixty. Eighty-
one-year-old Benjamin Franklin was the oldest delegate, while the
youngest was New Jersey's Jonathan Dayton, who was still twenty-
seven.

James Madison declared that "there never was an assembly of
men, charged with a great & arduous trust, who were more pure in
their motives, or more exclusively or anxiously devoted to the object
committed to them than were the members of the Federal Convention of 1787, to the object of devising and proposing a constitutional
system which would . . . best secure the permanent liberty and happiness of their country." He called them "the best . . . talents the
States could make for the occasion."[5] Franklin called them "the most
August and respectable assembly" he had ever encountered.[6]

Only fifty-five delegates actually attended the Convention.
They sat five to six hours a day, six days a week, from May 25 until
September 17, except for a nine-day adjournment between July 29
and August 6 to let a committee arrange and edit the resolutions
into a readable draft of a constitution. New Hampshire's delegates
failed to arrive until July 23 and contributed nothing to the first
draft. Rhode Island did not elect any delegates and sent none. Two
of New York's three delegates walked out after about six weeks, leaving the state without enough delegates to vote.

Under Convention rules, each state had one vote, determined by
a majority of delegates in that state. An even division was recorded
as "divided" and would not count—nor would a vote from any state
with fewer than two delegates. Of all the rules adopted, the two most
important were the secrecy rule and a rule allowing delegates to
reconsider any previously accepted issue and change their votes.

Under the secrecy rule, only the secretary could keep the journal
of the Convention proceedings—with one exception. For reasons
that remain undocumented—and there is no record of a debate
or vote—the Convention allowed James Madison, one of Virginia's

delegates in the Confederation Congress, to take and transcribe notes of the proceedings and all speeches. To help prepare them for the Convention, Madison had produced two reports for delegates before the proceedings got under way: one on the history of confederacies from ancient times to the present, and the other on the problems of the Confederation of American States. He found it difficult to determine the reasons for the failure of most confederacies because they had either failed to keep or had lost the records of their proceedings. He determined, therefore, "to preserve as far as I could an exact account of what might pass at the [Constitutional] Convention" to provide for future generations "the fund of materials for the History of a Constitution on which would be staked the happiness of a people great even in its infancy, and possibly the cause of Liberty throughout the world." The Constitutional Convention obviously agreed.

Madison nonetheless kept his notes secret for his entire life to prevent enemies of constitutional government from taking any of the ideas discussed at the Convention out of context or distorting them to attack either the delegates who expressed them or the document they produced. In the course of Convention debates, many delegates changed their minds on various issues, accepting compromises in some cases or yielding to stronger arguments in other cases. The secrecy rule allowed them to do so freely, without fear of political or social consequences. As Madison put it, "In general it had appeared to me that it might be best to let the work be a posthumous one; or at least that its publication should be delayed till the Constitution should be well settled by practice & till a knowledge of the controversial part of the proceedings of its framers could be turned to no improper account." Madison died in 1836, after outliving all other delegates. His *Notes* were not published until 1840.[7]

"In pursuance of the task I had assumed," the Princeton-educated Virginian explained, "I chose a seat in front of the presiding member, with the other members on my right & left hands. In this favorable position for hearing all that passed, I noted in terms legible & in abbreviations & marks intelligible to myself what was read from the Chair or spoken by the members; and losing not a moment unnecessarily between the adjournment & reassembling of

James Madison. Often called the "father of the Constitution,"
Madison recorded *Notes of Debates in the Federal Convention of 1787*,
which provide the only complete record of the arguments and
compromises that led up to ratification. With Alexander Hamilton
and John Jay, he coauthored *The Federalist*, writing twenty-six of
the eighty-five essays affirming the benefits of the Constitution.

the Convention I was enabled to write out my daily notes. . . . It
happened also that I was not absent a single day, nor more than a
cassual [sic] fraction of an hour in any day."[8]

It was fortunate that Madison sat in the middle of the front
row—sometimes with his back to the president—to better see and
hear the delegates as he took notes. Had he sat elsewhere, many delegates might never have noticed him. Only five feet, two inches
tall according to some estimates (others say five feet, four inches),
Madison was so thin and shy that he all but dissolved in a crowded
room. Some ladies found him "mute," "cold," and even "stiff" at
social functions,[9] but his male colleagues hailed him as "a gentleman
of great modesty—with a remarkable sweet temper. He is easy and

unreserved among his acquaintance, and has a most agreeable style of conversation."[10]

Son of a prosperous Virginia planter with ten thousand acres and more than a hundred slaves, Madison had been a frail, sickly child who compensated by becoming a compulsive student. He completed his bachelor's degree at Princeton in two years instead of three, but paid the price for his exertions with a bout of depression that lasted a year and left him pale, timid, sullen-looking, and somewhat priggish. Intellectually, however, he towered over others. He knew it and so did they. Constitutional Convention delegates who didn't know him stared in disbelief at his childlike appearance beside Washington's massive frame, which stretched a foot above the little intellectual. But it was to Madison that Washington had turned to synthesize his ideas for a national government into a cohesive plan for presentation to the Convention. As a member of the Confederation Congress, Madison had railed at the national government's impotence, and he eagerly joined with Washington and other nationalists in seeking to give Congress powers to force states to pay their share of national expenses. In characterizing Madison, Georgia's William Pierce noted that "every Person seems to acknowledge his greatness. He blends together the profound politician and the scholar . . . and tho' he cannot be called an Orator, he is a most agreeable, eloquent, and convincing speaker . . . he always comes forward the best informed Man of any point in debate . . . he perhaps has the most correct knowledge of . . . the affairs of the United States . . . of any Man in the Union."[11]

The secrecy rule had a number of unintended consequences at the Constitutional Convention. In addition to sealing delegate lips as they left the hall, it also sealed all windows and doors as they entered and, within minutes, transformed the State House into a hothouse and added new meaning to the term "heated debate." The buzzing flies trapped at the windowpanes did not add to delegate comfort. The hall proved particularly uncomfortable for older delegates such as Franklin, whose crippling arthritis and gout made it excruciatingly painful to extricate himself from his seat and walk out for fresh air and other needs. To prevent eavesdropping, Washington posted sentries outside the doors of the hall, where they had a clear view of all windows.

There were many other important rules, of course. One called for strict decorum, with "each delegate to address only the Chair and whilst he shall be speaking, none shall pass between them, or hold discourse with one another, or read a book, pamphlet or paper, printed or manuscript—and of two members rising at the same time, the President shall name him who shall be heard first."[12] Still another rule set reasonable limits on debate, with no member allowed to speak more than twice on the same question "without special leave . . . and not the second time, before every other, who had been silent, shall be heard, if he choose to speak on the subject."[13]

Most of the delegates did their best to obey the rules. Washington did so to the letter, even writing in his diary, "Attending in Convention and nothing being suffered to transpire [and] no minutes of the proceedings has [sic] been, or will be inserted in this diary."[14] But some delegates could not resist leaking news—sometimes just a kindhearted word to wives, relatives, and friends, but more often a politically motivated communication to avowed opponents of nationalism. From the opening day, New York's Robert Yates kept Governor George Clinton informed of the proceedings, while Virginia's George Mason arranged for details of the proceedings to reach Patrick Henry and Richard Henry Lee. Although the *Pennsylvania Herald* complained that "circumspection and secrecy mark the proceedings,"[15] the *Herald* as well as other newspapers routinely reported week-to-week progress of the Convention and the main issues under debate—if not the bitter words. Antinationalists tried provoking public disturbances outside the State House by calling the Convention a "dark conclave" where the "wealthy and ambitious . . . think they have the right to lord it over their fellow creatures."[16] Philadelphia newspapers, however, published enough nationalist material to counter such charges. "It is agreed on all hands, that our Convention are framing a wise and free government for us," wrote "Civis" in the *Pennsylvania Packet* a month after the Convention had started. "The present Federal Convention," wrote the *Philadelphia Independent Gazetteer* two days later, "is happily composed of men who are qualified from education, experience and profession for the great business assigned to them."[17]

On Tuesday, May 29, Washington ensured presentation of the Virginia Plan as the first business of the Convention by recognizing

Virginia governor Edmund Randolph. Randolph was slow to rise and, once on his feet, he hesitated for what seemed an eternity before beginning his oration. The consummate Virginia gentleman, Randolph despised and avoided conflict, seeking instead to promote calm accord with his "harmonious voice . . . and striking manners."[18] Born to a long line of English noblemen who had served as kings' attorneys, he had attended the College of William and Mary and studied law under his father, who later fled to England with his close friend Lord Dunmore, Virginia's last British governor, after the outbreak of the Revolution. Edmund moved into the home of his renowned uncle Peyton Randolph, Virginia's first attorney general and the first president of the Continental Congress. The then twenty-two-year-old Edmund went to Cambridge, Massachusetts, to serve as an aide to George Washington, but a year later, Edmund's uncle died, and as the oldest living Randolph male, he returned to Virginia to assume leadership of his family's vast properties, as well as the "natural" role of Randolph elders in state political affairs. Though only twenty-three years old, he assumed his uncle's position as state attorney general and, at the same time, served as mayor of Williamsburg—then the state capital. In 1786, at age thirty-three, he won election as governor of Virginia, and a year later he came to Philadelphia favoring a few revisions of the Articles of Confederation and a limited expansion in the powers of the Confederation Congress. Assuming that Washington, Madison, and the other Virginians had come with the same intent, he had attended social functions while Madison and other Virginia delegates had met for two to three hours each day drawing up details of the plan Washington wanted Randolph to present to the Convention.

When Randolph saw the plan for the first time, he blanched. It called for nothing less than scrapping the Articles of Confederation and replacement of the Confederation with an entirely new government. Although shocked by the document, Randolph realized he could not refuse to present it without creating an embarrassing scene. Instead, he scribbled some conciliatory remarks and all but apologized to the Convention for what he was about to present to them. According to Madison, Randolph "expressed his regret that it should fall to him . . . to open the great subject of their mission. But . . . his colleagues . . . had imposed this task on him." Couching his presentation in the most elegant language of the Virginia aristocracy, Randolph began by enumerating the defects of the Articles of Confederation, showing how those defects and the impotence of the unicameral Confederation Congress had placed the country at risk.

"In speaking of the defects of the Confederation," Madison said of the ever-cautious Randolph, "he professed a high respect for its authors, and considered them, as having done all that patriots could do, in the then infancy of the science, of constitutions, & of confederacies."[19]

In presenting the fifteen resolutions of the Virginia Plan, Randolph diluted the harsh tones of the first resolution to read, "Resolved that the Articles of Confederation ought to be so corrected & enlarged to accomplish the objects proposed by their institution; namely, common defence, security of liberty and general welfare."[20]

He left the remaining fourteen resolutions intact, however. They had evolved from the "Washington Plan" that Washington had formulated during the Revolutionary War and that Madison subsequently embraced, expanded, and refined. They called for replacing the unicameral congress with "a *national* government . . . consisting of a *supreme* Legislative, Executive & Judiciary."[21] The national legislature in the new government was to be a bicameral body and the most powerful of three branches of government, with sole power to elect both the executive and the judges sitting on the Supreme Court and all lower courts. Of the two houses of Congress, the lower house would be elected by the "people of the several states," with the number of congressmen (and consequently their votes) proportionate to the number of each state's "free inhabitants." The lower house, in turn, would elect members of the upper house, choosing from nominees selected by each state legislature, thus leaving each state government with some say in the makeup of the new central government. The executive in the new government would serve only one term in office; judges would serve indefinitely "during good behaviour."

The Virginia Plan also proposed a "council of revision," made up of members of the executive and judiciary branches and empowered to veto legislation and temporarily check congressional powers, but Congress could override the veto. Above all, the Virginia Plan empowered the new Congress "to negative all laws passed by the several

Edmund Randolph. Virginia governor Randolph
came to the Constitutional Convention a
committed Federalist and introduced the Virginia
Plan, which eventually formed the basis for the
finished Constitution.

States contravening . . . the articles of Union; and to call forth the
force of the Union agst any member of the Union failing to fulfill its
duty under the articles thereof."[22] The laws of Congress would be
supreme, and Congress could use military force, if necessary, to
enforce them in every state. The plan was Washington's revenge for
the fiscal mistreatment he and his army had suffered with the refusal
of state legislatures to provide his army with adequate funding during
the Revolutionary War.

"Persuaded I am," Washington wrote to his son-in-law David
Stuart,* "that the primary cause of all our disorders lies in the different State Governments, and in the tenacity of that power which

---

*Stuart had married Eleanor Calvert Custis, the widow of John Parke Custis, Martha
Washington's son by her first marriage, and Washington's stepson.

pervades the whole of their systems. Whilst independent sovereignty is so ardently contended for . . . incompatibility in the laws of different States, and disrespect to those of the general government must render the situation of this great Country weak, inefficient and disgraceful. It has already done so, almost to the final dissolution of it—weak at home and disregarded abroad is our present condition, and contemptible enough it is."[23]

Convention delegates sat in silence after Randolph's presentation, stunned by the sweep of his proposals. Randolph himself was none too happy. The Virginia Plan represented nothing less than the overthrow of the legally constituted American government. In proposing an entirely new government, it went well beyond the mandate of Congress to revise the Articles of Confederation. It would not only establish a new federal government, it would also strip the states of their sovereignty—and many delegates at the Convention of their powers to rule their states and profit from tax collections.

Southerners and northerners alike cringed at the word "supreme" to describe the national government. Southern planters envisioned federal troops marching across their lands as the British had done, and northern merchants shuddered at the vision of federal customs officers funneling import-export duties into the national treasury instead of state repositories. Rather than risk permitting a vote on the plan, the Convention resolved to convert itself into "a Committee of the Whole House . . . to consider the propositions moved by Mr. Randolph."[24] The parliamentary maneuver moved the debate out of the Convention into a committee—albeit a "committee" made up of every Convention delegate—but nonetheless a committee, with powers limited to "reporting" its recommendations to the Convention rather than enacting them. In effect, the move prevented any votes on the Virginia Plan from becoming final. Each vote in committee could be changed, giving delegates time to reconsider before their final vote in the Convention. The tack was cunning, complex, and clever; many Founding Fathers may well have been farmers, but they were brilliant farmers. Washington was delighted by the maneuver, because it relieved him of having to preside and allowed him to take a seat among the delegates. All he did, though, was listen, smile when he approved and scowl when he disapproved, and delegates seldom failed to glance at the former commander in chief to gain a sense of his sentiments on an issue.

Washington spent that evening at a concert, but at a party the following evening, he was able to obtain the tenor of delegate feelings. "The business of this Convention is as yet too much in embryo to form any opinion of the result," he wrote to Thomas Jefferson in Paris.

> Much is expected from it by some—but little by others—and nothing by a few—That something is necessary, all will agree; for the situation of the General Governmt (if it can be called a governmt) is shaken to its foundation—and liable to be overset by every blast. In a word, it is at an end, and unless a remedy is soon applied, anarchy & confusion will inevitably ensue.[25]

When delegates reconvened the following morning as a committee of the whole, South Carolina's wealthy Charles Pinckney, a Revolutionary War hero and prominent attorney, demanded "to know of Mr. Randolph whether he meant to abolish state government altogether." Randolph was devastated by the attack, but did not know how to extract himself from the center of the controversy. He could not suddenly disassociate himself from Washington and the other Virginians without humiliating himself. Pinckney's second cousin, the equally wealthy Charles Cotesworth Pinckney—also an attorney and war hero—challenged Randolph's right to propose the Virginia Plan, all but shouting that "the act of Cong[ress] recommending the Convention" did not "authorize a discussion of a System founded on different principles from the Federal Constitution [i.e., the Articles of Confederation]." The Virginia Plan, he argued, violated the mandate of Congress to "revise" the Articles of Confederation. To violate that mandate would represent a usurpation of authority not granted by Congress or the Articles of Confederation.

Elbridge Gerry, a Massachusetts merchant who had signed the Declaration of Independence, agreed, protesting that "it is questionable not only whether this convention can propose an government totally different or whether Congress itself would have a right to pass such a resolution as that before the house. The commission from Massachusetts empowers the deputies to proceed agreeably to the recommendation of Congress. This [is] the foundation of the convention. If we have a right to pass this resolution [the Virginia Plan] we have a right to annihilate the confederation."[26]

Scattered applause greeted Gerry as delegates suddenly realized that Washington and the Virginians had redefined the mission of the Convention. It was clear that they indeed intended to "annihilate the Confederation" and replace it with a new, "supreme" federal government.

"I cannot conceive of a government in which there can exist two supremes [state and federal]," Pennsylvania's Gouverneur Morris declared in support of the Virginia Plan. "A federal government which each party may violate at pleasure cannot answer the purpose. . . . We had better take a supreme [federal] government now than a despot twenty years hence—for come he must."

One by one, delegates began attacking various elements of the plan. Elbridge Gerry challenged the idea of popular voting. Harvard-educated, the forty-three-year-old Gerry had inherited his father's mercantile and shipbuilding enterprise that controlled the great fishing fleet out of Marblehead in northern Massachusetts. As a member of the Continental Congress, he had signed the Declaration of Independence and put his fleet to work privateering and smuggling arms to patriot forces during the Revolution. A longtime member of Congress, he earned the admiration of colleagues for his fervent patriotism and steadfast gentlemanliness, but some disdain for his inconsistency. On first hearing, he had expressed strong support for the Virginia Plan, but now suddenly reversed course inexplicably, declaring that it would grant too much authority to the people.

"The evils we experience," Gerry argued, "flow from the excess of democracy. The people do not want [lack] virtue, but are the dupes of pretended patriots . . . daily misled into the most baneful measures and opinions by false reports circulated by designing men."[27]

Enraged delegates jumped to challenge Gerry, with Virginia's George Mason arguing "strongly for an election of the larger branch [of Congress] by the people. It was to be the grand depository of the democratic principle of the Gov[ernmen]t. It was so to speak our House of Commons." Mason went on to demand that the Convention add a bill of rights to the document that would "attend to the rights of every class of people." A plantation owner who depended on slaves, he assumed what seemed to be an incongruous position, expressing

> wonderment at the indifference of the superior classes of society
> . . . considering that however affluent their circumstances or ele-
> vated their circumstances might be, the course of a few years not
> only might but surely would distribute their posterity throughout
> the lowest classes of Society. Every selfish motive therefore . . .
> ought to recommend such a system of policy as would provide no
> less carefully for the rights and happiness of the lowest than of the
> highest orders of Citizens.[28]

Southern planters cheered his disingenuous position, knowing that if slaves were counted as part of the population on which representation in Congress would be based, their owners would gain a majority in the lower house of the new government. As Connecticut's Oliver Ellsworth would later comment, "Mr. Mason has himself about three hundred slaves, and lives in Virginia, where it is found by prudent management they can breed and raise slaves faster than they want for their own use, and could supply the deficiency in Georgia and South Carolina."[29]

And that was just the beginning of the struggle.

In the days that followed, they argued about every resolution and almost every word and punctuation mark, including whether to include the word "supreme" in the phrase "supreme Legislative, Executive & Judiciary." They finally agreed on popular election of the lower house, but not on ways to elect the upper house. Some insisted that state legislatures elect members of the upper house; others demanded that the lower house elect the upper house. Unable to reach a compromise, they scowled at each other angrily and finally postponed voting.

Then came the explosive question of how many votes to give each state in each house. All agreed on proportionate representation for the lower house, and the big states all favored the same system in the upper house. But the concept of proportionate representation in both houses outraged delegates from small states, each of which had parity under the one-state, one-vote rule in the Confederation Congress. George Read threatened to pull Delaware out of the Convention before allowing any change, and Gunning Bedford—also from Delaware—went a step further, charging the big states with trying to "crush the smaller states."

"Sooner than be ruined," he pledged, the smaller states would find "foreign powers who shall take us by hand. I say this not to threaten or intimidate, but that we should reflect seriously before we act."[30] Taken aback by the obvious threat of civil war, Washington bunched his eyebrows and nodded to his friend the brilliant Gouverneur Morris of Pennsylvania to intervene and calm the tone of the debate. Although unrelated by blood, Morris was a close friend of and had worked with Robert Morris at the Bank of North America, a national bank of sorts that Congress had chartered to help finance the Revolution.

"This country must be united," Morris pleaded in his hypnotic, mellifluous voice. "If persuasion does not unite it, the sword will. . . . The scenes of horror attending civil commotion can not be described, and the conclusion of them will be worse. . . . The stronger party will then make traytors of the weaker; and the Gallows & Halter will finish the work of the sword. How far foreign powers would be ready to take part in the confusions, [I] would not say." Although he represented the large state of Pennsylvania, Morris urged all delegates to "take out the teeth of the serpents" from the debate and accommodate their ideas "to the true interest of man, instead of being circumscribed within the narrow compass of a particular Spot. . . . Who can say whether he himself, much less whether his children, will the next year be an inhabitant of this or that State."[31]

The issue of lifetime appointments for judges provoked a chorus of objections that provoked Franklin to rise from his seat, slowly, painfully. The old man's voice crackled that lifetime appointments of judges had worked well in Scotland. He explained that by selecting the ablest members of their profession as judges for life, lawyers "get rid of the best lawyers and can then share their practice among themselves."[32] After the roars of laughter subsided, the Convention approved lifetime appointments for the Supreme Court.

3
The Great Compromise

WITH THE CONVENTION STALEMATED over congressional voting, Roger Sherman, the mayor of New Haven, Connecticut, proposed a compromise. The son of a farmer, Sherman had started life as a shoemaker, but "despising the lowness of his condition, he turned Almanack maker" and built an enormously prosperous mercantile enterprise that earned him enough political influence to win appointment as a judge. At sixty-six he was the second-oldest delegate after Franklin, but one of the least popular—indeed, "the oddest shaped character I ever remember to have met with," according to Georgia's William Pierce. "He is awkward, un-meaning, and unaccountably strange in his manner." Pierce called Sherman's train of thinking "deep and comprehensive," but "the oddity of his address, the vulgarisms that accompany his public speaking and that strange New England cant . . . make everything that is connected with him grotesque and laughable."[1] Pierce and others resented Sherman's presentation of his every idea as if it were a revelation from God:

"Let voting in the lower house be proportionate to each state's population," Sherman suggested in his distinctive, Solomon-like tones, "and give each state parity—one vote—in the upper house. Otherwise a few large states will rule. The smaller states would never agree to [a] plan on any other principle than an equality of suffrage in this branch."[2]

Incredibly, the delegates voted down the former shoemaker by one vote—more, perhaps, because of personal dislike of the man than of his suggested compromise. As all sides refused to budge, New

Roger Sherman. A Connecticut shoemaker who built a prosperous mercantile enterprise and became a mayor and a judge, Sherman was a voice of compromise at the Constitutional Convention.

York's Alexander Hamilton rose to call for voting by proportionate representation in both houses. His motion carried by one vote, but Elbridge Gerry of Massachusetts made it clear that the motion would not stand.

"Why," he asked, "should the blacks, who were property in the South, be in the rule of representation more than the Cattle & horses of the North?"[3] Rufus King, also of Massachusetts, agreed, saying that the four New England states had more white people than the southern states and fewer representatives and that "no principle would justify giving them [the southern states] a majority."[4] Gouverneur Morris moved that voting be based on only free inhabitants, but went on to condemn slave states for the misery and poverty they inflicted. When the applause subsided, South Carolina's governor, John Rutledge, the owner of a great plantation and a hero of the Revolution, stood and proclaimed that humanity had nothing to do with the question. "The true question at present is whether the Southern States shall or shall not be parties to the Union. If the Northern States consult their interest, they will not oppose the increase of Slaves which will increase the commodities of which they will become the carriers."[5]

The Convention also divided on whether to invest executive powers in one man or three or more. Veering away from his fellow Virginians, Edmund Randolph called a single executive the "fetus of monarchy," while Charles Pinckney said a one-man executive would render the office "a monarchy of the worst kind;"[6] Gerry favored a multiple executive, saying that a Council [would] give weight & inspire confidence."[7] The Convention again postponed a decision and turned instead to the executive's term of office—three years, seven, nine. . . . No decision.

"The *mode of appointing* the Executive was the next question," Madison scribbled in his notes.[8] Pennsylvania's James Wilson, a Scot by birth, called for popular elections. He lost. Congress would elect the executive—for seven years.

But at what salary? the Scot retorted.

Although too weak to stand, Franklin nonetheless gained recognition and began to argue for limiting executive pay to "necessary expenses" and not paying any "salary, stipend fee or reward whatsoever for their services." The old man stopped suddenly and seemed unable to continue.

"He said that being very sensible of the effect of age on his memory," Madison jotted in his notes, "he had been unwilling to trust to that for the observations which seemed to support his motion, and had reduced them to writing, that he might with the permission of the [Convention] read instead of speaking them." The Convention agreed, but it was evident that his eyes were not up to the task, and his colleague James Wilson offered to read the old man's words. They were eloquent—more so, perhaps, because of Wilson's pronounced Scottish accent:

> Sir, there are two passions which have a powerful influence on the affairs of men. These are ambition and avarice; the love of power and the love of money. . . . And this alone occasioned great convulsions, actual civil wars, ending either in dethroning of the Princes, or enslaving the people. Generally . . . the revenues of princes constantly increas[e], and we see that they are never satisfied, but always in want of more. The more people are discontented with the oppression of taxes, the greater need the prince has of money to distribute among his partizans and pay the troops that are to suppress all resistance and enable him to plunder at pleasure.
>
> It may be imagined by some . . . an Utopian Idea . . . [but] have we not seen, the great and most important of our offices, that of General of our armies executed for eight years together without

Benjamin Franklin. The oldest delegate to the
Constitutional Convention, Franklin injected much-
needed humor into the debates, but is said to have
"shed a tear" when he signed the finished document.

the smallest salary, by a Patriot whom I will not now offend by any
other praise. . . . * And shall we doubt finding three or four other
men in all the U.States, with public spirit enough to bear sitting in
peaceful Council for perhaps an equal term, merely to . . . see that
our laws are duly executed. Sir, I have a better opinion of our
Country. I think we shall never be without sufficient number of
wise and good men to undertake and execute well the office in
question.[9]

---

*George Washington had refused "pecuniary considerations" as commander in chief of
the Continental Army during the Revolutionary War, asserting to Congress, "I do not
wish to make any profit from . . . this Arduous employment."—Address to the Continental Congress, June 16, 1775.

Although New York's Alexander Hamilton was quick to second Franklin's proposal, the Convention postponed the issue. "It was treated with great respect," Madison commented, "but rather for the author of it, than from any apparent conviction of its expediency and practicability." The Convention was concerned with the future and had relegated Franklin to history.

The debate over the Virginia Plan raged for two weeks, with delegates lunging, parrying, dodging, and retreating like swordsmen: "Mr. Wilson renewed his declarations . . ."; "Col. Mason favors the idea but thinks it impracticable . . ."; "Mr. Williamson asks . . ."; "Mr. Gerry doubts . . ."; "Mr. Madison disliked . . ."; "Mr. Bedford opposed . . ."; "Mr. Rutledge was by no means disposed."

"The words 'one or more' were struck out."

"The people will think we are leaning too much towards monarchy."

"But why might not a Cataline or a Cromwell arise in this country?"[10]

One of the most explosive debates centered on use of force by the national government on a "delinquent" state that failed to submit to "supreme" rule of national government. Madison condemned the provision as unjust "when applied to people collectively and not individually. A union of States containing such an ingredient seemed to provide for its own destruction. The use of force against a State would look more like a declaration of war than an infliction of punishment, and would probably be considered by the party attacked as a dissolution of all previous compacts by which it might be bound." At Madison's urging, delegates postponed further debate.[11]

In the heat of debate—and the hall—some delegates lost their patience—none more than Washington, who discovered that one delegate had carelessly let his notes on the Virginia Plan fall from his pocket in the hallway of the State House, where Pennsylvania's Thomas Mifflin—a general during the Revolution—had found them and turned them over to his former commander in chief as they walked into the Convention. Washington was furious.

"Gentlemen," he growled when he took his place, "I am sorry to find that some one Member of this Body, has been so neglectful to the secrets of the Convention as to drop in the State House a copy of their proceedings, which by accident was picked up and delivered to me this Morning. I know not whose Paper it is, but there it is." Washington tossed the paper on the table brusquely. "Let him who owns it take it," he snapped, and, according to Georgia's William Pierce, "bowed, picked up his Hat, and quitted the room with a dignity so severe that every Person seemed alarmed."[12] No one ever dared reclaim the notes.

Washington took his mind off the infuriating events at the Convention by writing longingly and lovingly to his beloved wife, Martha, whom he always addressed as "My Dearest," and then to his nephew George Augustine Washington, who was overseeing affairs at Mount Vernon in his uncle's absence. Washington missed the farm almost as much as he missed his family. He wrote page after page, each an ever more satisfying distraction from the grueling business of the Convention. An entire page cautioned "against turning the furrow from the drilled Corn, especially after it has got to any size. I think the drilled Corn at Morris's last year was injured thereby—and to this it was, that I inclined so strongly to the harrows; as I expected they would both weed, and stir the ground without throwing it ei[ther] from, or to the corn."[13]

As debate raged over the shape of the new government, delegates grew increasingly mean-spirited, often losing their tempers—and almost their sanity. They rejected good motions, yielded to bad ones, postponed both good and bad. On Wednesday, June 13, the Committee of the Whole, consisting of all Convention delegates, finally reported on the Virginia Plan to the Convention—that is, themselves. It was a wearying process, and Washington's behind-the-scenes efforts to produce agreement—at City Tavern and at various dinners at the Morris mansion—yielded few results. The committee agreed "that a National Government ought to be established, consisting of a supreme Legislative, Executive & Judiciary" and that the Legislature would consist of two branches—one of them popularly elected, the other elected by the state legislatures. Both branches could originate legislation, and all national laws would supersede or "negative" state laws. Voting in both houses would be "in proportion to the whole number of white & other free citizens & inhabitants of every age sex and condition, including those bound in servitude . . . & three fifths of all other persons [i.e., slaves] . . . except Indians not paying taxes in each State." The national legislature would elect the national executive "to consist of a single person . . . for a term of seven years . . . ineligible for a second time & removeable on impeachment and conviction of malpractices or neglect of duty—to receive a fixed stipend." The national judiciary would consist of "one supreme tribunal," with judges appointed by the upper house of the national legislature. The legislature would be able to create lower courts at its discretion. The report asked that provisions be made for amending the Articles of Confederation.

Before anyone could respond, New Jersey attorney general William Paterson shot to his feet to lead the small states, whose delegates refused to countenance the loss of voting parity with big states in the new Congress. Princeton-educated like Madison, Paterson proposed his own New Jersey Plan as a substitute for the Virginia Plan. Instead of creating a new government, the New Jersey Plan adhered strictly to the original congressional mandate to the Constitutional Convention, with nine proposed resolutions that would leave the Confederation in place, with voting parity among the states in Congress. But the plan gave Congress new powers—to raise taxes and to regulate foreign and interstate commerce. It also added a multiple executive with no veto powers over legislation. Like the Virginia Plan, it called for Congress to elect members of the court and the executive. It also espoused the principle of supremacy of national over state laws and, assuming that Washington himself would be the first president and never misuse his powers, it gave the national executive the right to use force to ensure state obedience to national law.

Now there was a second plan of government on the floor— before the Convention had voted on the first or even resolved what parts of the first plan to accept or reject. The process of the Convention was spiraling into the same abyss of futility that had emasculated the Congress of the Confederation it was trying to replace. Washington, Hamilton, Madison, and the others who had worked so hard to organize the Convention raged at the prospect of failure. All knew they had to act to save it.

After Paterson presented the New Jersey Plan, Hamilton cast a glance and instantly gained Washington's eye. Each knew the other intimately; they had maintained a close, virtually familial relationship for more than ten years. Although Washington had met Hamilton during the retreat from Harlem Heights, it was after the twenty-two-year-old artillery captain proved his valor at successive battles in Trenton and Princeton that Washington invited him to join his general staff. After Hamilton's daring helped capture more than one thousand Hessians and two hundred British troops, Washington is said to have exulted, "It is a fine fox chase my boys,"[14] and soon made Hamilton his "principal and most confidential aide."[15]

Like Washington himself, Hamilton had lost a parent at twelve. Born on the island of Nevis in the Caribbean, he came to New York alone, with no family, and Washington, in his heart, "adopted" him, treating him like a son and eventually giving him a key field command at the decisive Battle of Yorktown. Hamilton was handsome, with correct dress and bearing, intelligent, hardworking, responsible, fearless, and brave under fire—every inch the soldier Washington had aspired to be as a young man and became. After the war, Hamilton studied law, then worked assiduously as a member of Congress to reform the Confederation, and Washington named him to the three-man committee that wrote the Convention's rules.

As Hamilton and Washington glanced at each other in the Convention, each knew the meaning of the other's facial expression—like any father and son: They would meet and confer. But how? Each plotted a possible way. They would be too conspicuous at the City Tavern; it would have to be a quick word or two, off to the side at one of the dinners or teas Washington attended each afternoon with other prominent delegates. Hamilton was convinced that only a bold move would shock the Convention out of its deadlock—akin to Washington's thrust across the Delaware, or Hamilton's own heroics at Princeton, Trenton, Monmouth, and Yorktown. Washington agreed and urged Hamilton to act. With Washington's plan of national union hanging in the balance, Hamilton asked Washington for the floor on Monday morning, June 18, and began a six-hour verbal barrage that created as much havoc among the delegates as any shots he had fired during the Revolution. His presentation was all the more startling because he had said next to nothing at the Convention until then. He even began his attack in soft, apologetic whispers of "respect to others whose superior abilities age & experience rendered him unwilling to bring forward ideas dissimilar to theirs." Motivated by what he called "the crisis . . . which now marked our affairs . . . it would be criminal not to come forward."

He then went on to insult both the Virginia and the New Jersey plans, and repeat all the arguments for and against each of them—all but mocking the delegates who had uttered them during the previous three weeks.

"The general power"—Hamilton's words sliced through the hall's thick atmosphere—"whatever be its form, if it preserves itself, it must swallow up the State powers. Otherwise it will be swallowed up by them."

Then, as if talking to recalcitrant children, he paused between each word: "Two . . . sovereign . . . powers . . . can . . . not . . . co-exist . . . within . . . the . . . same . . . limits."

Delegate arguments—he sighed after a long pause—had "led him to despair that a Republican Government could be established. . . . Give all power to the many, they will oppress the few; give all power to the few, they will oppress the many."

But Hamilton had a solution. Calling the English model of government "the best in the world," he said he doubted "whether anything short of it would do in America." He urged indirect election of a monarch to serve for life and creation of a bicameral legislature, with the Senate, or upper house, chosen for life by electors, and an Assembly "elected by the people to serve for three years." He suggested creating an inferior federal court in each state and a Supreme Court with twelve judges serving for life on good behavior. He urged abolition of all state military forces, with "the Militia of all the States to be under the sole and exclusive direction of the United States, the officers of which to be appointed by them."[16]

Most delegates sat silently after Hamilton's speech—stunned, red-faced with rage at the impudence of the thirty-two-year-old New Yorker—indeed, one of the youngest delegates there—and foreign-born at that. Only Pennsylvania's Gouverneur Morris applauded, his

Alexander Hamilton. A brave and trusted aide of Washington
during the Revolution, Hamilton proposed a constitutional
monarchy at the Constitutional Convention and shocked
delegates into accepting the compromises that led to ratification.
Coauthor of *The Federalist* with James Madison and John Jay,
Hamilton wrote fifty-one of the eighty-five essays that affirmed
the benefits of the new Constitution.

solitary clapping reverberating eerily across the hall. A New York–
born aristocrat who out-Britished the British in his tone of voice and
cutting wit, he had been the victim of a horrible scalding as a child
that left him with a crippled arm and kept him out of the army during the war. To make matters worse, a terrible carriage accident as a
young man forced him to undergo amputation of his leg at the knee.
While recovering and learning to maneuver his wooden peg leg, a
friend tried to console him by predicting that "an event so melancholy . . . would have a good effect on his morals."

"My good Sir," Morris snapped back, "you argue . . . so clearly the advantages of being without legs, I am tempted to part with the other."[17]

Born at the Lordship of Manor of the three-thousand-acre Morrisania, on the mainland north of Manhattan Island, Morris was superbly well educated, superbly rich, and superbly aristocratic, agreeing with every Tory principle except the British monarch's right to tax Morrisania. With his friend John Jay, he earned a bachelor's degree from King's College (later, Columbia), went on to study law, then helped Jay write the New York State constitution and became a leader in abolishing slavery in New York.

"Mr. Gouverneur Morris," said Georgia's William Pierce, "is one of those Genius's in whome every species of talents combine to render him conspicuous and flourishing in public debate:—He winds through all the mazes of rhetoric, and throws around such a glare that he charms, captivates, and leads away the senses of all who hear him. . . . No Man has more wit."[18] The embodiment of a bon vivant, Morris loved fine foods, fine wines, laughter, good fellowship, and women—especially women.

"I have naturally a taste for pleasure," he admitted to all, and, for reasons only he and they could know, ladies had naturally a taste for him. He was seldom without a lady friend. Indeed, gossips insisted that his carriage accident had resulted from his hasty retreat from a lady's home at the unexpected arrival of her husband. "I have heard," John Jay is said to have teased his friend, "that a certain married woman after much use of your legs was the occasion of your losing one."[19]

A fierce supporter of Washington and the patriot cause during the Revolution, Morris made a courageous visit to Valley Forge to ascertain the army's needs for the Bank of North America and report to Congress. His effort—and their laughter-filled dinner together—endeared him to Washington for life. Despite his republican rhetoric, Morris, like many "republicans" at the Convention, loathed the idea of popular rule and responded enthusiastically to Hamilton's speech, calling it "the most able and impressive" he had ever heard.[20] He was all but alone in his opinion. Hamilton not only received almost no support, his enemies would use his speech against him the rest of his life to charge him with supporting the return of

Gouverneur Morris. The brilliant New York–born lawyer used his writing skills to produce the final, almost poetic version of the Constitution, including a clever closing paragraph that made the Constitutional Convention vote seem unanimous.

monarchism and, worse, the British monarchy. But Hamilton knew exactly what he was doing and, in the end, his courage in adopting so Swiftian a debating tactic had its desired effect. It startled delegates into recognizing that they would either have to shift positions toward a compromise in which each would win and each lose something, or they would all lose and win nothing. To the delight of Madison and the Virginians, the Convention responded to Hamilton's speech by rejecting the New Jersey Plan and returning its focus to the Virginia Plan—in effect, accepting Washington's demands for a second American Revolution, with an overthrow of the existing Confederation and its replacement by a new and powerful federal government.

On June 29, a month after the Convention had started, Hamilton returned to New York temporarily to attend to his law office and found himself the target of vicious rumors in the press. One rumor had him leading a plot by nationalist delegates at the Convention to raise England's duke of York* to power in America. Hamilton retaliated in New York's *Daily Advertiser* with a venomous attack on New York governor George Clinton for plotting to undermine the work of the Convention for personal gain and exhibiting "greater attachment to his *own power* than to the *public good.*"[21]

Federalist newspapers joined the attack, with Philadelphia's *Independent Gazetteer* declaring that "our Convention are framing a wise and free government for us.—This government will be opposed *only* by our *Civil Officers,* who are afraid of new arrangements taking place, which shall jostle them out of office.—If these men are wise, they will be quiet, by which means they may succeed to their old offices—but if they are not, they may, probably, share the fate of the loyalists in the beginning of the late war."[22] A week later, the newspaper printed a warning that officeholders who continue "to excite prejudices against the new federal government" should "expect to wear a coat of tar and feathers."[23]

*   *   *

---

*The duke of York is the king's (in this case, George III's) second son.

Three days after Hamilton had left for New York, the small states and large states reentered the Convention lists to battle over voting parity in the proposed upper house, and Washington let it be known that unless they began compromising, he would quit the Convention and issue a report to the American people charging delegates with incompetence and lack of patriotism—an accusation that would almost certainly renew farmers' rebellions in many states. The delegates not only stood to lose their power, many might see their palatial mansions burned to the ground—much as some British governors had seen their properties destroyed at the beginning of the Revolution.

"I *almost* dispair of seeing a favourable issue to the proceedings of the Convention, and do therefore repent having had any agency in the business," Washington wrote to Hamilton, repeating the frightening words he had whispered to delegates at City Tavern.

> The Men who oppose a strong & energetic government are, in my opinion, narrow minded politicians, or are under the influence of local views. The apprehension expressed by them that the *people* will not accede to the form proposed is the *ostensible*, not the *real* cause of the opposition. . . . I am sorry you went away—I wish you were back. The crisis is equally important and alarming, and no opposition under such circumstances should discourage exertions till the signature is fixed.[24]

Theorizing that Washington may well have helped author Hamilton's "monarchic" proposals, some delegates began edging toward compromise. As their first step, they reconsidered Roger Sherman's Connecticut Compromise, which they had rejected on June 11. As three large states—Virginia, Massachusetts, and Pennsylvania—edged toward compromise with three small states—Connecticut, New Jersey, and Delaware—New York's two remaining delegates—both Antifederalists—stomped out in protest, leaving only ten states in attendance. To make matters worse, the two New Yorkers violated the secrecy rule of the Convention by reporting all details of Convention proceedings to New York governor George Clinton, whom Hamilton blamed for the walkout. Clinton had, in fact, held his office for ten years and accumulated enormous power and wealth that he feared he would lose if a strong national government acceded to office.

On July 16 the remaining delegates in Philadelphia put aside their personal dislikes of the man and adopted Roger Sherman's Connecticut Compromise and solved the hitherto insoluble problem of voting in the two houses by establishing proportionate representation in the lower house and parity in the upper house, but giving the lower house sole right to originate appropriations legislation. Each state in the lower house would cast votes proportionate to the total of its free population and three-fifths of its slave population, while each state in the upper house would have but one vote, giving the small states parity with large states. But the South wanted more—a requirement of a two-thirds vote in the Senate for ratification of all treaties with foreign nations. Southerners had not forgotten that only two years earlier, northern states in Congress had almost ceded American navigation rights on the Mississippi River to Spain—rights that were "essential to the prosperity and happiness of the western inhabitants" of Virginia and the other southern states, whose western portions extended to the Mississippi River. Although the northern majority in Congress had approved the treaty by a bare majority, the Articles of Confederation had protected southern interests by requiring approval by nine of the thirteen states to ratify treaties. The South insisted on—and won—the same protection in the new Constitution.

With the most contentious issues resolved, delegates hammered out twenty-three other "fundamental resolutions" in the next week and submitted the rough draft of a constitution to a five-man "Committee of Detail" to polish. With a collective sigh of relief, the delegates adjourned for a week, and after catching up with his voluminous correspondence, Washington rode off with Gouverneur Morris to fish at Trout Creek, near the Valley Forge wartime encampment, where Robert Morris and his wife joined them to celebrate what Washington called their Convention "successes."

"Whilst Mr. Morris was fishing," Washington wrote in his diary, "I rid over the old Cantonment of the American [army] of the Winter of 1777, & [177]8. Visited all the Works, wch. were in Ruins; and the Incampments in woods where the ground had not been cultivated."[25] Cloaked in green, its new young trees sprouting beneath a warm sun, Valley Forge stood in stark contrast to the frozen barren of 1778's desperate winter.

Torrential rains sent him and all the Morrises back to Philadelphia the next day, but they had enjoyed each other's company so much that the reappearance of the sun two days later lured them off on another fishing trip—this time up the Delaware River to Trenton, where Washington could reminisce about another of his Revolutionary War exploits. Washington caught no fish the first evening, but the following morning, he "fished again with more success for perch."[26]

Washington reconvened the Convention on Monday, August 6, to listen to the refined draft of the Constitution. After each delegate had received a copy, South Carolina's John Rutledge took the floor and read it aloud, beginning with the preamble:

"We the people of the States of New Hampshire, Massachusetts, Rhode-Island and Providence Plantations, Connecticut [he read the names of all thirteen states] . . . do hereby declare, and establish the following Constitution for the Government of ourselves and our Posterity."

Even his sonorous voice could not make the phrases sing. The fifteen resolutions of the Virginia Plan had metamorphosed into twenty-three articles—some with as many as a dozen sections, printed on seven large pages each the size of a broadsheet, with ample margins for delegates to scribble notes or proposed changes. The reading took up the entire day. When they reconvened the next morning, however, delegates were in a good mood. They believed they were making progress toward agreement and immediately demonstrated their belief with rapid-fire approval of the preamble and the first three articles of the Constitution: Article I named their new government "The United States of America"; Article II gave it "supreme legislative, executive, and judicial powers"; and Article III vested legislative powers in "a Congress to consist of 2 separate & distinct bodies of men: a House of Representatives & a Senate."[27]

Their spirit of compromise vanished on the second day, however, and they would need a month to finish debating the twenty other articles. One of the most bitter debates centered on slaves, with

Pennsylvania's Gouverneur Morris reiterating his ardent condemnation of slavery, and South Carolina's John Rutledge repeating his equally fervent belief in the institution. In an effort to sustain the atmosphere of cordiality and compromise that his colleague Roger Sherman had created, Connecticut's Oliver Ellsworth, also a judge on his state's Superior Court, declared, "Let every State import what it pleases. The morality or wisdom of slavery are considerations belonging to the States themselves. What enriches a part enriches the whole, and the States are the best judge of their particular interest." South Carolina's Charles Pinckney agreed wholeheartedly, but nonetheless added a stern warning:

> South Carolina can never receive the plan if it prohibits the slave trade. In every proposed extension of the powers of the Congress, that State has expressly & watchfully excepted that of meddling with the importation of negroes. If the States be all left at liberty on this subject, S. Carolina may perhaps by degrees do of herself what is wished.[28]

To keep the South in the Union, the North agreed not to allow Congress to interfere with the importation of slaves for twenty years, but almost every delegate objected to other elements of the Constitution, which some predicted would provoke civil war once it went to the states for ratification. The delegates found something to debate to the very last day, including how many states should have to ratify the Constitution for it to take effect among those states. Maryland argued for all thirteen; Pennsylvania's James Wilson retorted in his Scottish accent, "It would be worse than folly to rely on the concurrence of the Rhode Island members of Congress in the plan. . . . New York has not been represented for a long time past in the Convention. . . . After spending four or five months in the laborious & arduous task of forming a Government for our Country, we are ourselves at the close throwing insuperable obstacles in the way of success."[29]

In the end, Washington brought the Convention to heel. "There are seeds of discontent in every part of the Union," he warned, "ready to produce disorders if . . . the present Convention should not be able to devise . . . a more vigorous and energetic government."[30]

The delegates compromised by requiring ratification of the Constitution by nine states for it to take effect.

By Wednesday, September 12, the "Committee on Stile," which depended largely on the brilliant writing skills of Gouverneur Morris, presented each of the delegates with a copy of the final draft. Clearly linked to and meant to be a sequel to the Declaration of Independence, the preamble was inspirational in its embrace of every citizen:

> We the People of the United States, in Order to form a more perfect Union, establish Justice, insure domestic Tranquility, provide for the common defence, promote the general Welfare, and secure the Blessings of Liberty to ourselves and our Posterity, do ordain and establish this Constitution for the United States of America.

What followed were seven articles, with the first three defining the shape, powers, and method of selecting the national legislature, the executive, and the judiciary, and the qualifications for serving (and removal) in each. It gave Congress, among other powers, the power to raise taxes and levy duties, to borrow money, to regulate foreign and interstate commerce, to maintain a standing army and navy, and to declare war. It gave the president power to make treaties—automatically stripping the states of any rights to deal directly with foreign powers. Article IV forced the states to recognize one another's laws and to give all citizens the rights of citizens in every state. The same article also provided for admission of new states and guaranteed "a republican form of government" in every state. Article V provided for amending the Constitution, and Article VI ranked laws by category. The Constitution and U.S. laws and treaties ranked highest as "the supreme law of the land," and local laws ranked lowest, with little or no consequence for the rest of the nation. Article VII required approval by ratification conventions in nine states for the Constitution to take effect among those states and create a new government.*

*   *   *

---

*See appendix A for the original Constitution as drafted by the Constitutional Convention.

In mid-September, four months after they had first come together in Philadelphia, the forty-two delegates still present heard the reading of the final draft. Three delegates scorned what they heard and refused to sign. According to Madison's notes, Virginia governor Edmund Randolph said "it would be impossible . . . to put his name to the instrument." He opposed the "indefinite and dangerous power" the Constitution gave Congress and predicted that "amendments might be offered by the State Conventions which should be submitted to and finally decided on by another general convention." He said his refusal to sign "did not mean he would oppose its adoption in his state, but he would not deprive himself of the freedom to do so."[31]

George Mason, Washington's neighbor on the bluffs overlooking the Potomac River in Virginia, agreed, all but shouting belligerently, "I would sooner chop off my right hand than put it to the Constitution as it now stands."[32] Insisting the document gave "dangerous power and structure to the Government," he predicted that without a bill of rights, it would end either "in monarchy or a tyrannical aristocracy. . . . This Constitution has been formed without the knowledge or idea of the people. . . . It was improper to say to the people, take this or nothing. . . . A second convention will know more of the sense of the people."[33]

Elbridge Gerry of Massachusetts also agreed, predicting that the Supreme Court was "a tribunal without juries, which will be a Starchamber." He complained that "three-fifths of the Blacks are to be represented as if they were freemen," and he objected strenuously to the power of Congress "to make what laws they may please . . . [and] raise armies and money without limit."[34] He moved to appoint a committee "to prepare a Bill of Rights." Mason promptly seconded Gerry's motion, and the Convention just as promptly defeated it. Later, Randolph moved for a second constitutional convention. Again Mason seconded, and again the Convention voted it down, arguing that the Constitution stated clearly that "We the People" had delegated specific powers to the central government—and nothing more, thus reserving all other powers to the states or the people. As written, the Constitution did not delegate any authority to the federal government to establish a state religion or to abridge freedom of speech or the press, or limit the right of peaceable assembly. More-over, seven states already had bills of rights in their constitutions, and every state protected freedom of religion, although five had established state religions. Every state guaranteed the right to trial by jury in criminal cases, and eleven states guaranteed freedom of the press. Eight states protected freedom of assembly, although only three guaranteed the right of free speech. As Connecticut's Roger Sherman would explain later, "The immediate security of the civil and domestic rights of the people will be in the government of the particular states.

> And as the different states have different local interests and cus-toms which can be best regulated by their own laws, it would not be expedient to admit the federal government to interfere with them. . . . The great end of the federal government is to protect the several states in the enjoyment of these rights, against foreign invasion, and to preserve peace and a beneficial intercourse among themselves, and to regulate and protect their commerce with for-eign nations. . . . The powers vested in the federal government are particularly defined, so that each State still retains its sovereignty in what concerns its own internal government, and a right to exer-cise every power of a sovereign state not particularly delegated to the government of the United States.[35]

Ignoring such logic, Gerry charged ahead, drawing battle lines that would divide the country for the next year and warning that "a Civil war may result" if the Convention ratified the Constitution without a bill of rights.[36] Ironically, even as Gerry called for adding a bill of rights to the Constitution, he argued against extending those rights to the West. "They will oppress commerce, and drain our wealth into the Western Country," he warned. Although he said he favored admitting a few new states in the West, he insisted on limit-ing their number "in such a manner, that they should never . . . out-number the Atlantic States. . . . They will, if they acquire power, like all men, abuse it," he predicted.[37]

At the very moment Gerry was warning the Constitutional Con-vention against western expansion, however, the Confederation Congress was drafting the most important document it would ever write: the Northwest Ordinance. The Northwest Ordinance provided that the vast Northwest Territory would be divided into no more than five new states as soon as sixty thousand people (about the population of Delaware at the time) had settled in any of them. Included in the Northwest Ordinance were a prohibition of slavery and a bill of rights guaranteeing freedom of the press, freedom of worship, the right to assemble peacefully, and other individual civil liberties—the very rights Gerry told the Convention he wanted added to the Constitution. He nonetheless joined Gouverneur Morris of Pennsylvania and, of all people, John Rutledge of South Carolina in moving "to secure the liberties of the States already confederated" by ensuring that the number of representatives in Congress from "the States which shall hereafter be established, shall never exceed in number the Representatives of the Atlantic Coast states."[38]

Again, it was Roger Sherman who injected a note of sanity into a senseless debate: "We are providing for our posterity," he cautioned, "for our children & our grand Children, who would be as likely to be citizens of new Western States, as of the old States . . . we ought to make no . . . discrimination."[39]

Then Benjamin Franklin struggled to rise with a speech in hand, but evidently in too much pain to proceed, he handed it to his fellow Pennsylvanian James Wilson, who had assumed the task of reading the old man's previous speeches—albeit with a distinct Scottish accent. Whether or not the two Federalists had rehearsed the scene, it made for effective drama:

> Mr. President
>
> I confess there are several parts of this constitution which I do not at present approve, but I am not sure I shall ever approve them . . . the older I get, the more apt I am to doubt my own judgment, and to pay more respect to the judgment of others. Most men indeed as well as most sects in Religion, think themselves in possession of all truth, and that wherever others differ from them it is so far error. Steele a Protestant in a Dedication tells the Pope, that the only difference between our Churches in their opinions of the certainty of their doctrines is, the Church of Rome is infallible and the Church of England is never wrong. But though many private persons think almost as highly of their own infallibility . . . few express it so naturally as a certain french lady, who in a dispute

with her sister, said, "I don't know how it happens, Sister, but I meet with no body but myself, that's always in the right—*Il n'y a que moi qui a toujours raison.*"

In these sentiments, Sir, I agree to this Constitution with all its faults, if they are such; because I think a general Government necessary for us, and there is no form of Government but what may be a blessing to the people if well administered. . . . I doubt too whether any other Convention we can obtain, may be able to make a better Constitution. For when you assemble a number of men to have the advantage of their joint wisdom, you inevitably assemble . . . all their prejudices, their passions, their errors of opinion, their local interests, and their selfish views. . . . It therefore astonishes me, Sir, to find this system approaching so near to perfection as it does. . . . Thus I consent, Sir, to this Constitution because I expect no better, and because I am not sure that it is not the best.[40]

Only thirty-nine of the forty-two delegates signed the document, but Gouverneur Morris's brilliant language made it seem otherwise. Even as he had changed the preamble's beginning from "We the States . . ." to the inspiring "We the People . . . ," he changed the last paragraph of the Constitution to the uplifting phrase, "Done in Convention by the unanimous consent of the states present." When the signers were finishing, Franklin looked toward the president's chair in which Washington had sat for the previous four months and pointed out the painting of a radiating sun on the back. During the Convention, he said, he had puzzled whether it was rising or setting, "but now at length I have the happiness to know that it is a rising and not a setting Sun."[41] It was said that he shed a tear at the signing—a bit of Federalist mythology that provoked a rash of poetry in the press that ranged from the cloyingly patriotic in the *Massachusetts Gazette*—

The god-like sage, revolving in his mind,
How many millions hell-forg'd fetters bind;
With tears of joy, survey'd the precious deed,
Which endless freedom to this clime decreed.
And while his aged hand subscrib'd
He reach'd the zenith of all human fame.

—to insulting condemnation in Boston's *American Herald:*

> The worn-out Sage too full of joy to speak,
> The puerile tear stole down his wrinkl'd cheek;
> He paused a moment—but alas, too late,
> He lent his Signet to his Country's fate,
> He grasped the trembling quil and signed his name,
> And damn'd the Laurels of his former fame.[42]

Washington was first to sign. Later he would warn Americans: "Should the States reject this excellent Constitution, the probability is . . . the next will be drawn in blood."[43] Then, after the other delegates had signed and the applause abated, he looked across the hall and displayed as broad a smile as his damaged teeth and painful gums allowed and declared the Convention adjourned.

"The Constitution," he wrote in his diary later that day, "received the Unanimous assent of 11 states and Colo. Hamilton's from New York. . . . The business being thus closed, the Members adjourned to the City Tavern together and took a cordial leave of each other."[44] As they said their good-byes, various state leaders assured Washington that they would deliver their states to the Union he was forging. Ironically, none of the Virginians could assure him that his own state would join that Union, and he had no power to manipulate Patrick Henry's Richmond political machine, which ran Virginia.

The following morning, Washington "took my leave of those families in wch. I had been most intimate. Dined early at Mr. Morris's with whom & Mr. Gouvr. Morris I parted at Gray's Ferry and reached Chester in Company with [Virginia delegate] Mr. [John] Blair who I invited to a seat in my Carriage 'til we should reach Mount Vernon."[45] The *Pennsylvania Packet* heralded what it called Washington's triumph:

> In 1775, we beheld him at the head of the armies of America, arresting the progress of British tyranny. In the year 1787, we behold him at the head of a chosen band of patriots and heroes, arresting the progress of American anarchy.[46]

4

"The Seeds of Civil Discord"

As WASHINGTON STEPPED OUT OF CITY TAVERN with the other delegates, he glowed over the manipulation of the final words of the Constitution to imply that "the proceedings of the Convention is handed from Congress by a unanimous vote (feeble as it is)."

"This apparent unity will have its effect," Washington gloated to James Madison and the others. "Not every one has opportunities to peep behind the curtain; and as the multitude often judge from externals, the appearance of unanimity in that body . . . will be of great importance."[1]

Powerful leaders of his own state, however—the sitting governor, three former governors, and several signers of the Declaration of Independence—opposed the Constitution as written, knowing that Convention delegates had not voted unanimously for ratification. For the first time Washington would have to stake his reputation as a patriot and leader against men who commanded almost as much popularity, if not reverence, in Virginia as he. Former governor Patrick Henry had preceded Washington as an outspoken champion of American independence, issuing his cry for "liberty or death" at the House of Burgesses in Williamsburg in March 1775—three months before Washington took command of the Continental Army. Former governor Thomas Jefferson, now American minister to France in Paris, had all but authored the Declaration of Independence, and with former governors Benjamin Harrison and Thomas Nelson Jr., had signed that document. So had Richard Henry Lee. Indeed, Lee was the first American leader to speak of national independence in a public forum when he proclaimed in the Continental Congress on June 7, 1776—a month before the Declaration of Independence—that the former British colonies "are, and of right ought to be, free and independent States."[2]

Washington harbored a bit of contempt for them all, however. With all their rhetoric and bombast, none had fired a shot during the Revolutionary War. Henry's inflammatory cry for "liberty or death" had helped provoke the nation to rebel, but when he had finished his performance, he stomped out of the chamber and rode to the safety of his mountain home, never to lift his own musket against the British enemy. Indeed, as governor and commander of the state militia, he not only resigned his military command, he failed to provide Washington's army with money or men to fight the war.

Henry was born on the frontier of western Virginia, and for him, as for most frontiersmen, *liberty* and *license* were all but indistinguishable; man was born free to acquire as much land, as many slaves, and as many other assets as he could—and keep *all* profits from his enterprise without sharing a penny with church or state. Many rejected humanist ideals that bound individuals to alienate personal liberties for the good of the greater community and had nothing but disdain for and deep suspicions of pious planters and merchant-bankers who controlled state government from their opulent mansions of the Chesapeake Bay tidewater region. They resented interference in their affairs by the distant state government in Williamsburg and had no intention of submitting to a new, even more powerful federal government in Philadelphia. Few Americans on the thriving Atlantic coast understood that Henry's cry for *liberty or death* in 1775 had been aimed at not only the British government but *any* government—American as well as British—that threatened to tax profits of American farmers or curtail their liberties.

Although he lacked the bluster and bravado of Patrick Henry, a planter in Mount Vernon, Virginia, best summed up farmer sentiments, saying simply that Parliament "hath no . . . right to put their hands in my pocket." The planter was George Washington.

Patrick Henry. A champion of individual liberty, the Virginia patriot loathed governments in general and national governments in particular, whether British or American. He led the unsuccessful Antifederalist campaign against ratification.

Henry had been Virginia's first governor before entering the state legislature and was almost as popular as Washington—more so in the state's mountainous Piedmont region, where Henry was born. One of eleven children, Henry had to scratch out his own living at fifteen. Desperate for income, he borrowed a digest of Virginia laws to practice a crude, albeit entertaining, frontier law in his father-in-law's tavern by the Hanover County Courthouse. With a fragmented grasp of legalities, but a spellbinding gift for "talking a long string of learning," Henry mesmerized local judges and juries with "the music of his voice" and the "natural elegance of his style and manner." In his first three years, he won almost twelve hundred cases—most on rhetoric rather than points of law. Henry left semiliterate farmer-jurors confused about law, but his histrionics proved so entertaining that in the end he convinced them that whatever he had said was right. He was one of their own: a fiddler, country dancer, hunter, and master of bawdy jokes. He not only defended them, he usually did so against "outsiders"—most of them lawyers cloaked in fancy clothes and even fancier words. Tidewater planters had sent many lawyers west to stalk courthouses and claim title to local farmlands by paying back taxes that semiliterate Piedmont farmers seldom even knew were overdue. Henry's arguments so fired up jurymen that after finding for a farmer, they often hoisted young Henry onto their shoulders and carried him from the courtroom into the streets—to the wild, adoring cheers of the townsfolk.

It was this sense of the individual's ability to govern his own affairs that provoked Henry's refusal to attend the Constitutional Convention and his deep suspicions of the document that emerged, which he called an "extreme danger to . . . rights, liberty, and happiness." Although Washington held Henry somewhat in contempt for his wartime inaction, he dared not alienate so popular a figure, and, indeed, he set about actively wooing Henry and the other former Virginia governors to the Federalist camp with gestures of courtesy and respect to each. The first thing Washington did after returning to Mount Vernon was to send a copy of the Constitution to Thomas Jefferson in Paris and to Patrick Henry, Benjamin Harrison, and Thomas Nelson in Virginia. Rather than defend the Constitution, Washington purposely empathized with the Antifederalist position by emphasizing Article V—the right of states to amend the Constitution.

"In the first moment after my return," he wrote to Henry, Harrison, and Nelson, "I take the liberty of sending you a copy of the Constitution, which the Fœderal Convention has submitted to the People of these States.

> I accompany it with no observations. Your own judgment will at once discover the good and the exceptionable parts of it; and your experience of the difficulties which have ever arisen when attempts have been made to reconcile such a variety of interest and local prejudices, as pervade the several States, will render explanation unnecessary. I wish the constitution, which is offered, had been more perfect; but I sincerely believe it is the best that could be obtained at this time. And, as a constitutional door is opened for amendments hereafter, the adoption of it, under the present circumstances of the Union, is in my opinion desirable.
>
> From a variety of concurring accounts it appears to me that the political concerns of this Country are, in a manner, suspended by a thread. That the Convention has been looked up to by the reflecting part of the community with a Sollicitude which is hardly

to be conceived, and that, if nothing had been agreed on by that body, anarchy would soon have ensued—the seeds being deeply sown in every soil.[3]

Benjamin Harrison's objections to the Constitution were far more moderate than Henry's. Harrison feared that "the seeds of civil discord are plentifully sown in very many of the powers given both to the president and congress, and that if the constitution is carried in to effect, the States south of potowmac will be little more than appendages to those to the northward of it." Harrison nonetheless agreed to withhold judgment until he heard "the reasons which operated in favor of the measures taken . . . and hearing from those who had a hand in the work."[4]

In an effort to reconcile differences with George Mason, Washington wrote a short note of commiseration over his poor corn crop and offered to join him in buying additional supplies from North Carolina and enable both men to save through bulk purchases. Knowing that Mason had injured his back in a carriage accident returning from Philadelphia, Washington added words of consolation: "I am sorry to hear you met with an accident on your return. I hope you experience no ill effect from it. The family here join me in compliments and good wishes to you, Mrs. Mason and Family."

After the bitterness he had engendered at the Philadelphia Convention, Mason was delighted with Washington's generous note of friendship, but his tactless answer only widened their differences and further alienated Washington.

> I take the liberty to enclose You my Objections to the new Constitution of Government, which a little Moderation & Temper, in the latter End of the Convention, might have removed. . . . You will readily observe, that my Objections are not numerous. . . . I am however most decidedly of Opinion, that it ought to be submitted to a Convention chosen by the people.[5]

Although neighbors for many years, Mason had always puzzled Washington—as he had many of his neighbors and, indeed, most members of the Convention. Educated privately by tutors in his family's plantation home, he remained a private, often unfriendly man throughout his life. Nourished with wealth that obviated any evident

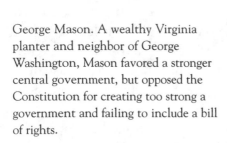

George Mason. A wealthy Virginia planter and neighbor of George Washington, Mason favored a stronger central government, but opposed the Constitution for creating too strong a government and failing to include a bill of rights.

basis for unhappiness, he nonetheless was far happier in the isolation of his study at home and preferred walking alone and contemplating in his boxwood garden than participating in public church services or civic assemblies. Although elected a burgess, he rarely attended—usually pleading ill health and submitting written papers, including his renowned draft of the Virginia Declaration of Rights and a draft for that state's first constitution. He did not serve in the war and, indeed, his first venture beyond the Potomac–Chesapeake Bay area was to attend the Constitutional Convention. By then, his extensive readings in the isolation of Gunston Hall, his magnificent Georgian home, had converted him into a self-professed—and annoyingly didactic—champion of individual rights. By the end of the Constitutional Convention, he had alienated most other delegates with his belligerent intolerance of views that disagreed with his own, and, after returning home, he not only alienated Washington, he so antagonized his neighbors that they rejected his candidacy to the Virginia ratification convention and forced him to run for election (and win) in a neighboring county.

In New York, meanwhile, the first copies of the Constitution had reached the Confederation Congress, which, according to the Articles of Confederation, had to approve the document before sending it to the states for approval. Article VII required ratification by specially elected ratification conventions in at least nine states to form the new union. Each of the remaining four states would be free to follow suit, become independent republics, or form their own confederation. Washington and everyone else in the political theater recognized that without the four most heavily populated states—Virginia, Massachusetts, Pennsylvania, and North Carolina—the new nation would be as fragile militarily and economically as the parchment on which the Constitution was engrossed. Virginia alone boasted the nation's largest economy and more than a fifth of the three million people in the thirteen states.

Less than two weeks after the Constitutional Convention had adjourned, Congress agreed to transmit the Constitution to each state legislature for submission "to a convention of Delegates chosen in each state by the people thereof." The resolution passed despite "a very serious effort . . . by R[ichard] H[enry] Lee and Mr. [Nathan] Dane from Massachusetts to embarrass it."[6] Though he had not sought to "embarrass" the Constitution, Lee was determined "to restrain and regulate the exercise of the great powers necessarily given to Rulers" by demanding that the Constitution "be bottomed upon a . . . Bill of Rights guaranteeing freedom of religion, freedom of the press, the right to trial by jury in criminal and civil cases, the right to free assembly, protection against unreasonable search and seizures."[7] Congress disagreed, saying it had no authority to change the Constitution—only to transmit it to the states, with or without a recommendation. Ignoring the Constitutional Convention's violation of its mandate, Congress abruptly dismissed Lee's proposal and, after two days of deliberations, agreed to transmit the document as written, without any recommendations. In effect, Congress effectively sounded the death knell for its own existence and that of the Confederation.

The harsh—indeed, rude—rebuff infuriated Lee. As old as Washington, he had been president of Congress—in effect, president of the Confederation of American States—only three years earlier. His age, rank, and family heritage demanded more respect, and the cavalier dismissal he suffered pushed him firmly into the Antifederalist camp. Descended from a line of Virginia's quasi-aristocratic planters, he was born at the family seat on Stratford Plantation, sent to England for his formal education, and raised to assume the traditional family role as a planter and dilettante burgess. After marrying an heiress from an equally wealthy family, he settled on Chantilly Plantation, adjacent to Stratford, and entered the House of Burgesses, gaining little attention until he joined Patrick Henry and Thomas Jefferson in opposing parliamentary taxation. At the Continental Congress he penned the resolution that led to the Declaration of Independence, but claimed illness to excuse his serving in the war. He did little of note in the decade that followed until he returned to Congress and faced the question of sending the new Constitution to the states for ratification. Balking once again at allowing a central government to tax private property, he joined in demanding a bill of rights to protect individuals (and the states) against government intrusion in their "natural" rights.

Lee set out to rally Antifederalists across the nation by sending copies of his proposed constitutional amendments and bill of rights to the governors of Massachusetts, Delaware, Pennsylvania, North Carolina, and Virginia, and to Antifederalist leaders such as Elbridge Gerry and Samuel Adams of Massachusetts, both signers of the Declaration of Independence with Lee. "I incline to think," Lee wrote to Gerry, "that unless some such alterations and provisions as those are interposed for the security of those essential rights of mankind without which liberty cannot exist, we shall soon find that the new plan of government will be far more inconvenient than anything sustained under the present government, And that to avoid Scylla we shall have fallen upon Charybdis."[8]

In his letter to Samuel Adams, Lee insisted that "universal experience" had proved it "necessary to protect the just rights and liberty of mankind from the silent, powerful and ever active conspiracy of those who govern." Lee listed what he called "precautions . . . necessary to restrain and regulate the great powers given to rulers:

> That the rights of conscience in matters of religion ought not be violated—That the freedom of the press shall be secured—That the trial by jury in criminal and civil cases . . . shall be held sacred—That standing armies in times of peace are dangerous to liberty . . . That the elections should be free and frequent;

Richard Henry Lee. His resolution in the Continental
Congress that the United States "are, and of right ought to
be, free and independent States" led to the Declaration of
Independence. He fought ratification of the Constitution
because it created a strong central government and lacked
a bill of rights.

That . . . justice be secured by the independency of judges; That
excessive bail, excessive fines, or cruel and unusual punishments,
should not be demanded or inflicted; That the right of the people
to assemble, for the purpose of petitioning the legislature, shall not
be prevented; that the citizens shall not be exposed to unreasonable searches, seizure of their persons, houses, papers or property.[9]

To Lee, "unreasonable . . . seizure of their . . . property" was syn-
onymous with taxation, and he was as determined to prevent taxation by the American government as he had been to prevent it by
the British government.

"It is under the strongest impressions of your goodness and can-
dor that I venture to make the observations that follow in this letter,"

Lee wrote to George Washington. Unlike the tactless Mason, Lee assured Washington that he felt it "among the first distresses" to dis-agree with his fellow Virginian, but "in consequence of long reflec-tion upon the nature of Man and government . . . I am led to fear the danger that will ensue to Civil Liberty from the adoption of the new system in its present form." Although he agreed with "the propriety of change in the present plan of confederation," he feared that the new Constitution gave the central government too much power and that a bill of rights was needed to secure individual liberties, along with a clause reserving to the states all powers not expressly dele-gated to the federal government. He said he believed it essential to impose the restrictions *before* ratification rather than *after,* by which time the new government may well have assumed dictatorial powers. Reaffirming his personal allegiance to Washington, Lee asked him to call a new Convention to permit "peaceable and fair discussion . . . of those objections that are fundamentally strong against the new Con-stitution which abounds with useful regulations."[10]

Although Lee made a special trip to Mount Vernon to try to impress Washington with the logic of his thinking, Washington re-jected the argument out of hand, saying proponents of a bill of rights could amend the Constitution after ratification and that any delay in establishing a strong federal government would allow anarchy to spread across the land. "The Constitution . . . is not free from imper-fections," Washington admitted,

> but there are as few radical defects in it as could well be expected considering the heterogeneous mass of which the Convention was composed and the diversity of interests that are to be attended to. As a Constitutional door is opened for future amendments and alterations, I think it would be wise in the People to accept what is offered to them . . . but this is hardly to be expected, because the importance, and sinister views of too many characters will be affected by the change. Much will depend on literary abilities, & the recommendations of it by good pens, should it be . . . attacked in the Gazettes.[11]

Washington's abrupt response only solidified Lee's opposition to the Constitution. "To say . . . that a bad government must be established for fear of anarchy," Lee scoffed, "is really saying that we must kill ourselves for fear of dying."[12]

Washington now recognized that reconciliation with the Henry-Mason-Lee triumvirate was impossible. None had fired a shot in the Revolutionary War; none had suffered a Valley Forge winter with an impotent Congress unable to supply troops with even subsistence levels of food, clothing, and ammunition. None, in Washington's mind, could understand the desperate need that he believed existed for a strong central government to ensure the nation's defense.

Although Washington abandoned efforts to lure Henry, Lee, or Mason from the Antifederalist camp, he did not despair of winning Jefferson and perhaps Randolph to his side. Both were deeply involved in Washington's cross-country waterway project to tie the Potomac and James rivers to the Ohio River, and he used their interests in that project to open a series of letters to each that inevitably touched on the Constitution—and a need for their particular skills in the new government.

"I am much obliged to you, my dear Sir," Washington wrote to Jefferson, "for the Acct. which you gave me of the general state of affairs in Europe . . .

> our situation is such as makes it . . . extremely imprudent to take a part in their quarrels. . . . I perfectly agree with you that . . . anything that will divert our attention from Agriculture must be extremely prejudicial, if not ruinous to us. but I conceive under an energetic general Government such regulations might be made . . . as would render this Country the asylum of pacific and industrious characters from all parts of Europe—would encourage the cultivation of the Earth by the high price its products would command—and would draw the wealth, and wealthy men of other Nations, into our own bosom, by giving security to property, and liberty to its holders. I have the honor to be with great esteem & regard Dear Sir Yr Most Obedt & Most Hble Servt.[13]

Jefferson's close friend James Madison also fired a barrage of letters to Paris and, within a month, Jefferson replied, "Were I in America, I would advocate it warmly till nine should have adopted it and then as warmly take the other side to convince the other four

Thomas Jefferson. Although he opposed the Constitution
because it lacked a bill of rights, Jefferson remained
relatively neutral in the fight over ratification because
of his deep loathing for Patrick Henry.

that they ought not to come into it till the declaration of rights is
annexed to it."[14]

In fact, Jefferson saw no reason for the Constitution, which he,
too, saw as a violation of the original congressional mandate to
revise the Articles of Confederation. As he wrote to John Adams,
then the American minister in Britain, "I think all the good of this
new constitution might have been couched in three or four new articles to be added to the good, old, and venerable fabric, which should
have been preserved as a religious relic. . . . Their president," he
added, after studying Article II, "seems a bad edition of the Polish
king."[15]

In a longer letter to his friend William Stephens Smith, who had
married Adams's daughter Abigail, Jefferson all but ridiculed the
Constitution—and George Washington's claim that it had been nec-

essary to stave off anarchy. "Yet where does this anarchy exist?" Jefferson asked.

> Where did it ever exist, except in the single instance of Massachusetts? . . . God forbid that we should ever be 20 years without such a rebellion. . . . We have had 13 states independent 11 years. There has been one rebellion. That comes to one rebellion in a century and a half for each state. What country . . . can preserve it's liberties if their rulers are not warned from time to time that their people preserve the spirit of resistance? Let them take arms. The remedy is to set them right as to facts, pardon & pacify them. What signify a few lives lost in a century or two? The tree of liberty must be refreshed from time to time with the blood of patriots & tyrants. It is its natural manure. Our Convention has been too much impressed by the insurrection of Massachusetts: and in the spur of the moment they are setting up a kite [chicken hawk] to keep the henyard in order.[16]

A few weeks later, however, Jefferson adopted a more tactful approach in a letter to Washington that included a brilliant two-thousand-word report on foreign affairs that all but doubled as an application to serve as Washington's foreign secretary. At the end of the report, he nonetheless expressed his reservations about the new Constitution. Knowing that Washington was as opposed to monarchic rule as he, Jefferson declared, "There are two things . . . which I dislike strongly . . . the want of a declaration of rights . . . [and] the perpetual re-eligibility of the President. . . .

> this I fear will make that an office for life first, & then hereditary. I was much an enemy to monarchy before I came to Europe. I am ten thousand times more so since I have seen what they are. there is scarcely an evil known in these countries which may not be traced to their king as it's source. . . . I can further say with safety there is not a crowned head in Europe whose talents or merit would entitle him to be elected a vestryman by the people in any parish in America. however . . . I look forward to the general adoption of the new constitution . . . as necessary for us under our present circumstances.[17]

Despite his strong reservations about the Constitution, Jefferson decided to adopt a position of tacit neutrality in Virginia's ratification debate. First, he was convinced that the Constitution would later be amended to include a bill of rights. Second—and of far greater influence on his decision—he loathed Patrick Henry. He considered Henry "avaritious and rotten hearted"—a virtual charlatan who used oratorical skills to disguise a rudimentary knowledge of law to lure the ignorant and poor into his political web. Jefferson's dislike for Henry rose to obsessive hatred when the latter moved to investigate Jefferson's failure as governor to make the "exertions which he might have for the defence of the country" at the time of the British offensive in Virginia in 1781. Henry's action was particularly loathsome in the wake of his own failure, as Jefferson's predecessor in office, to make any "exertions" to defend Virginia against the British. Indeed, Henry had resigned as commander of the militia. For Jefferson, therefore, the choice between allying himself with Henry or Washington in the ratification debate was a simple one.[18]

Virginia governor Edmund Randolph would prove more difficult to lure away from the Antifederalists, however. Although Randolph had joined Antifederalists Mason and Gerry in refusing to sign the Constitution in Philadelphia, Randolph made it clear that he had not rejected federalism, and, indeed, he suggested that the states study, modify, and resubmit the document to a second "general Convention [to] reject or incorporate them" into a final document. For the often indecisive governor, the suggestion seemed a fine way to postpone the inevitable—perhaps indefinitely.

On October 10, less than a month after the end of the Convention, Randolph published a pamphlet with a long, rambling, and at times contradictory letter addressed to the Speaker of the Virginia House of Delegates: "I disdain to conceal the reasons for withholding my subscription [to the Constitution]," Randolph declared. He insisted that the Constitution be altered so that "all ambiguities" would be "precisely explained" and that the president be "ineligible after a given number of years" and be deprived of "the power of nominating to the judiciary offices or of filling up vacancies which may there happen [sic] to be during the recess of the senate." He called for "drawing a line between the powers of congress and individual States . . . so as to leave no clashing of jurisdictions nor dangerous disputes" and "limiting and defining the judicial power."[19]

Three weeks after Washington had sent him a copy of the Constitution, Patrick Henry rejected Washington's effort at reconciliation and fired his first salvo against ratification of the Constitution:

> I was honored by the Receipt of your Favor together with a Copy of the proposed federal constitution . . . for which I beg you to accept my thanks. They are also due to you from me as a Citizen, on account of the great Fatigue necessarily attending the arduous Business of the late Convention.
>
> I have to lament that I cannot bring my mind to accord with the proposed Constitution. The Concern I feel on this account is really greater than I am able to express. Perhaps mature Reflections may furnish me Reasons to change my present Sentiments into a Conformity with the opinions of those personages for whom I have the highest Reverence. Be that as it may, I beg you will be persuaded of the unalterable Regard & attachment with which I ever shall be, dear Sir, Your obliged & very humble Servant.[20]

With political battle lines drawn in Virginia, Henry stood in the legislature a week later to oppose calling a state ratification convention. Blocking the call to convention would, he knew, effectively block ratification or delay the call long enough to build support for amending the Constitution at a second national convention before presentation to the states for ratification. A state convention, Henry warned the Virginia Assembly, would only have the power to accept or reject the Constitution as written—not to amend it—despite the "errors and defects" it contains.

George Mason, who had won election by running in a neighboring county, shot to his feet to support Henry. As one who had been "honored with a seat at the Federal Convention," Mason proclaimed, he had weighed every article of the Constitution and had "refused to subscribe to their proceedings." He declared that "no man was more completely federal . . . than I . . . that from the east of New Hampshire, to the south of Georgia, there was not a man more fully convinced of the necessity of establishing some general government." After careful consideration, however, he concluded that he could not approve the Constitution.

> I thought it wrong, Mr. Chairman—I thought it repugnant to our highest interests—and if with these sentiments I had subscribed to

it, I might have been justly regarded as a traitor to my country. I would have lost this hand before it should have marked my name to the new government.[21]

Federalist supporters tried to trivialize Antifederalist criticisms, with the *Pennsylvania Gazette* reporting, "We hear from Virginia that George Mason has been treated with every possible mark of contempt and neglect, for neglecting to sign the Fœderal Constitution." The *Pennsylvania Herald* carried a similar report: "The citizens of Virginia have expressed the most pointed disapprobation of the conduct of those delegates to the convention who have refused to concur in the new plan of government." And the *Pennsylvania Journal* added, "We hear from Virginia, that on the arrival of Mr. Mason at Alexandria, he was waited on by the Mayor and Corporation of that Town, who told him, they were *not* come to return him their thanks for his conduct in refusing to sign the Fœderal Constitution, but to express their abhorrence to it, and to advise him to withdraw from that town within an hour, for they could not answer for his personal safety, from an enraged populace, should he exceed that time." The newspaper article claimed that Elbridge Gerry had received much the same treatment in his home state of Massachusetts, having been "not only censured by the public in general, but by his best friends, for not signing the Constitution."[22]

Mason responded to newspaper attacks by assailing the Constitution. "In the name of God," he pleaded to readers of the *Virginia Independent Chronicle*, "look well before you leap,

> consider . . . whether you would rather be a sovereign or a sharer in sovereignty. . . . Consider that if you pass the Fœderal Constitution in toto, you subject yourselves to see the doors of your houses, the impenetrable castles of freeman, fly open before the magic wand of the exciseman, and, you will be dragged for trial before a distant tribunal, and there, perhaps, condemned without the benefit of a jury from your vicinage, your unalienable birthright as a freeman.[23]

After the fireworks of the Henry-Mason oratory in the Virginia Assembly subsided, thirty-two-year-old John Marshall, a self-educated country lawyer like Patrick Henry, stood to defend the people's right to consider the Constitution themselves and moved that it be "submitted to a convention of the people for full and free investigation and discussion."[24] Unlike Henry and Mason, Marshall had served bravely in the Continental Army at Brandywine, Germantown, and Valley Forge. He was a fervent nationalist who revered Washington and envisioned him as the nation's first president.

A master at parliamentary delay, Henry stood to assure the Assembly that he supported calling a convention—indeed that, like Mason, "no man is more truly federal than myself." He had but one objection, though: the limitation of the convention's choice to adopting or rejecting the Constitution, without giving it the option of proposing amendments.[25] It was the first of many changes to the resolution proposed by Henry to delay calling a ratification convention in Virginia. Henry's delaying tactics elated George Mason but infuriated James Madison. "Mr. Henry is the great adversary who will render the event precarious," Madison wrote to Thomas Jefferson in frustration. "He is, I find, with his usual address, working up every possible interest into a spirit of opposition."[26]

Henry managed to delay the call to convention until October 31, when he exhausted the last of his parliamentary tricks—a motion that Mason seconded to give the ratification convention "the power of proposing amendments." But Washington's Federalists in the legislature had a few parliamentary tricks of their own. Not only did they reject Henry's motion, they made one that rigged election rules for the ratification convention to offset the overwhelming popular majority of Antifederalists in Virginia. The rules not only limited voting to property holders, it expanded the number of eligible candidates to include all freeholders and officeholders—a rule that allowed judges, legislators, and other community leaders to run. More often than not, they were Federalists such as Madison, Justice Edmund Pendleton, John Marshall, and Henry ("Light-Horse Harry") Lee. Although the majority of ordinary Virginians were Antifederalists, the new voting rules would make it difficult for them to win even a slim majority of delegates to the state ratification convention.

Stunned by the setback, Patrick Henry nonetheless convinced the Assembly to delay elections for the ratification convention until the following March—long after most other states—and to postpone holding its convention until June 2, by which time he hoped that at least four or five other states would have doomed the Constitution. Even if most other states ratified, Henry believed that with Mason, Lee, and Governor Randolph on his side, he could prevent ratification in Virginia, and if Antifederalist allies such as Governor George Clinton in New York and Elbridge Gerry in Massachusetts succeeded in defeating ratification in their states, the Union would not survive. To encourage that eventuality, Henry resorted to clever political horse-trading and managed to amend the act that called for a ratification convention with an order to the governor to invite other states to join Virginia in securing amendments to the Constitution. For reasons he kept to himself, Governor Randolph delayed sending copies of Henry's amendment to his counterparts in other states until it could have no effect. Although he dated his letter of transmission December 27, 1787, the letters would not reach their destinations until eight states had already ratified the Constitution. Randolph's letter to Governor Clinton of New York did not reach him until March 7, 1788.

At the same time, Randolph sent Washington a warm letter enclosing a copy of the pamphlet he had sent to the Virginia House of Delegates explaining his objections to the Constitution. Still hoping to woo Randolph from the Antifederalist camp, Washington replied with equal warmth, calling Randolph's note "a fresh instance of your friendship and attention." Washington acknowledged that, like Randolph, "some things . . . I am persuaded never will obtain my cordial approbation: but I . . . do most firmly believe that, in the aggregate, it is the best Constitution that can be obtained at this Epocha; and that this, or a dissolution of the Union awaits our choice. . . . I pray your forgiveness for the expression of these sentiments."[27]

5

The Road to Ratification

As copies of the constitution traveled the long, rough road to ratification, people in every state except Rhode Island eagerly awaited the chance to reprise the exciting drama of the Constitutional Convention at their own state conventions—and in their streets, taverns, and homes. As in the original Convention, popular debate pitted country people against city people, farmers against merchant-bankers and shipping interests, small states against large, North against South, East against West, abolitionists against slave-owners, and sometimes even brother against brother and father against son.

"The Constitution is now before the Judgment Seat," Washington warned Henry Knox. "It has . . . its adversaries and supporters . . . the former, more than probably will be most active, as the major part of them will, it is to be feared, be governed by sinister and self important motives." Washington dismissed criticisms that a wealthy, powerful elite had usurped authority at the Constitutional Convention and violated the congressional mandate to revise the Articles of Confederation. He insisted that only "simple questions" underlay the debate over ratification:

1. Is the Constitution preferable to the Government (if it can be called one) under which we now live?
2. Is it probable that more confidence would be placed in another Convention . . . than was placed in the last one, and is it likely that a better agreement would take place therein?

3. Is there not a Constitutional door open for alterations or amendments? and is it not likely that real defects will be as readily discovered after as before trial; and will not our successors be as ready to apply the remedy as ourselves?[1]

Washington predicted that "the refusal of our Govr. [Edmund Randolph] and Colo. Mason to subscribe to the proceedings of the Convention will have a bad effect in this state." He said they would clothe their objections "in most terrific array for the purpose of alarming; some things are already addressed to the fears of the people and will no doubt have their effect."[2]

But Antifederalist alarms were already sounding far beyond Virginia's borders and dividing the nation with conflicting fears. Several states had approached the verge of dismemberment for nearly a decade, as back-country farmers, trappers, and other settlers united to combat exploitation by merchant-bankers and shipping interests in coastal cities, who dictated market prices, taxes, and legislative and judiciary proceedings. To appease rural interests, Virginia had moved its capital inland, from Williamsburg closer to the center of the state at Richmond in 1780; South Carolina moved its state capital from the coastal city of Charleston to the small, midstate rural town of Columbia; and New York's capital shuttled back and forth between New York City and Poughkeepsie, 85 miles north on the east bank of the Hudson River in the heart of the farm belt.* Pennsylvania's western counties—three of them named Washington, Greene, and Lafayette—were threatening to secede from what they angrily called "the state of Philadelphia." Like other inlanders across the nation, they felt helpless to protect their interests against easterners. Exploitation of farmers went beyond price fixing. A late mortgage payment or tax remittance allowed unscrupulous Philadelphia bankers to declare a farmer hundreds of miles away in default and begin foreclosure proceedings in a Philadelphia court. Antifederalists warned farmers that a strong federal government, with

---

*New York would later move its capital to Albany, 120 miles north of New York City on the opposite bank of the Hudson River.

unlimited taxing powers and a standing army to collect taxes, would allow eastern interests to send federal troops to seize farms at will. Ninety percent of Americans were farmers, and in a barter economy, where few people dealt in cash, taxation was the cruelest hardship they faced—tantamount to confiscation of their property, their sweat, their blood. Although Shays and his rebel farmers had taught state officials a lesson in Massachusetts, farmers feared they would not be able to oppose federal might.

Ironically, Antifederalists in coastal cities were sending an opposite, though equally frightening message, warning that westward expansion would create a powerful bloc of rural states and agricultural monopolies that would crush coastal merchant-banking interests. Antifederalist hawkers stood on street corners, handing out imitation constitutions and crude effigies of Federalist leaders for mobs to burn. Federalist and Antifederalist gangs—many of them bought and paid for by varying commercial interests—fought and rioted in New York, Philadelphia, Boston. Propaganda flooded the press with vitriol that overflowed onto streets and into taverns and homes.

"Beware! Beware!" a writer in the *Massachusetts Centinel* warned Federalists. "You are forging Chains for yourself and your children—your liberties are at stake."[3] A writer calling himself "Centinel" warned readers of Philadelphia's *Independent Gazetteer* that the Constitution would create "a *permanent* ARISTOCRACY. . . . Of all *possible* evils, that of *despotism* is the *worst* and the most to be dreaded."[4] *Freeman's Journal*, another Philadelphia paper, railed against the unlimited "power [of Congress] to lay and collect taxes." It called taxation "*impolitic* and *unjust*; it is a tax upon population, and falls indiscriminately upon the poor and the rich; the helpless who cannot work, and the robust, who can."[5] And Elbridge Gerry, hoping to prevent the Massachusetts legislature from calling a ratification convention, warned that if the Constitution were adopted, "it will lay the foundation of a Government of *force & fraud*, that the people will bleed with taxes [at every] pore, & that the existence of their liberties will soon be terminated. the wealth of the Continent will be collected in pennsylvania, where the Seat of the fœderal Government is proposed to be."[6]

Massachusetts poet Mercy Warren—a close friend of both Abigail Adams and Martha Washington—cried out that the Constitution "threatens to sweep away the rights for which the brave sons of America have fought."[7]

Federalist Rufus King fired back, calling those who supported that position "a detestable faction . . . desperadoes" for issuing a "malicious . . . piece of bombast and declamation . . . [an] attempt of the antifederal JUNTO to poison the publick mind."[8]

Other Federalists parried Antifederalist arguments by insisting that a strong federal government with the power to enforce laws was the only solution to anarchy and rebellion that was sweeping the nation, threatening to dismember states, and opening the frontier to attack by Indian raiders and conquest by foreign armies. To those who demanded a bill of rights, Federalists responded that Washington and Franklin, the nation's most revered heroes, were devoted to the defense of American rights and that Washington would almost certainly become first president and effect a smooth transition to federalism.

"George Washington, Esq., has already been destined, by a thousand voices, to fill the place of the first President of the United States, under the new frame of government," declared the *Philadelphia Gazette*, America's most widely read newspaper. In an article that would be reprinted several dozen times in seven other states, the Federalist newspaper stated,

> While the deliverers of a nation in other countries have hewn out a way to power with the sword, or seized upon it by stratagems and fraud, our illustrious Hero peaceably retired to his farm after the war, from whence it is expected he will be called, by the suffrages of three millions of people, to govern that country by his wisdom . . . which he had previously made free by his arms.—Can Europe boast of such a man?—or can the history of the world shew an instance of such a voluntary compact between the *Deliverer* and the *delivered* of any country, as will probably soon take place in the United States.[9]

Washington's own words confirmed the newspaper's faith: "The power under the Constitution will always be in the People," he pledged. "No man is a warmer advocate for *proper* restraints and *wholesome* checks in every department of government than I am."[10]

Washington's reassurances were enough to calm many Americans, but not all. Although opponents of the Constitution conceded that some taxing powers were essential to the nation's common defense and welfare, they demanded safeguards against misuse of such powers. "I am one of those who have long wished for a federal government, which should have power to protect our trade and provide for the general security of the United States," wrote "An Old Whig" in Philadelphia's *Independent Gazetteer*. Admitting that the Articles of Confederation did not give Congress "power sufficient for the purposes of the union," he pointed out that they nonetheless restricted Congress from exercising "any power or authority that is not in express words delegated to them . . . we find no such clause in the new Constitution. . . . The new constitution vests Congress with such unlimited powers as ought never to be entrusted to any men or body of men." Like many would-be Federalists, "Old Whig" opposed adoption of the new Constitution without specific language "to secure to the people their liberties."[11]

Opponents of the Constitution had other objections as well. They feared that without term limits, a four-year term would allow a president to consolidate power, become a tyrant, and serve for life. And they decried giving the nation's highest court the power to override state court decisions and try cases without juries from a fixed seat far from the jurisdictions of the persons involved. But most of their criticisms were reserved for the legislative branch. With no more than one representative for every thirty thousand people, small states feared domination in the House by the four most heavily populated states—Virginia, Massachusetts, Pennsylvania, and North Carolina. Virginia alone claimed at least a fifth of the nation's *total* population of about 4 million. In addition to the objections of small states, the northern states—both big and small—feared that the South would gain disproportionately large representation in the House because of its slave population. With three-fifths of the estimated 250,000 slaves in the South counted as part of the population, the Constitution would allow a handful of southern planters to derive at least five additional representatives in the House from the slaves they owned. Moreover, the South would be able to import additional slaves, expand the slave population, and increase the number of southern votes in the House for twenty years, until 1808. Northerners feared that inclusion of slaves in the population count to determine representation in the House would encourage the South to perpetuate slavery indefinitely.

Just as the small states feared domination by large states in the House, large states feared that with two votes for each state in the Senate, states with small populations would combine to defy the will of the majority of the American people. Opponents of the Constitution also condemned the vice president's dual role as president of the Senate, where, in the event of a tie, his state would gain one vote more than any other on potentially critical issues.

With critics flooding the press with their objections, the Constitution faced massive public opposition from almost the moment it emerged from Congress on its way to the various state legislatures. In early America, disagreements of any sort invariably meant violence. Indeed, the collegiality that had pervaded the Constitutional Convention was an aberration. Philadelphia's *Independent Gazetteer* playfully described a discussion in a "beer house" on the Saturday night following the end of the Constitutional Convention:

> *A Sea Captain.* By George, if we don't adopt the Federal Government we shall all *go to wreck*.
>
> *His Mate.* Hold, hold Captain, we are in no danger, *Washington* is still *at the helm*.
>
> *A Continental Army Lieutenant.* If we don't adopt the new government . . . well, *promotion is always most rapid in a civil war*.
>
> After the men had consumed more beer, a baker ventured, "Let me see the man that dares oppose the federal government, and I will soon *make biscuit of him*." A butcher replied, "And I would soon *quarter the dog*." To which the barber added, "And I would shave the son of a ____."
>
> *A Cook.* And I would *break every bone* in his body.
>
> *A Joiner.* And I would make a *wooden jacket* for him.
>
> *A Potter.* And I would grind his dust afterward into a *chamber pot*.[12]

The most thoughtful Americans often held two opinions about the new Constitution. "The New Government will abridge the powers of State legislatures," wrote a prominent Philadelphia merchant and broker, "& I suppose in some measure will impair their Constitutions—These things I am afraid the people will not readily consent to, and yet if they do not I am of opinion America cannot exist as one nation; So I see great difficulties every way."[13]

Those difficulties began the day after the Constitutional Convention adjourned. In one of the worst political blunders of his career, Franklin led Pennsylvania's delegation from the Constitutional Convention into the Pennsylvania Assembly to urge an immediate call for a ratification convention. He hoped that if Pennsylvania became the first state to ratify, Philadelphia would become the most eligible site for the new federal capital.

"Dr. Franklin," commented Georgia's William Pierce, "is . . . the greatest phylosopher [scientist] of the present age . . . the very heavens obey him, and the Clouds yield up their Lightning to be imprisoned. But what claim he has to the politician, posterity must determine. It is certain that he does not shine much in public Council."[14]

Far from shining, in fact, Franklin's political image grew tarnished by his very participation in a Constitutional Convention delegation that failed to include a single representative from the vast territory outside Philadelphia. The delegates in that gathering that he now led into the State Assembly were all prominent Philadelphia bankers, lawyers, and merchants—the very men that farmers across the state believed had been exploiting and cheating them. Among them was the treacherous Thomas Mifflin, the Speaker of the State Assembly. A prominent Philadelphia merchant, Mifflin had been quartermaster general during the Revolutionary War and had reaped unsavory profits by withholding food and clothing supplies from Valley Forge in his own warehouses until prices reached exorbitantly high levels. Accused later of embezzlement, he resigned from the army, but bought his way into Pennsylvania politics and the Speaker's post in the Assembly. It was he who read the new Constitution to the Pennsylvania Assembly and an audience of cheering Federalists on Friday morning, September 28, 1787, just as the Confederation

Congress in New York resolved to transmit the Constitution to the various states for ratification.

By the end of the day, the Federalist-dominated Pennsylvania Assembly compounded the errors their delegates had made at the Constitutional Convention by resolving to call a state ratification convention—without permitting debate by the nearly two dozen assemblymen from Pennsylvania's back country. The following morning, the angry inlanders refused to appear, leaving Mifflin and his Federalists two assemblymen short of a quorum to vote on a time and place for the convention and the means of electing delegates. Mifflin ordered a sergeant at arms and a clerk to find at least two absent members and order them to the hall. A crowd of rowdy Federalists followed them to the boardinghouse where many Antifederalists lodged. The mob broke into the house and dragged two protesting assemblymen onto the street back to the State House and into the Assembly hall, where sentries forced them to remain while Federalists attempted to vote on holding elections to the state ratification convention.

"I have been forcibly brought into the Assembly room contrary to my wishes," protested Assemblyman James M'Calmont, who represented the Franklin County hill country two hundred miles west of Philadelphia. M'Calmont demanded that he be allowed to leave.

"I hope," responded Federalist William Lowrey of Lancaster, "as the gentleman says he was forcibly brought, he will give some reason why force was necessary to make him do his duty. . . . Surely his being brought by force and against his wishes is not a reason that he should be suffered to go off again."[15]

Scottish-born Hugh H. Brackenridge, a Federalist from Westmoreland County (the Pittsburgh area) and founder of the *Pittsburgh Gazette,* thought it "proper for the House to discuss, whether their officers by force have brought this member here. . . . But if the member has been conducted by the citizens of Philadelphia to his seat . . . it must lie with him to obtain satisfaction. . . . Now, if the gentleman can show that his life will be endangered by staying with us . . . we may grant him the indulgence he asks for—waiving the whole story of his coming."[16]

M'Calmont demanded a reading of the rules, one of which imposed a fine of five shillings on a member who, by failing to answer the roll, leaves the Assembly without a quorum. M'Calmont rose from his seat, put his hand in his pocket, and threw some coins on the Speaker's table. "Here is your five shillings, so let me go." As the gallery roared with laughter, the Speaker rejected the coins, saying that the member appointed to receive fines was absent. M'Calmont nonetheless headed for the door.

"Stop him; stop him!" cried the gallery.

When the Speaker had restored order, Philadelphia assemblyman Thomas FitzSimons intervened, and after whispering with M'Calmont said that the Franklin County assemblyman had "occasion to go out and was willing to go in company with the sergeant at arms." As the gallery responded with catcalls, the Speaker put the question to the Assembly, which voted almost unanimously that he control his private functions and remain in the chamber. In rapid succession, the Assembly then fixed the first Tuesday in November for elections to the ratification convention, which was to convene two weeks thereafter, on November 20. As the gallery cheered, M'Calmont hurried out of the hall to attend to personal needs.[17]

The Assembly's conduct did not inspire confidence in Federalist plans for ending mob rule and anarchy under the Constitution—or assuage fears that the Constitution might produce tyrannical rule. The *New York Morning Post* described the day's events in Philadelphia as an "outrageous FRACAS . . . in consequence of a virtuous minority of the Legislature refusing to vote against their conscience;—an Event perhaps unparalelled [sic] in any Age or Country."[18]

But the *Pennsylvania Herald* blamed "the wanton desertion of *nineteen* [Antifederalists] of its members . . . [for] the scandal to which our legislature was . . . exposed."[19] The *Pennsylvania Gazette* hailed the Assembly: "From the time [of] the resolution of Congress till its adoption by the State of Pennsylvania was only *twenty* hours. Such is the zeal of Pennsylvania to show her attachment to a vigorous, free, and wise frame of national government. In consequence . . . the bells of Christ Church rang. . . . Many hundreds of citizens of the first character attended in the lobby, and at the door of the State House . . . and testified their joy . . . by three heartfelt cheers."[20]

News of the events in Philadelphia elated Virginia's George Mason, who wrote to Elbridge Gerry in Massachusetts, predicting, "shou'd many of the States pursue such intemperate & violent Measures as the Legislature of Pennsylvania has done, it requires no great Degree of Penetration to foresee the Consequences—a federal System will be defeated by the rash & improper means taken to support it, & the People of these United States involved in all the Evils of Civil War. Indeed the precipitation with which the City of Philadelphia, & that party in their Legislature, are attempting to force the new Government upon the People, betrays their Consciousness of it's not bearing the Test of impartial examination—they dread a thorough Knowledge & public Discussion of the Subject, & wish to hurry it down."[21]

But in a report to his foreign minister, French consul Louis-Guillaume Otto blamed "the conduct of both factions" for the Assembly debacle:

> The public was still busy examining the new Constitution and seemed, on the whole, to admire it, when the legislative Assembly of Pennsylvania imprudently . . . revived the jealousy and anxiety of democrats. In a blunder that is difficult to explain, Pennsylvania limited its delegation at the Constitutional Convention to Philadelphians; the other counties, whose interests have always been different from those of the capital were hardly satisfied. . . . In forcing the minority to ratify the new government without debate, the legislature acted so harshly and precipitously as to render any new government very suspect. . . . It could strike a fatal blow . . . the alarm is sounded, the public is on guard and they are now examining in detail what they would have adopted almost blindly.[22]

Philadelphia lawyer James Wilson, perhaps the most reasonable Pennsylvania delegate to the Constitutional Convention, tried to calm things down. Called by his contemporaries "a genius [who] understands all the passions that influence . . . Man,"[23] Wilson went before a large crowd in the Pennsylvania State House Yard and denied Antifederalist charges that "the federal constitution [was] designed . . . to annihilate . . . state governments.

> I will . . . prove that upon their existence, depends the existence of the fœderal government. . . . The president is to be chosen by elec-

tors, nominated . . . [by] the legislature of each state . . . so that if
there is no legislature, there can be no electors, and consequently
the office of president cannot be supplied. The senate is to be composed of two senators from each state, chosen by the legislature;
and therefore if there is no legislature, there can be no senate.

Wilson went on to crush every Antifederalist argument, calling a
federal bill of rights superfluous because most state constitutions already contained similar provisions. The new Congress, he said, could
not abrogate freedom of the press, because the Constitution did not
give it power to do so. As for the taxing powers of Congress, he
stated that "the dignity of the union" depended on the ability of the
government "to discharge debts contracted upon the collective faith
of the states for their common benefit." Wilson called Antifederalist
fears of tyranny "mere effusion of a wild imagination, or a factious
spirit." Wilson charged that any person who opposes the Constitution does so "not because it is injurious to the liberties of his country,
but because it affects his schemes of wealth and consequence.

> I will confess indeed that I am not a blind admirer of this plan of
> government, and that there are some parts of it, which if my wish
> had prevailed, would certainly have been altered. But, when I
> reflect how widely men differ in their opinions . . . I am satisfied
> that any thing nearer to perfection could not have been accom-
> plished. If there are errors . . . the seeds of reformation are sown in
> the work itself, and the concurrence of two thirds of the congress
> may at any time introduce alterations and amendments. Regarding
> it then, in every point of view . . . I am bold to assert, that it is the
> best form of government which has ever been offered to the
> world.[24]

Although his listeners had interrupted him several times with
applause, they roared with approval as he ended his speech. The
Pennsylvania Herald printed an "extra" edition with the speech, because, as editor Alexander J. Dallas* explained, "It is the first author-
itative explanation of the principles of the New Federal Constitution,

---

*Dallas was a Scottish-born lawyer who would later become James Madison's treasury
secretary.

and . . . may serve to obviate some objections, which have been raised to that system."[25]

Benjamin Franklin was elated, and sent a copy of the Constitution to a friend in Paris. If it succeeds in America, he posited, "I do not see why you might not in Europe carry the Project . . . into Execution, by forming a Federal Union and One Grand Republick of all its different States & Kingdoms; by means of a like Convention; for we had many Interests to reconcile."[26]

6

"Unite or Die"

THE BLUNDERS OF PHILADELPHIA FEDERALISTS in suppressing debate over the Constitution had harsh consequences in the farm country to the west. Incensed by the abuse their Antifederalist representatives had suffered in Philadelphia, farmers and frontiersmen muttered about armed revolt, secession—even unification with Canada and restoration of ties to Britain. Although rumors of their dissent filtered eastward with traders bringing goods to market, Federalists dismissed such reports disdainfully as emanating from a tiny minority of ever-present malcontents and social outcasts in the frontier population. Citing the ease with which the Massachusetts militia had crushed similar dissent by Shaysites, Federalists focused instead on good news.

"Your good Angel, I am persuaded, will not desert you," wrote David Humphreys, another of Washington's many devoted wartime aides-de-camp. A graduate of Yale College, Humphreys was back in New Haven and sent his former patron an optimistic assessment of Connecticut's political status. Beset economically by Boston and New York port taxes and terrified by Shays's Rebellion in neighboring Massachusetts, Connecticut Federalists were second only to those in Pennsylvania in their rush to call a ratification convention. Unlike Antifederalists elsewhere who opposed all taxes, Connecticut Antifederalists damaged their cause and all but assured Federalist success by embracing taxation, but urging assessment according to individual wealth. The proposal united all the powerful families of the state with almost every farmer and property owner. "All the different Classes in the liberal professions will be in favor of the proposed Constitution," Humphreys assured Washington. "What will tend, perhaps, more than any thing to the adoption of the new System, will be an universal opinion of your being elected President of the United States, and an expectation that you will accept it for a while."[1]

With Connecticut's nine newspapers refusing to publish articles by Antifederalists (only one newspaper acknowledged that there were any Antifederalists in Connecticut), the Federalist majority in Connecticut's House of Representatives voted without debate to call for town meetings across the state on November 12 to elect delegates to a ratification convention to be held on January 3, 1788.

Massachusetts was the next state to consider a call to convention, with Governor John Hancock delivering a copy of the Constitution to a joint session of both houses. Although he opposed ratification of the Constitution as written, he all but ordered the legislature to call a ratification convention without debate, saying that neither he nor the legislature had the prerogative "to decide this momentous affair." The legislature agreed and set January 9, 1788, for the ratification convention, with election of delegates to be held in various towns from November 19 through January 9. Only then did Speaker of the House James Warren, a Plymouth merchant and farmer, read the letter he had received from Elbridge Gerry:

"I have the honor to inclose, pursuant to my commission, the constitution proposed by the federal convention," Gerry wrote. "To this system I gave my dissent." He cited his principal objections:

> the people . . . have no security for the right of election—that some powers of the legislature are ambiguous, and others indefinite and dangerous—that the executive is blended with, and will have an undue influence over, the legislature—that the judicial department will be oppressive—that treaties . . . may be formed by the president with . . . two-thirds of a quorum of the senate . . . and that the system is without the security of a bill of rights.
>
> As the convention was called for "the sole and express purpose of revising the articles of confederation . . ." I did not conceive that these powers extended to the formation of the plan proposed.[2]

Both Warren and Gerry knew it was pointless to propose constitutional amendments in the legislature, which had no authority to consider such proposals. Like Hancock, they would save their efforts to change the Constitution until the ratification convention. If, together with Virginia and New York, Massachusetts voted against ratification, they would effectively block formation of the new union and its powerful central government.

Over the next two weeks, Georgia, New Jersey, and Delaware in quick succession issued their calls to convention. From the first, the Constitution had found widespread popular support in most of the underpopulated states, particularly poor rural frontier states such as Georgia. Beset by Indian raids and incursions by Spanish troops on their southern and western borders, Georgians welcomed the prospect of a central government with a standing army to protect its frontiers. As Washington put it to Samuel Powel, "If a weak State with the Indians on its back and the Spaniards on its flank does not see the necessity of a General Government, there must I think be wickedness or insanity in the way."[3] New Jersey, on the other hand, was beset by port duties imposed by New York and Pennsylvania on its imports and exports through New York City and Philadelphia. It looked to the new federal government to strip the states of powers to tax international trade. And Delaware, with its tiny population and exposure to the ocean, was eager for federal protection against invasion by foreign powers—including Pennsylvania!

In early November, the Rhode Island legislature outraged Washington and the Federalists by doing what no other state had dared contemplate: after having refused to send a delegate to the Constitutional Convention, it now refused to call a ratification convention to permit citizens of the state to consider the Constitution. Dominated by a handful of powerful merchants, "Rogue Island,"[4] as Federalists called it, had long been a leading commercial center. Narragansett Bay allowed ships to avoid the long voyage around Cape Cod to Boston and therefore captured much of the ocean and coastal trade to and from eastern Connecticut and southern Massachusetts. The result was a huge, steady flow of portside duties for the state and profitable freight forwarding fees for Rhode Island merchants. Neither the state nor its merchants were eager to share their bounty with a federal government.* "From the proceedings of our Legislature," complained a Rhode Island Federalist, "*our rulers* have not yet compleated their diabolical Schemes. How far they mean to carry their vile plans, time alone must make known. A viler and more abandoned sett of beings never disgraced any Legislative, Judicial or Executive Authorities since the Fall of Adam."[5]

In early November, Pennsylvania's propertied men became the first Americans to vote for delegates to their state's ratification convention, and before the end of the year, Maryland, North Carolina, and New Hampshire would bring to nine the number of states that had decided to hold ratification conventions. One of the four that had yet to call a convention was New York, where Antifederalist governor George Clinton seemed prepared to use his militia, if necessary, to keep his state out of the Union. He believed there could be no effective union without New York's geographic link between New England and the mid-Atlantic and southern states.

Ironically, Clinton had been a staunch nationalist as a general in the Revolutionary War, when the Continental Congress had frustrated him as much as it had Washington by its lack of taxing powers and consequent failure to provide the army with adequate supplies. Elected governor of New York in 1777, he grew ever more frustrated as efforts to strengthen Congress by delegates from his own state and from New Hampshire, Massachusetts, and Connecticut met nothing but opposition from mid-Atlantic and southern states. By the time the last British troops evacuated New York at the end of 1783, Clinton had lost all faith in the Confederation and its national legislature.

With the British gone, New York began collecting $100,000 to $250,000 a year (about $2 million to $5 million in today's dollars) in duties on goods flowing through the port of New York. The total amounted to one-third to one-half the state's annual income—more than enough to keep property taxes low and ensure Clinton the solid political support of Dutch-origin owners of the large estates that

---

*Rhode Island's opposition to the Constitution also stemmed from the federal government's policy of paying off state debts with paper money.

George Clinton. The governor of New York ran his state like
a private fiefdom and seemed prepared to secede rather than
accede to the Constitution and see the federal government
deprive his state of revenues from import-export duties.

lined the Hudson River north of New York City. By the time he
heard the call to the Constitutional Convention, Clinton had
turned New York into a personal fiefdom and become one of America's most powerful—and richest—governors. In office for ten years,
he had wooed and won the unfailing political loyalty of small farmers by engineering the transfer of the state capital, for part of the
year, from the merchant-banking center in New York City to the
heart of the farm belt in Poughkeepsie, 85 miles up the Hudson
River opposite Ulster County and Clinton's own home. Ulster was a
particularly large farming area bordered by the Hudson on the east and
the Delaware River on the west; its county seat of Kingston had been
one of several New York capitals until British troops burned it in 1777

to avenge earlier losses along the Hudson River Valley. Although Clinton eschewed public displays of wealth and prided himself as a herald of republican simplicity, he nonetheless had eight slaves and wallowed in wealth. With the capital rooted in his own section of the state for part of the year, Clinton extended his political power by dispensing hundreds of jobs and local judgeships to farmer friends, along with shares in more than $4 million in Tory properties the state had confiscated at the beginning of the Revolution.

Federalist Gouverneur Morris, whose three-thousand-acre Morrisania estate lay in what is now the Bronx, bitterly attacked Clinton and "the wicked Industry of those who have long habituated themselves to live on the Public, and cannot bear the Idea of being removed from the Power and Profit of State Government, which has been and still is the Means of supporting themselves, their Families and Dependents."[6]

Undeterred, Clinton appointed his political henchman John Lamb as collector of the impost, to divert enough port duties to his political and, indirectly, his personal benefit to create a network of sinecures that became the gears of America's first great political machine. The state constitution vested him with "supreme executive power and authority" and the right to call the legislature into special session or prorogue it for as many as sixty days. His three-year term in office was the longest of any governor in America, with no limit on the number of consecutive terms he could serve. As governor— in effect, ruler—of the state, he carried the title "His Excellency, the Governor-General and Commander-in-Chief of all militia, and Admiral of the Navy of the State of New-York." Ironically, it was John Jay and other Federalists who had written the state constitution to gain control of state government themselves, but yeoman farmers voted for Clinton and his allies, who later formed the core of the Antifederalist movement that now threatened the proposed new federal Constitution.

Clinton had not started life with such wealth and honors. He was the son of a frontier farmer in Ulster County, New York, who supplemented his meager income from the land by surveying. His work came to the attention of the colonial governor, who rewarded him by giving his nine-year-old son George a sinecure for life as clerk of the Court of Common Pleas of Ulster County, a position he would hold for fifty-three years.

Although he had started life as a farmer, young Clinton went to sea on a privateer to expand his opportunities. On his return, he fought briefly in the French and Indian War; became a lawyer; and, like Patrick Henry in Virginia, married into a wealthy, politically powerful family. A member of the Continental Congress when it declared American independence, Clinton was elected both governor and lieutenant governor the following year, and he served as a militia general and Continental Army brigadier general during the remainder of the Revolutionary War. He gained national fame when he rode alongside Washington into New York to take control of the city after the British evacuation in 1783. The flow of income from customs duties collected in New York's harbor restored the state's economic health—and inflated his political power (and, some would argue, his personal wealth) to levels matched by only a few other men in America. He was not about to cede that power and the state's income to a federal government. Hoping to slow or undermine the Constitutional Convention, he limited his state delegation to three men, two of whom were Antifederalist allies who abruptly walked out after only about six weeks, arguing—correctly—that their mandate had been to revise the Articles of Confederation, not to write a new constitution or create a new government. Their departure left New York with but one delegate, Alexander Hamilton—not enough, under Convention rules, for the state to cast a vote on any issue or on the Constitution itself. Although Hamilton signed the document, he could not vote for it.

When Congress sent the Constitution to the states for ratification, New York's legislature was not in session, and Clinton decided against asking his political allies in the legislature to hold a special session to vote on calling a state ratification convention. Instead, he decided to wait until the legislature held its regular annual session at the beginning of 1788 and use the interim to campaign against the Constitution. Like Patrick Henry, Clinton planned to prevent ratification by blocking the call to convention in the legislature. If he failed there, he would organize a majority in the convention to vote against ratification. At the same time, he would join Patrick Henry in urging other states and the Confederation Congress to call for a second constitutional convention to amend the existing document or write a new one. Federalists claimed that as a last resort, Clinton was prepared to form a separate "middle confederacy" with Virginia and other dissenting states and leave the United States.

Hamilton was outraged and again accused Clinton of having "greater attachment to his own power than to the public good." David Humphreys called Clinton one of the "popular demagogues who are determined to keep themselves in office at the risque of everything."[7]

Even before Congress sent the Constitution to the states for ratification, the full text of the document began appearing in newspapers across America. As the official printers of the Convention, the publishers of the *Pennsylvania Packet* printed five hundred copies of a special six-page publication containing the full text, which the Convention gave to delegates and sent to political leaders across the nation. All nine New York newspapers published it, and it appeared in pamphlet editions in New York City and elsewhere in the state— including German and Dutch editions. On September 27—the day before Congress had sent the document to the states—Clinton began his assault with an article in the *New York Journal*. Writing under the pseudonym "Cato"—a standard practice then*—Clinton warned "the Citizens of the State of New York . . . to recollect that the wisest and best of men [a reference to Washington] may err, and their errors, if adopted, may be fatal to the community."[8] Clinton ordered John Lamb to recruit Antifederalists and flood nearby states with leaflets assailing the Constitution—a tactic Federalist Noah

---

*Pseudonymous and anonymous works date back centuries with early criticisms of church and state by authors who would otherwise have faced punishment by imprisonment, torture, and/or death if they revealed their identities. Pseudonyms allowed authors in seventeenth- and eighteenth-century Britain and America to avoid arrest for criticizing government and government officials and to avoid libel suits and duels for criticizing other individuals. They also allowed authors to present independent social and political ideas and avoid judgment based on their political affiliations and social status. Pseudonyms and anonyms also provided vehicles for women to publish their works.

Webster's *New York Magazine* compared to treasonable activities during the Revolution. "Nothing . . . can equal the meanness of the Antifederalist junto in America," Webster declared, "but the low arts of our enemies during the war. Like them the Anti-Federal men are circulating hand-bills, fraught with sophistry, declamation and falsehoods, to delude the people and excite jealousies."[9]

The prominent Hartford, Connecticut, merchant and ardent Federalist Jeremiah Wadsworth confirmed that "a pamphlet is circulating here . . . written with Art & tho by no means unanswerable . . . is calculated to do much harm—it came from New York under cover."[10]

Hamilton and John Jay agreed that they could not allow Clinton's sallies to remain unchallenged, and they decided to write a series of essays under the pseudonym "Publius," a reference to Publius Valerius Publicola, a Roman consul from 509 to 507 B.C., whom some reference works credit with implementing popular anti-monarchical measures in the early Roman Republic.* The pseudonym would permit them to write without Hamilton's risking accusations of having violated the Constitutional Convention's rule of secrecy.[11] "The constitution . . . has in this state warm friends and warm enemies," Hamilton explained to Washington. "The first impressions every where are in its favor; but the artillery of its opponents makes some impression."[12]

With other responsibilities weighing heavily on each, neither Hamilton nor Jay had much time for the project; Hamilton was a congressman and a practicing attorney, and Jay was secretary for foreign affairs. They invited Gouverneur Morris and other Federalists to contribute, but they were equally busy. Only James Madison agreed to collaborate. As a southerner in Congress, he had fewer professional distractions in New York and hoped to use the essays to combat Antifederalists in his home state as well as in New York. "It was

---

*According to James Madison, Hamilton had originally planned addressing *The Federalist* "to the people of New York under the signature of a Citizen of New York." Because of Madison's subsequent participation, however, the authors found what they believed was an appropriate pseudonym.—James Madison to James Kirk Paulding, July 23, 1818, Rives Collection of the Madison Papers in the Library of Congress.

understood," he recounted, "that each was to write as their respective situations permitted, preserving as much as possible an order & connection in the papers successively published . . . the printer was to keep his newspaper open for four numbers every week."[13]

For newspapers, of course, the war of words over the Constitution proved a windfall of profits, increasing circulation to levels beyond the wildest ambitions of some printers—and even provoking the *Albany Gazette* to publish "The News-Mongers' Song," a poem that included the following among its fifteen verses:

> Good news, brother dealers in metre & prose!
> The world has turn'd *buffer* and coming to blows;
> Write *good sense* or *non sense*, my boys, it's all one,
> All persons may fire when the battle's begun.
>
> Much joy, brother printers! the day is our own,
> A time like the present sure never was known:
> Predictions are making-predictions fulfil,
> All nature seems proud to bring grist to our mills.[14]

A reader in Albany, New York, expressed a different point of view, arguing that newspapers had "*troubled* this part of the country with *false* alarms . . . in abundance.—The paper on which these things are printed, however, is of a *soft* texture, and answers the good people a very *necessary* purpose."[15]

"The Federalist I," as Hamilton labeled the first of his essays, appeared in the New York *Independent Journal* on October 27, 1787. Jay wrote the next four, and when Jay fell ill, Hamilton picked up the burden of the work for all but two of the next thirty-one essays— until the New York State Legislature convened in early January, when Clinton presented the Constitution to the people of New York and their representatives. Hamilton sent his first essay to Washington, but it was Madison who, after reading Hamilton's and Jay's work, decided to use their writings to fight Patrick Henry in Virginia as well as Clinton in New York. Madison sent the first seven essays to Washington, urging him to put them "in the hands of some of your confidential correspondents at Richmond who would have them reprinted there."[16] Washington was elated at the prospects of a new weapon to fire incognito from the isolated woods of Mount Vernon against Patrick Henry's Antifederalists in Richmond. Washington immediately forwarded them to his son-in-law David Stuart, then serving in the Virginia House of Delegates.

"If there is a Printer in Richmond who is really well disposed to support the New Constitution," Washington wrote, "he would do well to give them a place in his Paper. They are (I think I may venture to say) written by able men; and before they are finished, will, if I mistake not, place matters in a true point of light. Altho' I am acquainted with some of the writers . . . I am not at liberty to disclose their names, nor would I have it known that they are sent by me to you for promulgation."[17]

With Madison writing numbers ten and fourteen, the first thirty-six essays of *The Federalist* appeared under the pseudonym "Publius" every week for the rest of the year in four New York City newspapers and twenty-one newspapers in nine other states, including the *Virginia Independent Chronicle*, which published twenty-four essays in Richmond. The initial essays also appeared in Connecticut, Massachusetts, and North Carolina and proved to be among the most effective weapons Federalists would have. A reasoned, superbly written, and refreshingly unemotional explanation of the new Constitution and how the new government would function, the essays proved critical in states where ratification was far from certain. In simplest terms, *The Federalist* laid bare the differences between *liberty* under a republican government ruled by elected representatives of the people, and *license* under a democracy ruled with unlimited powers by a majority of the people themselves—that is, the masses. It demonstrated how the new republican government would protect liberty and prevent license—a task the Confederation had demonstrably failed to do.

"After an unequivocal experience of the inefficacy of the subsisting Federal Government," Hamilton addressed "the people of the State of New-York" in "The Federalist I," "you are called upon to deliberate on a new Constitution for the United States of America.

> The subject speaks its own importance; comprehending in its consequences nothing less than the existence of the UNION . . . an empire, in many respects, the most interesting in the world. It has been frequently remarked, that it seems to have been reserved to

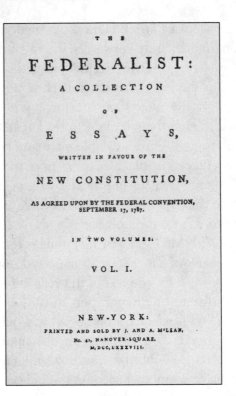

THE

FEDERALIST:

A COLLECTION

OF

E S S A Y S,

WRITTEN IN FAVOUR OF THE

NEW CONSTITUTION,

AS AGREED UPON BY THE FEDERAL CONVENTION,
SEPTEMBER 17, 1787.

IN TWO VOLUMES.

VOL. I.

NEW-YORK:

PRINTED AND SOLD BY J. AND A. M'LEAN,
No. 41, HANOVER-SQUARE.
M, DCC, LXXXVIII.

The Federalist. The title page of a bound volume of the first two dozen essays of this publication, a series of eighty-five essays by Alexander Hamilton, James Madison, and John Jay expounding the benefits of the proposed federal constitution. Authorship of three essays remains in dispute.

the people of this country, by their conduct and example, to decide the important question, whether societies of men are really capable or not, of establishing good government from reflection and choice, or whether they are forever destined to depend, for their political constitutions, on accident and force. If there be any truth in the remark . . . a wrong election of the part we shall act, may . . . be considered as the general misfortune of mankind.

Among the most formidable of the obstacles which the new Constitution will have to encounter, may readily be distinguished the obvious interest of a certain class of men in every State to resist all changes which may hazard a diminution of the power, emolument and consequence of the offices they hold under the State-establishments—and the perverted ambition of another class of men, who will either hope to aggrandize themselves by the confusions of their country, or will flatter themselves with fairer prospects of elevation from the subdivision of the empire into several partial confederacies, than from its union under one government.[18]

There was no way for Hamilton, Madison, or Washington to measure the immediate impact of *The Federalist*, although Washington grew convinced the essays would have "a good effect . . . in this State [Virginia] . . . as there are certainly characters in it who are no friends to a general government—perhaps I might go further, & add, who would have no great objection to the introduction of anarchy & confusion." As he mailed the letter, however, he received disturbing news from his son-in-law in Richmond: "I am sorry to inform you that the Constitution has lost ground so considerably that it is doubtful whether it has any longer a majority in its favor."[19]

It remained a foregone conclusion, however, that Federalists would dominate the ratification conventions scheduled during the remainder of 1787. On December 7, Delaware was first to ratify—unanimously (30 to 0). Its small size and disproportionately large shoreline made union with other states essential to its defense. Although Pennsylvania's ratification convention had convened more than two weeks earlier, Federalist mobs had terrorized the city, throwing stones through the windows of Antifederalist homes and lodging houses of visiting Antifederalists. When the ratification convention began, Antifederalists immediately accused the Federalist majority of trying to stifle debate—as they had in the Assembly in September. Federalists yielded and agreed to allow each delegate to speak as often as he wished before bringing the Constitution to a vote. In a captivating speech on November 24, the eloquent Scot James Wilson reiterated what the Constitution represented:

> America has it in her power to adopt either of the following modes of government: she may dissolve the individual sovereignty of the states and become one consolidated empire; she may be divided into thirteen independent, and unconnected commonwealths; she may be erected into two or more confederacies; or, lastly, she may become one comprehensive federal republic. . . . Of these [first] three . . . I must observe that they obtained no advocates in the Federal Convention. . . . The general sentiment in that body, and, I believe, the general sentiment of the citizens of America, is expressed in the motto which some of them have chosen, UNITE OR DIE.[20]

Antifederalists reiterated their opposition to the Constitution: that the Constitutional Convention had exceeded its authority by creating a new government instead of reforming the old, that the Constitution contained no bill of rights to protect individual liberties and private property, and that the creation of a federal government with "supreme" powers would destroy state sovereignty. "In the Preamble," argued one Antifederalist, "it is said, 'We the People,' and not 'We the States,' which therefore is a compact between individuals . . . and not between separate states enjoying independent power and delegating a portion of that power for their common benefit."[21]

"Ah-ha!" shouted James Wilson triumphantly as he stood to rebut. "The secret is now disclosed, and it is discovered to be a dread, that the boasted state sovereignties will under this system be disrobed of part of their power. . . .

> Upon what principle is it contended that the sovereign power resides in the state governments? . . . my position is that the sovereignty resides in the people; they have not parted with it; they have only dispensed such portions of power as were conceived necessary for the public welfare. This Constitution stands upon this broad principle . . . that its existence depends upon the supreme authority of the people alone.[22]

After Sunday's day of rest, the renowned Philadelphia physician Benjamin Rush opened Monday's debate on December 3 by assailing the concept of state sovereignty. "This plurality of sovereignty is in politics what plurality of gods is in religion—it is the idolatry, the heathenism of government. We sit here as representatives of *the people*—we were not appointed by the legislature. A passion for state sovereignty dissolved the union of Greece. Britain—France—enjoyed more advantages *united* than *separate*," he said, his voice filled with passion. "The sovereignty of Pennsylvania is ceded to the United States. I have now a vote for members of Congress. I am a citizen of every state."[23]

Irish-born John Smilie stood and scoffed in his Irish brogue. "I never heard anything so ridiculous except a former [statement] by the same gentleman," purred the Antifederalist from Fayette County in western Pennsylvania, where farmers had talked of seceding from "the state of Philadelphia."

Benjamin Rush. America's most renowned physician,
he declared himself "a citizen of every state" in
heralding the ratification of the Constitution by his
state (Pennsylvania).

"We wish alterations made in the Confederation," Smilie demanded in charming but forceful singsong phrases, "but we wish not
to sacrifice the rights of men to obtain them. Rights of conscience
should be secured."[24]

Federalist delegates and their supporters in the gallery began
shouting Smilie down and, as a Federalist delegate stood to defend
the Constitution, they roared their approval. Smilie shouted back,
"Those who clap and laugh are not the people of Pennsylvania. If
the gallery were filled with bayonets, it would not intimidate me."[25]

An explosion of catcalls filled the hall. "Mr. President," Smilie
continued his counterattack, his face flushing red, "I confess that . . .
the gentlemen on the other side have, indeed, an argument which
surpasses and supersedes all others—a party in the gallery prepared
to clap and huzza in affirmation of their speeches. But, sir, let it be
remembered that this is not the voice of the people of Pennsylvania . . . and were this Convention assembled at another place, the

sound would be of a different nature, for the sentiments of the citizens are different indeed."[26]

Infuriated by Smilie's remarks, Wilson demanded to know how "the honorable gentleman from Fayette claimed for the minority, the merit of contending for the rights of mankind . . . what then are the majority contending for? Who are the majority in this assembly? Are they not the people? Are they not the representatives of the people, as well as the minority? Were they not elected by the people as well as the minority?"[27]

Unlike Wilson, Rush never replied to Smilie's insult. A brilliant scientist, he had received a bachelor's degree from the College of New Jersey (later, Princeton) and his medical training at the College of Philadelphia (later, the University of Pennsylvania) and the University of Edinburgh. Despite the honors and wealth that devolved from his professional career, he had risked all to proclaim his allegiance to American independence, and now, once again, he jeopardized his professional future by publicly supporting the Constitution. Before he could respond to Smilie's insult, however, their debate became moot. With a two-thirds majority, Federalists ratified the Constitution by a vote of 46 to 23. To Franklin's disappointment, however, the three-week debate had delayed ratification long enough to prevent Pennsylvania from being the first state to ratify. Although he had not been a delegate himself, he nonetheless led Federalist delegates and other notables to Epple's Tavern the following day to offer thirteen toasts—the first to "The People of the United States" and the last to "Peace and free governments to all the nations in the world."[28]

As Christmas of 1787 approached, Pennsylvania's submission to federal rule so elated New Jersey delegates that they ratified the Constitution unanimously (38 to 0), trusting that a new federal government would lift the crushing burden that Philadelphia customs duties exacted on New Jersey consumers of imported goods. Washington, too, was ecstatic and began to believe that ratification was approaching a certainty. He called the opponents of the Constitution "so small a proportion to its friends that there is little doubt of its [ratification] taking place.

"Three states," he wrote to a friend in Ireland who had supported the American struggle for independence, "have already decided in its favor . . . from every information the others will be found pretty fully in sentiment with them. The establishment of an enerjetic [sic] Government will disappoint the hopes and expectations of those who are unfriendly to this Country."[29]

To the dismay of Federalists, however, the Antifederalist minority at the Pennsylvania ratification convention refused to accept the majority's decision. Outraged by Federalist suppression of all debate at the state ratification convention, twenty-one of the twenty-three members who had voted against ratification signed a document titled *Dissent of the Minority*, which Philadelphia's *Independent Gazetteer* published on December 18. In addition to the now-ubiquitous attacks on the secrecy of the Constitutional Convention and its lack of authority to write a new constitution, *Dissent* assailed the force used to obtain a quorum at the Pennsylvania Assembly as an example of the type of tyranny Americans could expect from the federal government if the Constitution were ratified. It also listed fourteen suggested amendments, most of which mirrored those of Richard Henry Lee, George Mason, Elbridge Gerry, and other critics of the Constitution: freedom of speech, freedom of the press, guaranteed right of trial by jury in civil cases, and so forth. But it added three others that fired up the passions of Antifederalists: one would have prohibited passage of any law "for disarming the people . . . unless for crimes committed"; a second allowed the states to retain their sovereignty, freedom, and independency; and a third left "the power of organizing, arming and disciplining the militia . . . with the individual states."[30]

Antifederalists circulated *Dissent of the Minority* across the nation. As copies drifted across the Appalachian Mountains to the west, talk of secession grew louder, laced with predictions that Philadelphia merchant-bankers who controlled state government would impose federal taxes, which, when added to state taxes, would force small farms into bankruptcy. Although secessionists in western Massachusetts had failed, settlers in the west country of other states had been more successful. Farmers in western North Carolina had already seceded from the state's eastern establishment and formed the independent State of Franklin. Kentucky settlers were in virtual rebellion from the rest of Virginia, as were farmers across the Allegheny Mountains in western Pennsylvania.

On the day after Christmas, farmers in Cumberland County at the eastern base of the Appalachian Mountains grouped on the edge of Carlisle, the county seat about 125 miles from Philadelphia. Church bells had called citizens to the public square, where Federalists prepared to celebrate ratification with a bonfire and thirteen shots from one of the town's cannons. Before they could begin, according to the local newspaper, "a number of men armed with bludgeons came in regular order from one quarter of the town, while others sallied forth from different streets armed in the same manner." The mob pummeled the unarmed celebrants, brutally beating the cannoneer and others before the celebrants managed to flee. The mob then lit the bonfire; destroyed the cannon and its carriage; burned a copy of the Constitution along with effigies of James Wilson and Thomas McKean, the state's chief justice; then shouted "loud huzzas, with damnation to the 46 members [who had voted for ratification in Philadelphia], and long live the virtuous 23 [who had voted against]."[31]

Federalists regrouped the following day at the courthouse, armed with muskets and bayonets and a new cannon, and determined "to repel, at the risk of their lives any attack which might be made on them.

> A bonfire was made, and the ratification of the Constitution by this state was read, accompanied by the acclamation of all the people present, repeated volleys of musketry and firing of cannon . . . although the mob made their appearance in several places, armed with guns and bludgeons, and even came close to where the Federalists were firing the cannon, and used threatening language, which was treated with every possible contempt, and no violence offered to them.[32]

Among the rioters were the presiding judge of the Cumberland County Court of Common Pleas—a clear indication that unlike Shays's Rebellion in Massachusetts, the resentments that motivated the Carlisle, Pennsylvania, riot embraced a far broader segment of the population. Pennsylvania's "aristocracy" had indeed ratified the Constitution, but a huge proportion of the population had not. Philadelphia's elite had agreed to join the new Union, but questions remained whether the rest of Pennsylvania would do the same. Across the state, printed flyers and pamphlets extolled the "virtuous 23" who had voted against ratification.

"You cannot conceive the violent language used here," a correspondent from Carlisle wrote to Philadelphia's *Independent Gazetteer*, "the whole county [Cumberland] is alive with wrath, and it is spreading from one county to another so rapid, that it is impossible to say where it will end, or how far it will reach, as the best and leading characters in all these counties, during the late war, are now the foremost in this unfortunate dispute." Antifederalists in western counties, the letter continued, "are forming themselves into societies and associations to oppose this new constitution."[33] The Carlisle violence raised the specter of full-scale civil war if the Constitution were ratified as written, without alterations.

On January 2, 1788, Pennsylvania comptroller general John Nicholson joined Philadelphia Antifederalists in drafting a petition to the State Assembly to censure Pennsylvania delegates to the Constitutional Convention for exceeding their authority under the congressional mandate. It asked the state assembly to vote against ratification. He further petitioned the Assembly to instruct Pennsylvania delegates in the Confederation Congress to vote against final ratification "in the said United States."[34] Across the state, *Dissent of the Minority* appeared in Antifederalist newspapers and in pamphlet form and transformed its authors—the "virtuous 23"—into heroes of the Antifederalist movement. On January 2, 1788, *Freeman's Journal* in Philadelphia predicted that "it is almost certain that we will have another convention . . . called in the state, for amending the proposed Constitution, and annexing a bill of rights thereto."[35]

7

"Words to My Brother Ploughjoggers"

On new year's eve of 1787, Georgia became the fourth state to ratify—the third to do so unanimously (26 to 0). Dirt-poor Georgia settlers prayed that the new federal government would send troops to protect them against atrocities by Indian raiders and incursions by Spanish troops. As Washington had predicted, "Nothing but insanity, or a desire of becoming the Allies of the Spaniards or Savages, can disincline them to a Government which holds out the prospect of relief from its present distresses."[1]

On January 1, Connecticut's ratification convention convened, with the state's merchants and farmers geared for bitter attacks on each other. A small group of landed "aristocrats"—the Trumbulls, Dwights, Wolcotts, Swifts, and the like—had ruled the state as their private barony for generations. Although the Trumbulls had attended Harvard, the rest had gone to Yale, where other students acknowledged fealty by addressing them each as "sir"—Sir Wolcott, Sir Dwight, and so on—while students from lesser families, usually farmers' sons, routinely split and fetched wood for them, tended their fireplaces, and performed other menial chores. Although Connecticut's rich soil had allowed both farmers and merchants to prosper during the Revolutionary War, each group assailed the other for profiteering. With war's end, however, farmers and merchants faced common enemies—New York and Massachusetts, both of which imposed heavy duties on imports that traveled to Connecticut and other nearby markets. As such duties devoured an increasing share of the Connecticut's gross revenues—almost one-third by 1787—the state plunged into deep economic depression. Writing under the thinly disguised pseudonym "Landholder," Federalist judge Oliver Ellsworth wrote a series of nine essays that appealed to both farmers and merchants to unite in supporting the federal Constitution, which would strip states of their powers to impose duties on imports.

"Our being tributaries to our sister states is in consequence of the want of a federal system," Ellsworth declared.

> The state of New York raises [about] £80,000 [nearly $5 million today] a year by impost [duties]. Connecticut consumes about one third of the goods upon which this impost is laid; and consequently pays one third of this sum to New York. If we import by the medium of Massachusetts, she has an impost, and to her we pay a tribute. If this is done when we have the shadow of a national government, what shall we not suffer when even that shadow is gone?[2]

Ellsworth's "Demosthenean energy"[3] succeeded in uniting Connecticut's "landed interest" with "the trading interest" and swayed the convention in favor of ratification.

"With great satisfaction," Jonathan Trumbull, the former governor's son, wrote to Washington, "I have the Honor to inform—that, last Evening the Convention of this State, by a great Majority, Voted to ratify & adopt the proposed new Constitution for the United States—Yeas 127—Nays 40. . . . The great Unanimity with which this Decision has been made . . . I hope will have a happy influence on the Minds of our Brethren in the Massachusetts—their Convention is now collecting & will be favored with this Information Tomorrow."[4]

The Massachusetts ratification convention did indeed begin the following day, January 9. By then, five states had ratified the Constitution, although four others besides Massachusetts had called conventions. Massachusetts was, however, the first state where the outcome of the convention was in doubt. Because of its large, widely scattered population, the state had needed seven weeks to elect delegates, with Federalists and Antifederalists firing a ceaseless barrage of accusations at each other in the press; Federalist newspapers even accused Antifederalists of godlessness—a heinous crime in Puritan Massachusetts.

"Has it come to this," asked an editorial in Boston's Antifederalist *American Herald*, "that no person of any denomination is a *Christian*, except those who pray for adoption of the proposed Federal Constitution? If that constitution is as good as its most zealous devotees can imagine, I can by no means suppose that it will be considered . . . as a test of Christianity. In a free government all such *scurrilous* reflections cannot be perused without horror."[5]

Massachusetts delegates would continue their bitter exchange in convention debates for a full month—longer than at any previous state ratification convention. "Our convention meets this morning," Benjamin Lincoln wrote to Washington. As a general under Washington, Lincoln had accepted the ceremonial sword at the British surrender of Yorktown, and it was he who led the state militia to crush Shays's Rebellion in western Massachusetts. "Whether it will be adopted or not, in this State, the most prophetic spirit among us cannot determine. . . . The constitution has very potent adversaries in this State."[6]

The most potent adversary was Elbridge Gerry, whose letter to the legislature explaining his refusal to sign the Constitution had fired Antifederalist passions. The riots in Carlisle, Pennsylvania, they argued, were proof of Gerry's prediction that civil war would ensue if the Constitution were ratified.

Federalists agreed that "Mr. Gerrys letter has done great injury to the proposed New Constitution, more than he will ever be able to do good by a whole life of repentance—every thing went on *firm* & *well* untill that *damn'd* Letter—he has his influence with a certain party. . . . however I don't despair yet, as all the liberal & most sensible men, are highly in favor of it. they stand as firm & unshaken as a Rock—the Insurgent int[e]rest, is the only influence against it—but this is pretty powerfull."[7]

A social radical in his early years, Gerry used his Harvard master's thesis to encourage American merchants to refuse to pay import duties, which he said necessarily raised costs of essential goods. His blind embrace of popular rule suffered a setback in 1774, however, when a mob yielded to hysterical fears and burned down a hospital

Elbridge Gerry. One of three delegates at the Constitutional Convention who refused to sign the document, Gerry called the document "ambiguous and dangerous" and feared that its failure to include a bill of rights would lead to civil war.

Gerry had built to administer smallpox inoculations. Falling under the spell of Samuel Adams, he joined the pro-independence movement, won election to the Continental Congress, signed the Declaration of Independence, and used his family shipping and trading operations in Marblehead, Massachusetts, to import and distribute military supplies to the Continental Army. He had just settled into an elegant mansion in Cambridge with his beautiful—and very rich—wife when Shays's Rebellion threatened to engulf the state in chaos and convinced him to reject democracy and embrace the concept of a stronger central government. At the Constitutional Convention, however, he wavered constantly, and his often inexplicable inconsistencies quickly alienated his colleagues. He embraced the Virginia Plan at first, then attacked it; he chaired the committee that approved the "great compromise" on congressional voting, and he voted with the majority—only to attack the compromise on the floor of the Convention. Described as "a nervous bird-like man," he was "a hesitating and laborious speaker"[8] who, in the end, angered many delegates to the Constitutional Convention by continually preaching compromise and then refusing to sign his name to the finished document. He seemed unable to define what form of government he favored. Although he feared democracy as a formula for mob rule, he wrote to the Massachusetts legislature that republican government as proposed in the Constitution was a formula for tyranny.

In addition to Gerry's letter to the Massachusetts legislature, George Mason's objections to the Constitution appeared in newspapers across Massachusetts. "There seems to be a Class of people among us, who wish for No Government at all," one Federalist responded to Mason's letter.[9] Another warned that Antifederalists were "secret enemies . . . like a venomous viper hugged in your bosom, if possible, will eat out your bowels, prey upon your vitals, and sap the foundation of your national security and happiness."[10]

In mid-October 1787, a squad of new Antifederalist writers—most of them public officials—began a concerted attack on the Constitution under a variety of pseudonyms, whose true identities remain somewhat of a mystery to this day—despite shrewd guesses by shrewd historians. Among the most effective pseudonymous authors was "Brutus," who produced a series of sixteen essays in the *New York Journal*. Four Massachusetts newspapers immediately reprinted the Brutus materials. A series of sixteen essays by "Agrippa" followed. Federalist replies labeled Agrippa variously as an "ignorant loggerhead" or an "ungrateful monster"; one offered "a reward of 500 pounds to anyone who could explain what 'Agrippa' is labouring to prove."[11]

Articles from other out-of-state newspapers also filled the Massachusetts press, while Federalist newspapers reprinted accolades for Washington, Franklin, Alexander Hamilton, and the Constitution and blistering attacks on George Mason, Patrick Henry, George Clinton, and Elbridge Gerry. One newspaper compared Gerry to Benedict Arnold. To counter the effects of Gerry's objections to the Constitution, the Federalist press printed the eloquent speech of Pennsylvania's James Wilson defending the Constitution at his state's ratification convention. Lurking in everyone's mind in Massachusetts, however, was Shays's Rebellion and the atrocities of the subsequent "farmyard wars." Even a few Shaysites grew convinced of the need for a strong federal government to crush anarchy and disorder.

The Antifederalist press, of course, carried opposite, though equally provocative, praise for those who opposed ratification, and condemnation of those who favored it. "Bribery & Corruption!" read a headline in the Boston Gazette. "The most diabolical Plan is on foot to corrupt the members of the Convention, who oppose the Adoption of the new Constitution. Large sums of money have been brought from a neighbouring State for that purpose, contributed by the wealthy."[12] Newspapers in other states immediately reprinted the story, with Philadelphia's Freeman's Journal embellishing the story by announcing "the arrival of a large sum of money [in Boston] from the southward" and asserting that "the rich and well-born [in Massachusetts] had contributed an additional sum, for the purpose of corrupting and bribing the members of their convention to vote for their scheme of power and office-making; as there appeared to be a majority against it . . . part of that money had been applied in hiring a mob of sailors, &c. to surround the seats of the members of convention, and to hiss, hoot and intimidate the country members."[13]

With Federalists planting rumors that Shaysites were remobilizing, the Massachusetts convention elected as its president the state's enormously powerful and popular governor, John Hancock. One of the wealthiest merchant-bankers in America and certainly the wealthiest in Massachusetts, the Harvard-educated Hancock had gained national renown as the president of Congress who was first to sign the Declaration of Independence, using a bold, oversized signature and pronouncing, "There! I guess King George will be able to read that!" Deeply disappointed at losing the appointment as commander in chief of the Continental Army to George Washington, he served as an efficient president of Congress during the early war years, and returned to Massachusetts in 1780 to help frame the Massachusetts constitution. Elected the state's first governor, he served for five years and ducked out of office just long enough to avoid dealing with Shays's Rebellion. After his successor Governor James Bowdoin absorbed all the blame for the Springfield debacle, Hancock returned to office in 1787 and quieted the turmoil by issuing full pardons to Shaysites and forcing through legislation that prevented creditors from seizing clothing, household goods, or tools of trade as security for overdue debt. In an effort to promote reconciliation across the state, Hancock cut government spending by eliminating sinecures and even cut his own salary to permit dramatic reductions in taxes.

Although the state legislature had set January 9 for the convention to begin, hundreds of citizens—Bostonians as well as farmers, Shaysites, and curious out-of-staters—streamed to the State House to view the proceedings, packing the galleries to capacity and stranding hundreds on the street. As cries for admission threatened to disrupt proceedings, the 360 delegates moved to the much larger Brattle Street Church, but poor acoustics made it so difficult for delegates to hear the chair that they moved back to the State House. Overcrowded galleries and poor ventilation in the dead of winter made the stench of humanity unbearable, however. According to Boston pastor Jeremy Belknap, "a mixture of all sorts of Characters" filled the gallery—"Some of [the] insurgents of last winter among them. Several of Shays's Captains & Counsellors."[14] Fearing violence in the packed gallery, convention leaders accepted Belknap's invitation to move to his Congregational Church on Long Lane, where the gallery could hold 600 to 800 spectators.

Recognizing that they faced long and bitter debates, the delegates had counted on John Hancock's renowned mediation skills to maintain order, and although the wily governor accepted the appointment, when it was time for him to bring the convention to order, he was nowhere to be seen. He had stayed home—in bed, he said—with painful gout.

"As soon as the majority is exhibited on either side," Federalist Rufus King predicted with a smile, "I think his health will suffice him to be abroad."[15] Hancock remained in bed for the next three weeks, until the end of the month.

With all its moves between the State House and two churches, the convention did not begin debating the Constitution until January 14, when it invited the controversial Elbridge Gerry to be seated to answer questions about his refusal to sign it. When he rose to

John Hancock. Famed for his bold signature on the Declaration of Independence, Hancock was the first governor of Massachusetts—and also his state's wealthiest, most powerful merchant-banker. He supported ratification of the Constitution on condition that a bill of rights be added.

speak, however, Federalist delegate Judge Francis Dana—ironically, a close friend of Gerry—protested "vociferously" that Gerry was not a delegate. Although Dana said Gerry could respond to specific questions by delegates, he had no right to address the convention. After the convention adjourned for the day, the two got into a fierce shouting—and shoving—match outside the hall. Delegates and spectators rushed to separate the two and restrain them. Gerry shook loose, stomped away angrily, and never returned—a snub that left Antifederalists at the convention without their most knowledgeable spokesman and at a disadvantage that gradually eroded their support in debates.

To keep track of the debates, Hancock asked both camps to brief him each day at Hancock House, his sumptuous mansion on top of Beacon Hill. As the wealthy and powerful head of a sovereign state, Hancock, like New York's George Clinton, did not want to see his own powers or those of his state reduced. On the other hand, a host of internal and external dangers threatened the nation, and, as former president of Congress, he was well aware that the Articles of Confederation gave Congress no powers to raise and support an army and navy. Hancock realized the United States would not survive—indeed, his own state might not survive—unless the states ratified the new Constitution. As a merchant, he knew that geography alone would not leave Massachusetts self-sufficient. In comparison to sea routes to Rhode Island, the long and circuitous route around Cape Cod created long delays for Boston-bound freight from mid-Atlantic and southern states and the Caribbean. If independent Rhode Island lowered its import duties enough, Boston harbor might well deteriorate into a helpless backwater if the state failed to ratify the Constitution and join the Union.

After a week of fruitless debate, Antifederalists maintained a solid majority; the Constitution faced its first defeat unless a second constitutional convention was called to add a bill of rights. "The intelligence from Massachusetts begins to be very ominous to the Constitution," Madison wrote to Washington from New York. "The antifederal party is reinforced by the insurgents, and by the province of Mayne [sic] which apprehends greater obstacles to her scheme of a separate Government, from the new system."[16]

Despite Federalist calls for his public support, Washington had been reluctant to intervene in state debates over the Constitution because of Antifederalist charges that the document assigned a tyrant's powers to the president of the proposed federal government. Even the marquis de Lafayette, an avowed friend of federalism, who called Washington "my adoptive father," confessed to Thomas Jefferson in Paris that he was skeptical about the powers the Constitution gave to the president. "I am afraid that our friends are gone a little too far on the other side—But Suppose it is the Case, and General Washington is the President, I know him too well not to think he will find the danger, and lessen the authority before he goes over."[17] Lafayette had written much the same in an earlier letter to Washington, saying that he approved of the Constitution but was "afraid of two things . . . the want of a declaration of Rights . . . [and] the Great Powers and Possible Continuance of the President, Who May one day or other Become a State Holder [*stathoudérat*, or dictator]. . . . In the Name of America, of Mankind at large, and Your Own Fame, I Beseech You, my dear General, Not to deny Your Acceptance of the office for the first Years—You only Can Settle that Political Machine."[18]

Not a soul in America, including Washington himself, doubted that he would be the first president if the nation ratified the Constitution. He feared that if he entered the debate over the Constitution, however, Antifederalists would attack him personally and taint public opinion about his motives. In any event, that was not Washington's style. Although fiercely ambitious even as a youth, he had long earlier discovered that the best approach to power was to prove himself indispensable by deed—and then feign disinterest. At the Continental Congress of 1775, he stated that "I do not think my self equal to the Command," but he was the only member dressed in military uniform and the only member with battlefield experience. Now, he believed, any display of ambition for the presidency would not only hurt his chances for that office, it might well hurt the chances for ratification of the Constitution and the creation of the office, which he believed essential to the survival of the country.

Madison, however, warned him that Massachusetts might not ratify without his support. A coalition of Gerry, Samuel Adams, and James Warren had won farmer support at the ratification convention and built a majority of 192 to 144 against the Constitution. Madison pleaded for Washington to support Massachusetts Federalists with "an explicit communication of your good wishes for the plan. . . . I have good reason to believe . . . it would be attended with good effects."[19] On January 23, the *Massachusetts Centinel* published "The illustrious WASHINGTON'S opinion of the federal Constitution.

> *Extract of a letter, of a late date, from the illustrious President of the late federal Convention. . . .*
>
> My *decided* opinion of the matter is, that there is *no alternative* between the *adoption* of it and *anarchy*. . . . All the opposition to it . . . is, I must confess, addressed more to the passions than to the

reason; and *clear I am*, if another federal Convention is attempted, that the sentiments of its members will be *more* discordant or *less* accommodating than the last. In fine, they will agree on no general plan. General government is now *suspended by a thread*. I might go further, and say it is *really at an end*, and what will be the consequence of a fruitless attempt to amend the one which is offered, before it is tried . . . does not in my judgment need the *gift of prophecy* to predict.

I am not a blind admirer (for I saw the imperfections) of the Constitution I aided in the birth of, before it was handed to the publick; but I am fully persuaded it is the *best that can be obtained at this time*;—(that it is free from many of the imperfections with which it is charged) and that *it* or *disunion* is before us to choose from. If the first is our election, when the defects of it are experienced, a constitutional door is open for amendments, and may be adopted in a peaceable manner, without tumult or disorder.[20]

The letter appeared in eight other Massachusetts newspapers over the next week and so elated Federalist leaders that they approached opposition leaders with a plan of compromise: in exchange for Antifederalist support for ratification of the Constitution as written, the Federalists agreed to "give way a little to those who are for Adopting it with Amendments."[21] They pledged to support "recommendatory amendments" to the Constitution and join Antifederalists in pressing to amend the Constitution with a bill of rights after the new federal government took office. The language and legalisms of the compromise were too complex for many delegates from the farm country. One asked that Federalists "not play round the subject with their fine stories, like a fox round a trap, but come to it. These lawyers, and men of learning, and monied men, that talk so finely and gloss over matters so smoothly, to make us poor illiterate people, swallow down the pill, expect to get into Congress themselves; they expect to be the managers of this constitution, and get all the power and all money into their own hands, and then they will swallow up all us little folk, like the great *Leviathan*, Mr. President; yes just as the whale swallowed up *Jonah*."[22]

As "learned" Federalists scratched their heads seeking an adequate response, an improbable speaker—Jonathan Smith of Lanesboro—gained recognition and stood:

Mr. President, I am a plain man, and get my living by the plough. I am not used to speak in public, but I beg your leave to say a few words to my brother ploughjoggers in this house. I have lived in a part of the country where I have known the worth of good government, by the want of it. There was a cloud that rose . . . last winter, and spread . . . and brought anarchy. People that used to live peaceably, and were before good neighbors . . . took up arms against the government . . . if you went to speak to them, you had the musket of death presented to your breast. They would rob you of your property, threaten to burn your house; oblige you to be on your guard night and day; alarms spread from town to town; families were broke up; the tender mother would cry, O my son is among them! What shall I do for my child! Some were taken captive, children taken out of their schools and carried away. Then we should hear of an action, and the poor prisoners were set in the front, to be killed by their own friends. . . . Our distress was so great that we should have been glad to snatch at anything that looked like a government. Had any person that was able to protect us come and set up his standard, we should have flocked to it, even if it had been a monarch, and that monarch might have proved a tyrant; so you see that anarchy leads to tyranny, and better have one tyrant than so many at once.

Now, Mr. President, when I saw this constitution, I found that it was a cure for these disorders. . . . I got a copy of it and read it over and over. . . . I did not go to any lawyer—we have no lawyer in our town, and we do well enough without. I formed my own opinion and was pleased with this constitution. My honorable old daddy there won't think that I expect to be a congress man and swallow up the liberties of the people. I never had any post, nor do I want one. But I don't think the worse of the constitution because lawyers and men of learning, and monied men are fond if it. I am not of such a jealous make. They that are honest men themselves are not apt to suspect other people. . . . I think those gentlemen who are so very suspicious that as soon as a man gets into power he turns rogue had better look at home.

We are by this constitution allowed to send ten members to congress. Have we not more than that number fit to go? I dare say if we pick out ten, we shall have another ten left, and I hope ten times ten, and will not these be a check upon those that go? Will they go to congress and abuse their power and do mischief when they know they must return and look the other ten in the face and be called to account for their conduct? . . . Brother farmers . . . suppose two or three of you had been at the pains to break up a piece of rough land, and sow it with wheat—would you let it lay waste because you could not agree what sort of fence to make? Would it not be better to put up a fence that did not please every one's fancy, rather than not to fence it at all or keep disputing about it until the wild beast came? . . . Some gentlemen say don't be in a hurry, take time to consider, and don't take a leap in the dark. I say . . . gather fruit when it is ripe. There is a time to sow and a time to reap; we sowed our seed when we sent men to the federal convention, now is the harvest, now is the time to reap the fruit of our labor, and if we wont do it now, I am afraid we never shall have another opportunity.[23]

Stunned by his simple eloquence, the convention sat silent until, one by one, the lawyers, the men of learning, and most of Smith's "brother ploughjoggers" stood to applaud, then cheer.

On January 30, five days after Smith's oration, Governor Hancock appeared in the hall and took control of the convention. Although he loathed ceding his vast powers as governor to a federal government, he did not want to risk a war between states or between factions within individual states—perhaps his own. Federalist leader Rufus King, an eloquent attorney who, like Hancock, was a Harvard graduate, assured Hancock that Federalists had placated enough farmers to prevent any rekindling of the fires of rebellion in western Massachusetts. Even more convincing—indeed irresistibly so—was King's assurance that if Massachusetts ratified the Constitution, Hancock would be the Federalist choice as vice president, and if Virginia failed to ratify, Washington would be ineligible to serve as president and Hancock would become the "only fair candidate for President."[24] With that sop, Hancock ordered his servants to carry him "wrapped in flannels" from his mansion into his resplendent coach. Arriving at the convention hall, his servants carried him into the meeting all, where he took the chair of the convention. Pledging to seek adoption of "Conciliatory Amendments" after the new federal government was seated, Hancock declared, "I give my assent to

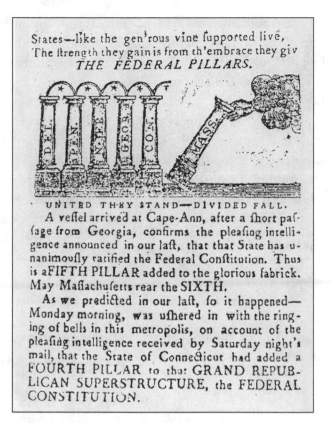

States—like the gen'rous vine supported live,
The strength they gain is from th'embrace they giv
THE FEDERAL PILLARS.

UNITED THEY STAND—DIVIDED FALL.
A vessel arrived at Cape-Ann, after a short paf-
fage from Georgia, confirms the pleasing intelligence announced in our last, that that State has u-
nanimously ratified the Federal Constitution. Thus
is a FIFTH PILLAR added to the glorious fabrick.
May Massachusetts rear the SIXTH.
   As we predicted in our last, so it happened—
Monday morning, was ushered in with the ringing of bells in this metropolis, on account of the
pleasing intelligence received by Saturday night's
mail, that the State of Connecticut had added a
FOURTH PILLAR to that GRAND REPUB-
LICAN SUPERSTRUCTURE, the FEDERAL
CONSTITUTION.

The Federal Pillars (Mass.). On January 16, 1788, *The
Massachusetts Centinel* published the first in what would be
a series of cartoons as each state, represented by a pillar,
ratified the Constitution and gradually built the federal
edifice to hold the "Great National Dome." The cartoons
made the *Centinel* the most frequently reprinted newspaper
in America in 1788.

the Constitution, in full confidence that the amendments proposed
will soon become part of the system."[25]

A week later, on February 6, delegates to the Massachusetts convention voted 187 to 168 that they "DO . . . *assent to*, and *ratify* the
said *Constitution for the United States of America*."[26] Boston erupted
in joy, as Federalists and trade leaders mounted a celebratory procession that broke with tradition by inviting the public to participate
instead of limiting marchers to public officials, the military, and

marching bands. Ridiculed by Antifederalists as a "childish parade and flummery," it was nonetheless one of the most widely reported events along the road to ratification, with full descriptions in thirty-five newspapers and two magazines in eleven states.

As church bells pealed and cannons boomed, a throng of farmers led the way, followed by members of every trade, each carrying tools of their trade and appropriate flags or decorations. Drummers, fifers, and other musicians joined in, along with the twelve Boston delegates to the state ratification convention. A "plough drawn by two horses and two yokes of oxen" led the procession, according to the *Massachusetts Centinel*, which published the "Order of Procession":

> A Brush-Harrow, drawn by a horse,
> A large Roler, drawn by a horse and pair of oxen,
> Four Reapers with sickles, &c.
> Four Mowers with scythes, followed by eighteen Hay-makers, with
>   rakes, &c.
> Eight Husbandmen, with hoes, spades and other Farming utensils,
> A Winnower, with a Fan.
> A Cart, drawn by a yoke of oxen, with Flax dressers at work,
>   and in working dresses,
> A yoke of fat Cattle, with killers, properly equipped,
> A Cart loaded with Beef, followed by eight master Butchers,
>   in clean frocks (with cleavers, &c.)

And that was but the beginning. Behind the farmers came more than five thousand marchers—seventy-three blacksmiths, forty-three shipwrights, seventy-five ropemakers, thirty mastmakers, thirty sailmakers, and on and on: coopers, painters, bakers, shoemakers, "taylors," hatters, carpenters, masons, printers, bookbinders, chairmakers, saddlers, tobacconists, and, most startling of all,

> The Ship FEDERAL CONSTITUTION,
> On runners, drawn by 13 horses,
> John Foster Williams, Esq. Commander,
> Lieut. Weeks, Lieut. Adams, Mr. La Moine, Master, Mr. E. Sigourney,
>   Purser,
> Manned by thirteen seamen and marines.
> With full colours flying—followed by Captains of vessels, 85 seamen,
> dressed in ribons, and about 150 of the principal merchants in town.

Twenty shipbuilders followed on a float decorated as "a work-yard, drawn by 13 horses, in which were 7 or 8 vessels, on the stocks, with the men at work."[27]

Although European parades routinely used ships on horse-drawn floats to symbolize a nation's far-reaching commerce, its empire, or its naval strength, Boston's *Federal Constitution* was the first appearance of such a display in America, and the widespread reporting of Boston's spectacular celebration assured its reappearance in similar celebrations across the land. Boston's procession began at 11 A.M. and continued until 4 P.M., when, according to the *Massachusetts Centinel,* "refreshment was liberally provided." According to Benjamin Lincoln, however, the newspaper description would "no more compare with the original than the light of the faintest star would with that of the Sun." Still feeling the effects of the celebration, Lincoln scribbled a letter to his friend George Washington:

> fortunately for us the whole ended without the least disorder and the town during the whole evening was . . . perfectly quiet—The Gentlemen provided at Fanuel Hall some biscuit & cheese four qrs Casks of wine three barrels and two hog[head]s of punch the moment they found that the people had drunk sufficiently means were taken to overset the two hogs.* of punch this being done the company dispirsed and the day ended most agreeably.[28]

With that, he drew a line through each of the lines he had just written.

Although Massachusetts ratified the Constitution unconditionally, the convention recommended that once in place, the new federal government approve nine amendments, the first of which "explicitly declared, that all powers not expressly delegated by the aforesaid Constitution, are reserved to the several States."[29] The other recommendatory amendments dealt with the judiciary, taxing powers, commerce, and titles of nobility, but curiously steered clear of the controversial bill of rights that Gerry, Samuel Adams, and other political opponents of John Hancock had demanded.

---

*The term "hogs" refers to "hogsheads," casks that held the equivalent of 62 modern U.S. gallons each. Two "hogs" held about 124 modern gallons.

8

"A Fig and a Fiddle-stick's End"

IN THE DAYS AND WEEKS FOLLOWING Massachusetts ratification, forty-nine newspapers and one magazine reprinted the extract of Washington's letter, which, with Hancock's recommendatory amendments, proved decisive at the Boston convention. In fact, the letter had first appeared in Virginia, and although Washington claimed he had nothing to do with its publication, he was delighted with its impact. Federalists now had a major weapon in their war to capture the minds, hearts, and votes of Americans who imagined Washington an oracle and at least a demigod, if not actually divine. "He comes, he comes, the hero comes," they sang on his arrival at every function.

> He comes! 'tis mighty Washington!
> Words fail to tell all he has done;
> Our hero, guardian, father, friend!
> His fame can never, never end.

And every man who had fought in the Revolution could sing of General Washington to the tune of "British Grenadiers," whose last four bars all but exploded "Hu-zza, hu-zza, hu-zza, hu-zza, for war and Wash-ing-ton!"

After their Massachusetts victory, Federalists tried to undermine Antifederalist strength in neighboring states by printing Washington's letter in all three New Hampshire newspapers, four Rhode

Island newspapers, and eight New York newspapers. In New York, Antifederalist governor George Clinton had used the four months between the Constitutional Convention and the regular session of the New York State legislature in January 1788 to conduct what he called "a campaign of education." Writing an endless flow of letters to newspapers under such pseudonyms as "Cato," he asked citizens of New York to "reject it [the Constitution] with indignation."[1] Charging that the Constitutional Convention had "exceeded the authority given to them," Cato insisted that any new government formed under the Constitution would be "founded in usurpation."[2] Clinton's aides and political allies joined Cato in attacking Washington's favorite and most frequent argument that failure to ratify the Constitution would provoke anarchy.

"How comes it," asked an anonymous writer in the *New York Journal*,

> that the goddess *Liberty*, lately so much adored in the United States, should now be reprobated under the name of *Anarchy*? Suppose that we were to treat this fair lady Liberty as the Poet [Matthew Prior] advises to treat another lady of much less consequence:
>
> > "Be to her *faults* a little blind,
> > "Be to her *virtue* very kind."
>
> Perhaps this moderation of temper may arrest the *haste* with which some people would force the new constitution upon us, without suffering amendments to be made or offered, although amendments may be *necessary* to secure our liberties from weak or wicked rulers.[3]

The writer conveniently neglected to cite the subsequent two lines of the poem, however:

> "Let all her Ways be unconfin'd
> "And clap your PADLOCK—on her mind."[4]

By early October 1787, Clinton learned of Patrick Henry's successful tactics in delaying a call to convention in the Virginia House of Delegates, and Clinton laid plans for his political allies in the New York legislature to do the same when that body reconvened in

January. To combat Clinton, Madison warned Washington that the "Government party" in New York was "hostile" to the Constitution and that "newspapers here begin to team with vehement & virulent calumniations of the proposed Govt."[5] Shortly thereafter, Hamilton offered Madison the opportunity to join in writing *The Federalist* essays. New York's *Independent Journal* published "The Federalist I" on October 27, the same day as Cato's third attack on the Constitution, warning the "Citizens of the State of New-York . . . [that] this new form of national government . . . will be dangerous to your liberty and happiness." All but calling for New York to secede, Cato insisted that the Constitution would consolidate the United States "into one government" and that southerners would use the votes of their slaves to gain control of the national legislature.

> The people . . . from the southern states . . . where slavery is encouraged, and liberty of course, less respected, and protected; who know not what it is to acquire property by their own toil, nor to œconomize with the savings of industry—will these men therefore be as tenacious of the liberties and interests of the more northern states, where freedom, independence, industry, equality, and frugality are natural to the climate and soil as men who are your own citizens, legislating in your own state, under your inspection, and whose manners, and fortunes, bear a more equal resemblance to your own?[6]

Publius struck back with a vicious attack on Clinton, declaring that "the most formidable obstacles which the new Constitution will have to encounter . . . [are] the obvious interest of a certain class of men in every State to resist all changes which may hazard a diminution of the power, emolument and consequence of the offices they hold under the State-establishments. . . .

> A dangerous ambition more often lurks behind the specious mask of zeal for the rights of the people, than under the forbidding appearance of zeal for the firmness and efficiency of government. History will teach us, that the former has been found a much more certain road to the introduction of despotism, than the latter, and that of those men who have overturned the liberties of republics the greatest number have begun their careers, by paying an obsequious court to the people, commencing Demagogues and ending Tyrants.[7]

Secretary for Foreign Affairs John Jay wrote the next four essays, then fell ill. Hamilton wrote the next four and Madison added his first contribution—a brilliant discourse on the differences between "democracy," where minorities have little protection from tyrannical rule by a majority, and a "republic," in which government is delegated to "a small number of citizens elected by the rest [that is, the entire population]."[8]

The essays drew so much attention that by early December, the printers of New York's *Independent Journal* received a commission to combine the first two dozen essays in a volume and publish five hundred copies. New York City's well-educated Federalists such as Noah Webster hailed *The Federalist* as "one of the most complete dissertations on government that ever has appeared," but Clinton was confident they would have little impact in the rural areas that represented his political base.

Under Clinton's direction, Antifederalists attacked what they called "the long-winded productions of Publius" for willfully deceiving the public about Antifederalist principles. Far from opposing "a confederated national government," Antifederalists claimed, they simply wanted to ensure an equitable balance of power between the states and the new federal government by validating existing state constitutions and limiting powers of the national government. The proposed Constitution, they insisted,

> positively expressed that the different state constitutions are repealed and entirely done away with. . . . And hence it was of the highest importance that the most precise and express declarations and reservations of rights should have been made. . . . Far from being true that a bill of rights is less necessary in the general constitution than in those of the states, the contrary is true.[9]

From his law office in New York City, Hamilton believed his essays would turn New York's political tide in favor of the Federalists, but upstaters disagreed. "Our Legislature have formed at Poughkeepsie," wrote an Albany state senator as the legislature gathered for its regular session on January 1, 1788, "and the first object of their attention will be the calling a Convention. This however will meet a warm opposition & 'tis doubted by the best friends to the New Government whether we shall have a Convention called by a Legislative

Act, the opposition are determined to make their first stand here—the Complexion of our Senate is unfavourable but the other house will pass a Bill for the purpose."[10]

Whether or not they learned of or intuited John Jay's authorship of some *Federalist* essays, Antifederalists took advantage of Jay's illness to plant assertions in the press that "Jay (a gentleman of the first rate abilities, joined to a good heart) who at first was carried away with the new plan of government, is now very decidedly against it, and says it is as deep and wicked conspiracy as has been ever invented in the darkest ages against the liberties of a free people."[11]

The article stunned Washington and indeed Jay himself, who was one of the most steadfast American leaders, with conservative views that had not changed dramatically since his childhood. Born in New York to a merchant family of exceptional wealth—his mother was a Van Cortlandt—he grew up with a self-confidence derived from thorough contentment with his life and circumstances. From earliest childhood he savored and devoured books. He graduated from King's College (later Columbia), became a lawyer, acquired a prosperous practice among wealthy merchant friends of his father, and, after marrying into the equally wealthy Livingston family, he prepared to spend a pleasant life among his social peers. He had no political ambitions and never once, throughout his life, sought an appointment or election to public office, accepting such offices only as an obligation to his country. A deeply pious man, he was sent to the Continental Congress by conservative New York merchants who feared independence would provoke mob rule. Once Congress had passed the Declaration of Independence, however, he used his talents to support the new nation and especially his own, then-sovereign state. After drafting the state's first constitution, he served as its chief justice and acquired so glowing a reputation for his disinterested objectivity and abilities as a mediator that Congress tapped him to join Franklin and Adams in negotiating the peace treaty with Britain and then to serve as secretary for foreign affairs. Thoroughly opposed to democracy and unrestricted majority rule, he remained a staunch supporter of the Constitution and least likely to have second thoughts about it. Madison immediately wrote to reassure Washington of Jay's steadfast support:

John Jay. A prominent New York jurist and ardent
Federalist, Jay was U.S. secretary of foreign affairs and
coauthored *The Federalist* with Hamilton and Madison,
writing five of the eighty-five essays advocating ratification.
Washington named Jay first chief justice of the U.S.
Supreme Court—a post he resigned after six years to
become governor of New York.

You did not judge amiss of Mr. Jay. The paragraph affirming a
change in His opinion . . . was an arrant forgery. He has contra-
dicted it in a letter . . . which has been published in the Philadelphia Gazettes. Tricks of this sort are not uncommon with the
Enemies of the new Constitution. . . . Docr. Franklin's concluding
speech . . . in one of the papers . . . is both mutilated & adulterated
so as to change both the form & the spirit of it.[12]

Astonished by the ruse, Jay denied "the change in sentiments"
and declared that "in my opinion, *it is adviseable for the people of America to adopt the constitution proposed by the late Convention.*"[13]

Shocked by the lack of ethics in the campaign, French consul Louis-Guillaume Otto sent an insightful report to his foreign minister in Versailles. In it he scolded everyone, including Washington. "The debates, My Lord, for and against the new Constitution continue to absorb public attention, and while the individual States are preparing to call conventions in order to adopt or reject this new plan, the two parties abuse each other in the public papers with a rancor which sometimes does not even spare insults and personal invectives.

> As is usual in these sorts of political commotions, the men and the issues usually disguise themselves so as to become unrecognizable. . . . According to one side Despotism will be the necessary consequence of the proposed Constitution; according to the other the united States will reach the summit of glory and power with this same Constitution. Indifferent Spectators agree that the new form of Government, well executed will be able to produce good results; but they also think that if the states really had the desire to be united the present Confederation would be adequate for all their needs. Meanwhile they are unable to conceal that after having excited this general ferment there is no longer a means to stop it, that the old edifice is almost destroyed, and that any fabric whatsoever must be substituted for it. In effect it was impossible to carry out a more violent coup to the authority of Congress, than in saying to all America, to the entire Universe, that this body is inadequate . . . and that the united States have become the laughingstock of all the powers. This principle repeated over and over by all the Innovators seems as false as the enthusiasm that generated it; the united States held the place among nations which their youth and means assigned them; they are neither rich enough, populated enough, nor well established enough to appear with more luster and perhaps one ought to reproach them only for the impatience of anticipating their future grandeur.[14]

Otto's report of insults and personal invectives in public papers was hardly an exaggeration:

One critic wrote to Publius that "as you appear to be much bloated . . . and not infrequently to have written like a Person, who considered himself as the sole Proprietor of all common Sense . . . permit me to remind you of the Fable of the Ox and the Frog, who, ambitious to make as great an appearance as the Former, kept straining its lankey Sides till it burst."[15]

A Federalist complained to New York's *Daily Advertiser* that "Anti-Federal men are circulating hand-bills, fraught with sophistry, declamation and falsehoods."[16] An Antifederalist responded in the same paper: "A fig and a fiddle-stick's end, Mr. Printer, for your fidderal or foderal nonsensikalities. I can smell a rat as quick, and see as far into a mill-stone as some others. I do now smell a plot; nay, I smell two plots. The southern bashaws are for establishing unfidelity; the eastern saints, double stilled high wine piritanism."[17] Eager to have the last word, a Federalist shot back: "Sir, you do not possess a single grain of understanding, inasmuch as all that region is closed upon you which is above the sphere of rationality, and that only is open to you which is below the rational."[18]

"I really pity you, Sir, I pity you,"[19] came the reply.

"Cato . . . is an hypocrite . . . not unlike the wooden heads exposed to view in a barber's shop,"[20] wrote a Federalist, who had previously charged Antifederalists with living "in a state of brutal ignorance . . . mere *orang outangs*—blockheads, numskulls, asses, monkeys, sheep, owls, and lobsters."[21]

Lack of a quorum prevented the New York State legislature from convening as scheduled on January 1. Poughkeepsie lay far enough north to make it a difficult winter trip for New York City's Federalists. By January 10, however, enough members had appeared for Governor Clinton to make his official opening address.

Despite Clinton's efforts to flood neighboring Connecticut with Antifederalist leaflets, it had ratified the Constitution the day before, bringing to five the number of states that had ratified the Constitution: Delaware, Pennsylvania, New Jersey, Georgia, and Connecticut. Four others—Maryland, North Carolina, New Hampshire, and Virginia—had already called ratification conventions, and Massachusetts had called its convention to order the previous day. Clinton had published another Antifederalist Cato essay—his seventh—the previous week, hoping to convince the New York legislature not to issue a call to convention. To no one's astonishment, therefore, he all but ignored the Constitution and the question of a ratification convention in his talk to the legislature. After discussing a few state matters, he added offhandedly, "I shall leave with you several official communications which have been made to me . . . the proceedings of the general Convention lately held in the City of Philadelphia, and an Act of the United States Congress for their Transmission to the Legislatures of the different States. From the nature of my Office . . . it would be improper for me to have any other Agency in the Business than that of laying the Papers . . . before you for your Information."[22]

Every legislator knew what he meant, and New York City Federalists grew concerned, with James Madison describing the legislature as "much divided. A majority of the Assembly are said to be friendly to the merits of the Constitution," he wrote to George Washington. "A majority of the Senators . . . are opposed to a submission of it to a Convention. . . . The decision of Massachusetts . . . will involve the result in this State."[23]

After three weeks, Clinton's Antifederalists proposed a new oath of allegiance for state officeholders—"that they should Swear never to consent to any Act or thing which had a *tendency* to destroy or *Alter* the present *constitution of the state*"[24]—an oath that would preclude delegates to a ratification convention from voting in favor of a federal constitution. Before they could vote on the oath requirement, however, word arrived from Boston that Governor John Hancock was about to announce his "assent" to the Constitution at the Massachusetts ratification convention. Knowing that New York would have to stand alone in the North if it remained outside the Union, a handful of moderate Antifederalists switched positions. After defeating the oath proposal, the New York legislature voted by the barest margin—27 to 25 in the Assembly and 11 to 8 in the Senate—to call a ratification convention.

Clinton's political machine salvaged many advantages from the apparent defeat, however. Antifederalists had delayed elections to the ratification convention until April 29. The convention would not take place until mid-June—after Virginia's ratification convention and late enough for Clinton to flood the state with propaganda describing terrifying scenes of federal oppression that would inevitably result if New York ratified the Constitution. Those descriptions had

an immediate effect on Ulster County—Clinton's home county—
where a mob estimated at six hundred by one observer but only one
hundred by another, burned a copy of the Constitution, along with
effigies of Hamilton and two local Federalists.

"Violence rather than modification is to be looked for from the
opposite party," Alexander Hamilton lamented in a letter to Gouverneur Morris. "Obstinacy seems the prevailing trait in the character of its leader. The language is, that if all the other states adopt,
this [state] is to persist in refusing the constitution. . . . Clinton has
in several conversations declared the UNION unnecessary."[25]

Besides delaying ratification, Antifederalists in the New York
State legislature also managed to suspend the state's voting eligibility
rules. Normally limited to adult male property owners, the polls for
the ratification convention extended the vote to *all free adult male*
citizens, including those who owned no property, thus ensuring a
populist—and usually Antifederalist—complexion to the ratification convention.

The delay in the New York State elections and ratification convention gave Clinton time to establish ties with Virginia Antifederalists
and build a national Antifederalist political movement—perhaps
even a separate confederacy. Called the "Federal Republicans," his
followers aimed at defeating ratification in the remaining states and
provoking reevaluation of the Constitution in states such as Pennsylvania and Massachusetts, which had already ratified but were
clearly unsettled by their decisions. Clinton appointed his political
lackey John Lamb, the customs collector for New York City and a
former Continental Army brigadier general, to chair the organization and recruit Antifederalist leaders in other states. Although
Clinton had wanted to write Patrick Henry personally, protocol
required him as governor of New York to write to his counterpart in
Virginia while Lamb wrote to Henry. Clinton assumed that Randolph, who had refused to sign the Constitution at the Constitutional Convention, was a dedicated Antifederalist who would rally
Antifederalists at the Virginia ratification convention. Indeed, the
Virginia state legislature had charged Randolph to invite other states
to join Virginia in proposing amendments. For reasons of his own, he

delayed doing so, and he now remained equally secretive about the letter from Clinton. Henry, on the other hand, was delighted by the letter from Lamb. "It is a matter of great consolation," Henry replied, "to find that the sentiments of a vast majority of Virginians are in unison with our northern friends. I am satisfied four-fifths of our inhabitants are opposed to the new scheme of government. Indeed, in the part of this country lying south of James River, I am confident nine-tenths are opposed to it." Henry told Lamb that George Mason had agreed to serve as chairman "of our republican society. . . . I can assure you that North Carolina is more decidedly opposed to the new government than Virginia. The people there seem rife for hazarding all before they submit."[26]

A week after the New York State legislature issued its call to convention, Massachusetts ratified the Constitution, and a week after that, General John Sullivan, a hero of the Revolution and now president (governor) of his state, called the New Hampshire ratification convention to order. A fierce Federalist, the gruff, quick-tempered Sullivan believed he would be able to bully his delegates into ratifying the Constitution as quickly as Philadelphia's Federalists had done.

"It is with real pleasure that we can announce the sentiments of his Excellency, President SULLIVAN, to be perfectly *federal*," crowed the state's major newspaper, the *New Hampshire Spy*. "He was bold to say, *It was one of the best systems of government that was ever devised*."[27] In an obsequious display of support to the powerful Sullivan, the *Spy* gave the Constitution its "greatest approbation.

> As *the heart panteth after the cooling water-brook*, so does every citizen of this state pant after a *reform in government*—not only a *local*, but a *federal* reform—and this, we have reason to hope, will be effected, notwithstanding the arts that are, or may be used in New-York and Rhode-Island to oppose it. The characters residing in these two states, who have uniformly opposed a federal reform—are well known—It would be well for them to desist from their nefarious schemes. The united force of America is against them . . . tremble ye workers of iniquity, and no longer oppose the *salvation* of your country, lest speedy *destruction* come upon you.[28]

Sullivan lost no time in ramroding the call to convention through a special session of the New Hampshire legislature. "I have carefully considered the plan," he told its members on December 5. "Permit me, gentlemen, to recommend to you unanimity and dispatch."[29] By December 31, the state's far-flung rural districts began electing their delegates to the ratification Assembly. Six weeks later, Henry Knox wrote to Washington with confidence:

"The Convention of New Hampshire assembled yesterday. About 20 days hence I hope to have the pleasure of informing You of the adoption of the constitution in that State."[30] James Madison echoed Knox's optimistic appraisal. "The Convention of N. Hampshire is now sitting. There seems to be no question that the issue there will add a *seventh* pillar, as the phrase now is, to the federal Temple.[31]

When, however, Governor Sullivan called the ratification convention to order in Exeter on February 13, New Hampshire's farm delegates refused to shy under his bullying. They stood squarely against ratification and were prepared to humiliate him. They opposed a new layer of super government that could tax them, seize their farms, try them in far-off courts without juries, and force them to leave their fields to fight in foreign wars.

Nor were these their only objections:

"We do not think ourselves under any obligations to perform works of supererogation in the reformation of mankind," John Atherton, of Amherst, cried out in a stirring appeal to the convention, "we do not esteem ourselves under any necessity to go to Spain or Italy to suppress the inquisition of those countries; or making a journey to the Carolinas to abolish the detestable custom of enslaving Africans; but, sir, we will not lend the aid of our ratification to this cruel and inhuman merchandise, not even for a day."[32]

After the applause died down, it was clear that New Hampshire was ready to vote against ratification by a substantial majority. Sullivan's Federalists could count only 30 to 48 of the 108 delegates as possible votes for the Constitution, and after nearly a week it became clear that "the only thing that can be done to prevent its rejection is to have an adjournment of the Convention."[33]

"Contrary to the expectation of almost ev'ry thinking man," former governor John Langdon explained to Washington, "a small majority . . . appeared against the system.

> This was the most astonishing to ev'ry man of any information, as Massachusetts had accepted it, and this State in particular had ev'ry thing to gain and nothing to loose, by the adoption of the Government and almost ev'ry man of properties and abilities for it . . . a report was circulated by a few designing men who wished for confusion . . . [that] the liberties of the people were in danger, and that the great men . . . were forming a plan for themselves . . . which frightened the people out of what *little* senses they had . . . the Convention adjourned to meet the third day of June next.[34]

In addition to forcing an adjournment, New Hampshire Antifederalists won a second victory by forcing the convention to reconvene sixty miles inland, at Concord, in the heart of the farming country. "Adjournment into the Wilderness augurs ill," admitted Boston Federalist Samuel A. Otis.[35]

As the first outright—albeit temporary—rejection of the Constitution, New Hampshire's adjournment sent shock waves across the nation, despite a flurry of Federalist letters to newspapers assuring readers that "the decisive question, respecting adoption of the federal constitution, was not voted upon. The only vote that was taken was for an adjournment, which was carried—yeas 57, nays 48."[36]

At heart, though, Federalists feared the New Hampshire adjournment would strengthen Antifederalist sentiment in states that had yet to ratify the Constitution and give new life to secessionist movements in states that had ratified. Rhode Island had yet to call a convention and might not do so in the aftermath of the New Hampshire adjournment.

"The conduct of the State of New Hampshire has baffled all calculation," Washington lamented at Mount Vernon in a letter to Henry Knox.

> Had it not been for this untoward event, the opposition in this State would have proved entirely unavailing, notwithstanding the unfair conduct (I might have bestowed a harsher epithet without doing injustice) which has been practiced to rouse the fears, and to inflame the passions of the people. What will be the result now, is

difficult for me to say. . . . The Kentucke district will have great weight . . . and the idea of its becoming an impediment to its sep-aration, has got hold of them; while no pains is spared to inculcate a belief that the Government proposed will . . . barter away the right of Navigation to the River Mississippi.

The postponement in New-Hampshire will also . . . give strength and vigor to the opposition in New York; and possibly will render Rhode Island more backward than she otherwise would have been, if all the New England States had finally decided in favor of the measure.[37]

As Washington feared, Rhode Island's legislature again refused to call a ratification convention and opted instead for a popular, statewide referendum.

"A viler and more abandoned sett of beings never disgraced any Legislative, Judicial or Executive Authorities since the fall of Adam," complained a disgruntled Rhode Islander to the *Pennsylvania Gazette*. "Every *conscientious* and *honest* man in our devoted republic is . . . devoutly wishing for the *speedy* adoption of the New Constitution, tho' their fears are occasionally on the alarm from the ill-founded suggestions of a G-r-y [Gerry]."[38] A second writer agreed that "all honest men in Rhode-Island, (who, alas, are not very numerous) are anxious for adoption of the new constitution."[39] But others dis-agreed, saying that "the new constitution . . . will not go down here— *nine-tenths* of the people are against it—in MY OPINION it is a DAMN'D *impudent* composition."[40]

On March 24, 1788, Rhode Island voters overwhelmingly re-jected the Constitution, 2,711 to 239.

As Federalists had feared, the effects of the New Hampshire adjourn-ment reached far beyond New England. In Pennsylvania, support mushroomed for Comptroller General John Nicholson's petition to the state Assembly not to confirm the results of the ratification con-vention and to instruct Pennsylvania members in the Confederation Congress to vote against final ratification. In addition to Pennsylva-nia newspapers, his petition appeared in newspapers in Boston, New York, and other cities, and by the end of March, it had received more than six thousand signatures in seven rural counties in Pennsylvania. Together they represented a tacit threat of secession if Philadelphia's political leaders continued leading the state along the Federalist road to ratification without taking cognizance of the needs of farmers and others in the interior of the state.

The Federalist majority in the Pennsylvania Assembly, however, continued debating the issue until the end of March, when it tabled the Nicholson petitions and adjourned, knowing that farmers would be too busy planting their fields to protest, let alone rebel. The issue of secession thus drifted away quietly in the spring breezes.

Three weeks later, Maryland's ratification convention came to order in Annapolis, with Antifederalist leader Luther Martin said to be boasting, "I'll be hanged if ever the people of Maryland agree to it." Weary of Martin's histrionics, Federalist leader Daniel of Saint Thomas Jenifer retorted, "I advise you to stay in Philadelphia lest you be hanged."[41] Within a week, the Maryland convention's overwhelming Federalist majority ratified the Constitution, 63 to 11, with no debate permitted. Backed by the state's huge shipbuilding, shipping, and merchant-banking industries, Federalists beat back attempts by Antifederalists to add amendments to the Constitution, declaring they had been elected "to ratify the proposed constitution . . . and to do no other act." To avoid postconvention recriminations that were dogging Pennsylvania delegates, Maryland Federalists defused a potentially explosive political confrontation by allowing Antifederalists to read their amendments and to recommend them to the Assembly. As in Boston, Federalists staged an enormous procession to celebrate ratification, complete with pealing church bells, cannon blasts, and floats carrying an allegorical federal ship, which was later delivered to Mount Vernon as a gift for Washington.

Maryland's ratification elated Washington, who predicted it would be "a thorn . . . in the sides of the leaders of opposition in this State [Virginia]. Should South Carolina give an unequivocal approbation of the system, the opposition here will become feeble; for eight affirmatives without a negative carries *weight* of argument, if not of eloquence along with it."[42]

In a letter to Gouverneur Morris on the same day, Washington all but claimed victory for the new government: "I . . . entertain more confidence since the ratification of it in Maryland by so large & decided a Majority. The *fury* of the opposition I believe is spent . . . the hopes of the leaders begin to flag."[43]

About two weeks after Maryland ratified, South Carolina's ratification convention came to order. The debate had been raging in the state since mid-January, when the state's House of Representatives first considered calling a convention. Former state president Rawlins Lowndes led Antifederalists by demeaning the proposed Constitution as a mere experiment.

"What!" he cried out. "Risk the loss of political existence, on experiment!" Predicting that the North would rule the South, he accused northern states of "jealousy of our negro trade" and called the slave-trade provision of the Constitution "*a stroke aimed at the prohibition of our negro trade* by an ungenerous limitation of twenty years, and this under the *specious pretext of humanity.*" According to the *Charleston City Gazette*, Lowndes declared "*this sort of traffick justifiable* on the principles of RELIGION, HUMANITY and JUSTICE, for certainly to translate a set of human beings from a bad country to a better, was fulfilling every part of *those principles.*" But the northern states, he continued, "don't like our slaves, because they have none themselves; and therefore want to exclude us from this great advantage."[44]

Lowndes's argument—the first and only public declaration favoring slavery as a "positive good"—found little support. Nor did another Antifederalist contention—that the president could be reelected indefinitely under the Constitution and establish a "tyrannical monarchy."

Federalists countered that far from prejudice against the South, the North had exhibited deep fraternal feelings during the Revolutionary War, never demanding assistance and willingly sending its forces to Virginia and the Carolinas to defend them. "It is the manifest interest of these states to be united," declared David Ramsay, a Charleston physician who had studied under Benjamin Rush in Philadelphia and was one of the first two Americans to write a history of the American Revolution:

Eternal wars among ourselves would most probably be the consequence of disunion. Our local weakness particularly proves it to be for the advantage of South-Carolina to strengthen the federal government; for we are inadequate to secure ourselves from more powerful neighbours. . . . When several parishes, counties or districts form a state, the separate interests of each must yield to the collective interest of the whole. When thirteen states combine in one government the same principles must be observed. These relinquishments of natural rights, are not real sacrifices: each person, county or state, gains more than it loses, for it only gives up a right of injuring others, and obtains in return aid and strength to secure itself in the peaceable enjoyment of all remaining rights.[45]

The South Carolina ratification convention met in Charleston on May 12, with Federalists in complete control. Four of them—the two Pinckney cousins, Charles Pinckney and Charles Cotesworth Pinckney; former governor John Rutledge; and Pierce Butler—had been to the Constitutional Convention and had signed the document without objections. The convention elected Governor Thomas Pinckney, brother of Charles Cotesworth, as president, and ten days later he steered the proceedings to a routine two-to-one Federalist victory for ratification—and the now-mandatory celebratory procession with federal ships sailing by on huge, horse-drawn floats, firing blank cannon blasts as they passed.

Washington was elated. He now entertained "good hopes of its adoption" in Virginia and wrote to Lafayette in Paris that "the plot thickens fast.

> A few short weeks will determine the political fate of America for the present generation, and probably produce no small influence on the happiness of society through a long succession of ages to come. Should every thing proceed with harmony and consent according to our actual wishes and expectations; I will confess to you sincerely, my dear Marquis; it will be so much beyond anything we had a right to imagine or expect eighteen months ago, that it will demonstrate as visibly the finger of Providence, as any possible event in the course of human affairs can ever designate it. It is impracticable for you or any one who has not been on the spot to realize the change in men's minds and the progress towards rectitude in thinking and acting which will then have been made.
>
> Adieu, my dear Marquis, I hope your affairs in France will subside into a prosperous train without coming to any violent crisis. Continue to cherish your affectionate feelings for this country and the same portion of friendship for me, which you are ever sure of holding in the heart of your most sincer[e] Friend.[46]

Henry Knox in New York was far less optimistic, however. Although eight states had ratified the Constitution, two of the states that had not—Virginia and New York—would now determine whether there would be a more perfect union—indeed, whether there would be any union at all. "Much will depend on Virginia," Knox wrote. "Her conduct will have a powerful influence on this state [New York] and North Carolina. In this state it appears to be conceded on the part of the federalists that numbers will be against them in the convention . . . the party against it in this state are united under the auspices of the Governor and he is supposed to be immoveable."[47]

John Jay presented a different scenario, however:

> There is much reason to believe that the Majority of the Convention of this State will be composed of antifederal Characters, but it is doubtful whether the Leaders will be able to govern the Party. . . . An idea has taken air, that the Southern part of the State will at all Events adhere to the union, and if necessary to that End seek a Separation from the northern. this Idea has Influence on the Party.[48]

Knox had good reason for concern about Virginia. The Antifederalist forces had what seemed like overwhelmingly powerful leadership at the convention: former governor Patrick Henry, current governor Edmund Randolph, congressmen James Monroe and William Grayson, and George Mason. Mason had served at the Constitutional Convention with Randolph and, like Randolph, had refused to sign. In the months before the convention, Mason had traveled "through the back Counties of [Virginia] . . . pointing out the dangerous effects or consequences which would inevitably flow from the new Constitution . . . [and] into North Carolina, on the same Business . . . to sound the alarm." Indeed, Mason had won assurances from North Carolina political leaders that if Virginia rejected federalism, they would follow suit and join Virginia in forming a vast, separate confederacy reaching from the Atlantic to the Mississippi. The new confederacy would embrace the large Antifederal territories west of the Blue Ridge and Appalachian mountains, including Kentucky and what had been the secessionist State of Franklin in western North Carolina.

Informed by intermediaries of Mason's and Henry's activities in Virginia and North Carolina, Washington grew anxious about the effects of their campaign but hoped that reason would prevail. "What I have mostly apprehended," Washington wrote to Madison, "is that the insidious arts of its [the Constitution's] opposers to alarm the fears and inflame the passions of the Multitude may have produced instructions to the Delegates that would shut the door against arguments and be a bar to the exercise of the judgment. . . . The ratification by eight States without a negative . . . is enough one would think to produce a cessation of opposition. . . . I think it is enough to produce some change in the conduct of any man who entertains a doubt of his infallibility."[49]

It was not enough to change the conduct of Patrick Henry, however. Unlike Washington, Henry had never entertained any doubt about his infallibility. As in 1775, he was prepared to combat what he perceived as tyranny—and renew his dramatic cry, *I know not what course others may take, but as for me, give me liberty or give me death*. Instead of revolution, however, his cry might well provoke civil war.

On Monday, June 2, 1788, sixty-seven-year-old Edmund Pendleton, Virginia's crippled but revered revolutionary leader—and the state's highest judge—called the Virginia ratification convention to order.

9
The Language of Secession

AN INCONGRUOUS COLLECTION OF DELEGATES shuffled into the Virginia ratification convention at the State House of Delegates. Elegantly dressed Tidewater planters in powdered wigs mixed uncomfortably with ill-clothed Kentucky frontiersmen with fearsome pistols in their belts. Onlookers described Patrick Henry as looking "like an eagle in an ill-fitting wig." Although only fifty-two, a long illness left him a bit hunched, his face drawn and coated with a sickly pallor. His piercing, deep-set eyes gave him the solemn look of a priest who had never smiled. In sharp contrast to the fashionably dressed delegates from the eastern Tidewater, Henry came to the ratification convention dressed like many of the frontiersmen in the galleries, in coarse black clothes—always black—made on his own loom and still covered with dust of the road to make him look like a farmer who had just stepped from his fields. His modest demeanor belied his position as master of some twenty thousand acres, more than forty slaves, and one of Virginia's largest mansions—an elegant sixteen-room structure ninety-six feet across and thirty-six feet deep.

In contrast, the diminutive James Madison, who still lived in his father's home, all but disappeared from view beneath his taller colleagues. Henry made no secret of his disdain for bookish scholars such as Madison, and few Federalists could resist the obvious comparison to David and Goliath as the learned little Madison prepared to face the oratorical blasts of the great Henry. As in Massachusetts, crowds of spectators had flocked to the capital, filled the building to overflowing, and forced the convention to adjourn to a much larger site—a French-American university called the Academy. Rumors circulated that "Mr. Henry is supposed to aim at disunion." Another asserted that "Mr. H. does not openly declare for a dismemberment of the Union, but his arguments in support of his opposition to the Constitution go directly to that issue. He says that three confederacies would be practicable, and better suited to the good of commerce than one."[1]

To Patrick Henry's dismay, Washington's powerful Federalist allies had managed to gain parity if not a clear majority of delegates through a legislative fiat that had allowed officeholders—largely Federalist judges and legislators—to run for election to the convention.

"Our affairs in the convention are suspended by a hair," wrote Antifederalist congressman William Grayson to Clinton ally John Lamb, the chairman of New York's Federal Republican Committee, which was trying to build a national movement to block ratification. "I really cannot tell you on which side the scale will turn; the difference . . . will be exceedingly small indeed. . . . The opposition . . . is firm and united; there are seven or eight dubious characters, whose opinions are not known, and on whose decisions the fate of this important question will ultimately depend."[2]

From the outset, Antifederalists were on the defensive. When Federalists nominated sixty-six-year-old Virginia Supreme Court president Edmund Pendleton as president, Antifederalists dared not voice opposition. Although he was a staunch Federalist, almost all Virginians venerated Pendleton for his impartiality as a jurist and his courage in coming to the convention with a painfully crippling hip condition that required him to hobble about on crutches.

Some Washington allies at the convention believed they had a majority of twenty, "which number they imagine will be greatly encreased," Washington wrote to John Jay in New York. James Madison, however, was less sanguine, reporting that the shifting Federal majorities ranged from "not more than six" to as low as "three or four. . . . I do not know that either party despairs absolutely."[3]

Patrick Henry was supremely confident, however. Besides George Mason, the Antifederalist hero who had refused to sign the Constitution, Henry's supporters at the convention included former governors Benjamin Harrison and Thomas Nelson Jr.; Congressmen James

Monroe and William Grayson, who helped defeat the Jay treaty with Spain; and, most importantly, the state's powerful sitting governor, Edmund Randolph, who, like Mason, had helped write elements of the Constitution but, in the end, refused to sign it. In addition, Henry fully expected support from another ex-governor—Thomas Jefferson, who was still in Paris as American minister to France. A letter from Jefferson opposing ratification that Henry could read to the convention would give him the ultimate weapon for defeating the Federalists—and the Constitution.

With the New York convention scheduled to begin two weeks after Virginia's, Madison and Alexander Hamilton established a private, express-courier service between Richmond, Mount Vernon, and Poughkeepsie, New York, to keep the Federalist triumvirate abreast of day-to-day developments and to influence delegates with whispered news, rumors, and gossip. Lamb's Federal Republicans set up an identical service linking New York's Antifederalists with those in Virginia.

When Pendleton opened the Virginia convention to discussion, Patrick Henry and George Mason charged into the debating lists first, aiming much of their initial rhetoric at fourteen delegates from the Kentucky back country, who Antifederalists and Federalists agreed held decisive votes. A child of the mountainous Piedmont region of Virginia, Henry had founded the so-called "people's party" in Virginia by exposing widespread corruption among the great plantation owners in the eastern Tidewater region who had dominated Virginia politics. He won national fame as an orator when he called for Virginia independence in the House of Burgesses at Williamsburg after the British had enacted the Stamp Act in 1765. Ruled out of order, Henry roared in protest: "Caesar had his Brutus; Charles the First his Cromwell; and George the Third may profit by their example." And when the Speaker and Tidewater plantation owners shouted "Treason! Treason," Henry dared his opponents to order his arrest: "If this be treason," he roared, "make the most of it!"[4]

Henry's spectacular success at Williamsburg left him undisputed leader of a new, radical party made up of a large rural rabble whose views had hitherto been ignored. As one of his political enemies put it, Henry returned "into the upper parts of the country . . . to recommend himself to his constituents by spreading treason, and enforcing firm resolutions against the authority of the British Parliament."[5]

The "upper parts" of Virginia elected Henry to the House of Burgesses every year for the next decade and helped Henry build an enormous, lucrative law practice and acquire tens of thousands of acres in land—some as payment for legal services, but most of it from complex, often colorful, and sometimes vicious courthouse deals. With early American wealth measured in fertile acreage, Henry's pursuit of land became as much a priority for him as public service. After his first wife died, in 1775, Henry married Dorothea Dandridge, the daughter of Martha (Dandridge) Washington's first cousin, who gave Henry a strong family tie to the Tidewater aristocracy—and a dowry of twelve slaves to add to his thirty. By now he boasted a ten-thousand-acre plantation, and ten thousand additional acres in the Kentucky wilderness. No longer a rough-hewn frontiersman, he reveled in riding in an elegant, expensive carriage, and, until the ratification convention, he was seldom seen "without a scarlet cloak, black clothes and a dressed wig." Some of his habits died hard, however, and he would have twelve more children by "Dolly," as he called her. Virginians often quipped that Henry's nineteen children and sixty grandchildren made him, not Washington, the father of his country.

In May 1776 Henry's rural supporters helped him win election as the state's first governor, but the state constitution frustrated his quest for personal power by limiting the governor's term to three successive terms of one year each. Once in the governor's chair, he immediately found himself constrained by term limits and a host of wartime problems that he had neither the time nor the qualifications to solve. Virginia, like Massachusetts and other states, faced a vast array of factional conflicts between franchised property owners and the disenfranchised; between farmers and merchants, debtors and creditors, eastern plantation owners and western farmers, and Anglicans and Dissenters. In the end, Henry was unable to raise a militia—or the taxes to pay for one. In effect, most of the poor refused to risk their lives in battle to support the interests of the rich, while the rich refused to pay taxes to support the poor. After three one-year terms without firing a shot against the British or causing one to be fired, Henry gladly ceded the office to Thomas Jefferson, who proved as incapable as Henry of recruiting an effective militia or collecting enough taxes to pay for one. Indeed, British troops over-ran most of Virginia and would have captured Jefferson, Henry, and the entire state legislature if local patriots had not warned them of the British approach. After the war, a close political ally of Henry stood in the House of Delegates and demanded an inquiry into what he called Jefferson's "cowardice" as governor in fleeing rather than defending the capital city against the British assault. Although the inquiry cleared Jefferson of the charges—indeed, offered its "sincere thanks . . . for his . . . attentive administration"—it provoked a life-long feud between the two Virginians, with Jefferson calling Henry "below contempt" for having inspired the inquiry.[6]

The end of the Revolutionary War plunged Virginia into bitter political turmoil over fiscal and social reform, and in 1784 Virginia put Henry back in the governor's chair for two more one-year terms. He spent most of that time fighting the attempts of northern gover-nors to convert the Jay-Gardoqui agreement into a treaty, which would have ceded Mississippi River navigation rights—and the rights of westerners to deposit goods in New Orleans for transfer to oceangoing vessels—in exchange for opening ports in Spain to northern and eastern shipping interests. Henry threatened Virginia's secession from the Confederation and exhorted James Monroe, Vir-ginia's senior member in Congress, to lead the fight against such a treaty. Congress nonetheless voted seven states to five in favor of the Jay agreement, but because the Articles of Confederation required a majority of nine states to enact a treaty into law, the Jay agreement was scrapped and Henry became the darling of farmers on the fron-tier beyond the Appalachians. As Kentucky's fourteen delegates arrived in Richmond, Henry reiterated his pledge to guard their "natural" rights to sail the Mississippi.

Fearing that Federalists would move—as they had in Philadel-phia—for a quick up-or-down vote on ratification without debate, Mason jumped to his feet for recognition after the convention had adopted the rules of order and, threatening the convention with "divine vengeance," demanded unlimited, clause-by-clause debate. To his astonishment—and to Henry's delight—both Federalists and

Antifederalists at the convention agreed, and Henry's political ally John Tyler moved for and won approval for the convention to metamorphose into a committee of the whole to begin arguments. With clause-by-clause debate, Henry enthused, he would be able to drag out convention deliberations for weeks—at least until June 23, when Virginia's state legislature was to reconvene. More than 60 of the 170 delegates of the ratification convention were members of the state legislature and would, by law, have to leave to attend to their legislative duties and force the convention to adjourn without having ratified the Constitution. Henry reasoned that if Virginia failed to ratify, New York would follow suit and provoke riot-torn Pennsylvania and Massachusetts to reconsider ratification and subscribe to holding a second constitutional convention to dilute government powers.

Federalists were equally pleased with clause-by-clause debate. Although Washington and Madison had long earlier conceded Henry's brilliant oratorical skills, they knew he was careless about studying and preparing his facts in legal arguments. Jefferson had characterized Henry as being "all tongue without either head or heart,"[7] and Madison believed that Henry's emotional rhetoric would be no match for reasoned argument. Madison, after all, had all but written the Constitution, knew every clause in every sentence—and the factual basis and arguments for and against each clause. Supporting him would be John Marshall and Francis Corbin, both brilliant young lawyers with suburb expository skills. And by shifting debate to a committee of the whole, the equally brilliant elder statesman Edmund Pendleton could leave his chair as president of the convention and debate as a Federalist delegate from the floor.

Henry, of course, had no intention of relying on legal arguments; he never had. His plan was to stir men's souls to rebellion, as he had in 1775. Two days after the Virginia convention began, debate on the Constitution opened in earnest, and Henry took quick control of the floor before anyone else could speak. His recent illness had made his face appear more gaunt than usual—a dramatic change that made his eyes more penetrating, even hypnotic. Six feet tall and about 160 pounds, he used his hands expressively, contorting his arms, shoulders, and facial elements to theatrical perfection, adding drama and excitement to his every word. As it turned out, he would speak on seventeen of the twenty-two days and provide 20 percent of convention verbiage. With Mason, Tyler, and Benjamin Harrison applauding and frontiersmen cheering his every word, Henry declared himself "extremely uneasy at the proposed change of Government. . . .

> I consider myself as the servant of the people of this Common-wealth, as a centinel over their rights, liberty, and happiness. . . . A year ago the minds of our citizens were at perfect repose. Before the meeting of the late Federal Convention at Philadelphia, a general peace, and an universal tranquility prevailed in this country; but since that period they are exceedingly uneasy and disquieted. . . . If our situation be thus uneasy, whence has arisen this fearful jeop-ardy. It arises from . . . a proposal to change our government:— A proposal that goes to the utter annihilation of the most sol-emn engagements of the States. A proposal of establishing 9 States into a confederacy, to the eventual exclusion of 4 states. . . . but, Sir, give me leave to demand, what right had they to say, *We, the People* . . . who authorized them to speak the language of, *We, the People*, instead of *We, the States?* . . . I have the highest respect for those Gentlemen who formed the Convention. . . . But, Sir, on this great occasion, I would demand the cause of their conduct.— Even from that illustrious man [George Washington] who saved us by his valor, I would have a reason for his conduct—that liberty which he has given us by his valor, tells me to ask his reason. . . . The people gave them no power to use their name. That they ex-ceeded their power is perfectly clear. . . . The Federal Convention ought to have amended the old system—for this purpose they were solely delegated: The object of their mission extended to no other consideration.[8]

To no one's surprise, Governor Edmund Randolph then took the floor. Henry and Mason smiled as they anticipated the governor's appeal to undecided delegates.

> Mr. Chairman. Had the most enlightened Statesman whom Amer-ica has yet seen [Washington] foretold but a year ago the crisis which has now called us together, he would have been confronted by the universal testimony of history: for never was it yet known, that in

so short a space, by the peaceable working of events, without a war . . . a nation has been brought to agitate on a question, and error in the issue of which, may blast their happiness.[9]

Delegates shifted in their chairs uncomfortably; Mason and Henry turned to each other with puzzled looks, clearly unable to follow Randolph's meaning or direction. Randolph plodded on: "trying exigency . . . proselytes by fire . . . mutual toleration." Then at last, he seemed to get to the point of his speech: "Before I press into the body of the argument"—applause spilled from the gallery for a moment—"I must take the liberty of mentioning the part I have already borne in this great question."

The applause turned to groans, but he continued undeterred, with no one following his reasoning until he looked up and declared forcefully, "I refused to sign, and if the same were to return, again would I refuse."

Henry, Mason, and the Antifederalists jumped to their feet to cheer.

"Wholly to adopt or wholly to reject, as proposed by the Convention," Randolph called out above the cheers, "seemed too hard an alternative to the citizens of America. . . . Amendments were consequently my wish; these were the grounds of my repugnance to subscribe." The applause faded away. His words continued to puzzle Henry and Mason—until Randolph turned and looked directly at Patrick Henry:

"I express my apprehension that the postponement of this Convention, to so late a day has extinguished the probability of [amendments] . . . without inevitable ruin to the Union, and the Union is the anchor of our political salvation, and"—Randolph looked at Mason now and mocked Mason's dramatic refusal to sign the Constitution in Philadelphia—"and I will assent to the lopping of this limb before I assent to the dissolution of the Union."

Henry and Mason flushed red with anger. Randolph resumed his attack on Henry:

I shall now follow the Honorable Gentleman in his enquiry. Before the meeting of the Federal Convention, says the Honorable Gentleman, we rested in peace. . . . Miraculous must it appear to those who consider the distresses of war, and the no less afflicting calamities which we suffered in the succeeding peace. . . . The members of the General Convention were particularly deputed to meliorate the confederation. On a thorough contemplation of the subject, they found it impossible to amend that system. What was to be done? . . . The dangers of America . . . suggested the expedient of forming a new plan. . . . The Honorable Gentleman . . . objects because nine States are sufficient to put the Government in motion. What number of States ought we to have said? Ought we to have required the concurrence of all the thirteen? Rhode-Island . . . notorious for her uniform opposition to every federal duty, would then have it in her power to defeat the Union . . . would it not be lamentable that nothing could be done for the defection of one State? . . . The Gentleman then proceeds, and inquires, why we assumed the language of "We, the People." I ask why not? The Government is for the people. . . . What harm is there in consulting the people on the construction of a Government by which they are to be bound? Is it unfair? Is it unjust? If the Government is to be binding on the people, are not the people the proper persons to examine its merits or defects? I take this to be one of the least and most trivial objections that will be made to the Constitution—it carries the answer with itself.

No one had ever confronted Patrick Henry so brazenly, condescendingly, but now it was Randolph's voice that soared:

In the whole of this business, I have acted in the strictest obedience to my conscience, in discharging what I conceive to be my duty to my country. I refused my signature, and if the same reasons operated on my mind, I would still refuse; but as I think that those eight States which have adopted the Constitution will not recede, I am a friend to the Union.[10]

Randolph's final words—they were actually Washington's words that Randolph had extracted from several letters—stunned delegates, left them sitting in silence and disbelief. Washington, they said to themselves, had evidently convinced Randolph to switch positions. Jefferson would later describe Randolph as "the poorest chameleon I ever saw, having no colour of his own and reflecting that [of the person] nearest him."[11]

But Madison exulted over Randolph's sudden switch in allegiance. "The Governor has . . . thrown himself fully into the federal scale," Madison rejoiced in a letter to Washington. "Henry & Mason made a lame figure & appeared to take different and awkward ground. The federalists are a good deal elated by the existing prospect. I dare not however speak with certainty. . . . Kentucke has been extremely tainted, is supposed to be generally adverse, and every piece of address is going on privately to work on the local interests & prejudices of that & other quarters."[12]

One of Washington's favorite nephews, Bushrod, also was a delegate. "Mr. Henry," Bushrod enthused in a letter to his uncle, "called upon the friends to point out the objections to the present federal constitution. This challenge, which was given with an appearance of great confidence, drew from the governor yesterday a very able and elegant harangue for two hours and a half; for I suppose you have been informed of Mr. Randolph's determination to vote for the proposed government without previous amendments. He . . . painted in a masterly and affecting manner the necessity of a more solid union of the States. . . . Mr. Madison followed, and with such force of reasoning, and a display of such irresistible truths, that opposition seemed to have quitted the field."[13]

Washington was overjoyed, though not entirely surprised, writing confidently to John Jay in New York that if Virginia becomes the ninth state to ratify, "it will, I flatter myself, have its due weight. . . . I will give you a few particulars which . . . you might not, perhaps, immediately obtain through any public channel of conveyance. . . . Governor Randolph . . . is reported to have spoken with great pathos . . . and . . . declared, that, since so many of the States had adopted the proposed constitution, he considered the sense of America to be already taken & that he should give his vote in favor of it without insisting upon previous amendments. . . . Mr. Randolph's declaration will have considerable effect with those who had hitherto been wavering. . . . Mr. Henry & Colonel Mason took different and awkward ground—and by no means equaled the public expectation in their Speeches . . . the leaders of the opposition appear rather chagreened & hardly to be decided in their mode of opposition."[14]

And that was but the beginning of the assault on Henry. On the following day, Federalists opened by picking apart Henry's arguments, one by one, with Pendleton pointing out that far from the "universal tranquility" Henry had described, the nation's commerce had decayed, "our finances [were] deranged, public and private credit destroyed. If the public mind was then at ease, it did not result from a conviction of being in a happy and easy situation. It must have been an inactive unaccountable stupor."[15]

After the laughter subsided, Pendleton went on to refute every point Patrick Henry had made, before turning over the floor to Revolutionary War hero Henry ("Light-Horse Harry") Lee. He began his response to Patrick Henry with flattery that cloaked his mockery of Henry's rhetoric.

> Mr. Chairman—I feel every power of my mind moved by the language of the Honorable Gentleman yesterday [Henry]. The eclat and brilliancy which have distinguished that Gentleman, the honors with which he has been dignified, and the brilliant tactics which he has so often displayed, have attracted my respect and attention. On so important an occasion and before so respectable a body, I expected a new display of his powers of oratory: But instead of proceeding to investigate the merits of the new plan of Government, the worthy character informed us of horrors which he felt, of apprehensions in his mind, which make him tremblingly fearful. . . . Mr. Chairman was it proper to appeal to the fear of this House? . . . I trust he is come to judge and not to alarm.[16]

Lee went on to describe the "imbecility" of the Confederation in its inability to collect needed revenue. Commerce had come to a halt, with not an American merchant ship to be found in coastal waters. He asked whether Shays's Rebellion was an example of what Henry had described as universal tranquility.[17]

Unabashed by the rhetorical thrashing, Henry recaptured the floor at about noon, and actually thanked Lee for his "encomium," before plunging into a spellbinding oration that began by predicting that the Constitution would cost Americans their "rights of conscience, trial by jury, liberty of the press, all your communities and franchises, all pretensions to human rights and privileges." As

Antifederalists cheered him on, Henry scaled the peaks of oratorical grandeur, asking,

> Is this tame relinquishment of rights worthy of freemen? . . . It is said eight states have adopted this plan. I declare that if twelve states and a half had adopted it, I would with manly firmness, and in spite of an erring world, reject it. . . . Is it necessary for your liberty that you should abandon those great rights by the adoption of this system? Is the relinquishment of the trial by jury, and the liberty of the press, necessary for your liberty? Will the abandonment of your most sacred rights tend to the security of your liberty? Liberty, greatest of all earthly blessings—give us that precious jewel, and you may take everything else.

He paused, looked away from the audience for a moment, and assumed a modest air:

> Twenty-three years ago I was supposed a traitor to my country. I was then said to be a bane of sedition, because I supported the rights of my country. . . . I say [now] our privileges and rights are in danger.

His voice rose to a crescendo:

> Guard with jealous attention the public liberty. Suspect every one who approaches that jewel. Unfortunately nothing will preserve it but downright force; whenever you give up that force you are inevitably ruined. . . .
>
> We are come hither to preserve the poor Commonwealth of Virginia, if it can possibly be done: Something must be done to preserve your liberty and mine: The Confederation; this same despised Government, merits, in my opinion, the highest encomium: It carried us through a long and dangerous war: It rendered us victorious in that bloody conflict with a powerful nation: It has secured us territory greater than any European Monarch possesses: And shall a Government which has been thus strong and vigorous be accused of imbecility and abandoned for want of energy? Consider what you are about to do before you part with this Government . . . the new form of government . . . will oppress and ruin the people.[18]

On and on he went, hour after hour.

"There was a perfect stillness throughout the House, and in the galleries," according to Judge Edmund Winston, a pro-Henry delegate. A spectator in the gallery is said to have been so stirred by Henry's vivid description of federal enslavement that "he involuntarily felt his wrists to assure himself that the fetters were not already pressing his flesh."[19]

"The Constitution is said to have beautiful features," Henry appealed to the audience in softer tones before assuming an accusatory look and turning almost angrily to the Federalist chairman, George Wythe.

> But when I come to examine these features, Sir, they appear to me horribly frightful. Among other deformities, it has an awful squinting; it squints towards monarchy. And does not this raise indignation in the breast of every AMERICAN? Your President may easily become King. . . .
>
> Where are your checks in this government? Your strongholds will be in the hands of your enemies. It is on a supposition that your AMERICAN governors shall be honest, that all the good qualities of this government are founded; but its defective and impœrfect construction puts in their power to perpetrate the worst of mischiefs, should they be bad men. . . .
>
> Show me that age and country where the rights and liberties of the people were placed on the sole chance of their rulers being good men, without a consequent loss of liberty. . . . If your American chief be a man of ambition and abilities, how easy is it for him to render himself absolute! The army is in his hands . . . the president, in the field, at the head of his army, can prescribe the terms on which he shall reign master, so far that it will puzzle any American ever to get his neck from under the galling yoke . . . and what have you to oppose this force? What will then become of you and your rights? Will not absolute despotism ensue?

Henry lashed out angrily at Federalist tactics in rigging earlier convention elections:

> Permit me, Sir, to say that a great majority of the people even in the adopting States are averse to this government. I believe it would be right to say that they have been egregiously misled. Pennsylvania has perhaps been tricked into it. If the other States

who have adopted it have not been tricked, still they were too much hurried into its adoption. There were very respectable minorities in several of them; and if reports be true, a clear majority of the people are averse to it. . . . This government has not the affection of the people, at present . . . and, Sir, you know that a Government without their affections can neither be durable nor happy. I speak as one poor individual—but when I speak, I speak the language of thousands.

With that, the gallery exploded into whoops and cheers. Antifederalist delegates rose to their feet to join the mass acclaim. "And," Henry tried shouting over the crowd: "and, Sir . . . and, Sir." The audience gradually grew quiet, and Henry forced himself to suppress a smile: "But Sir, I mean not to breathe the spirit nor utter the language of secession."

Again the gallery erupted, and after the chair restored order, Henry stood silent in a dramatic pose, looking down into the space between him and the first row of delegates. Then he looked up and all but whispered, "I have trespassed so long on your patience." Henry looked at his watch and realized he had held the floor for seven hours. "I have, I fear, fatigued the Committee, yet I have not said the one hundred thousandth part of what I have on my mind, and wish to impart." Henry then tapped the reservoir of veneration that most Virginians held for him.

"Having lived so long—been so much honored—my efforts, though small are due my country. I have found my mind hurried. I did not come prepared to speak on so multifarious a subject. . . . I trust you will indulge me."[20]

After a long silence, a voice rang out impatiently: "Mr. Chairman!" Governor Randolph had had enough of Henry and stood to protest. The dinner hour had long since passed. "Mr. Chairman! If we go on in this irregular manner . . . instead of three or six weeks, it will take us six months to decide this question. I shall endeavor to make the Committee [of the Whole] sensible of the necessity of establishing a national government [but] it is too late to enter into the subject now."[21]

IO

On the Wings
of the Tempest

PATRICK HENRY HAD BEEN TALKING ENDLESSLY on the floor of the Virginia ratification convention—cleverly trying to extend proceedings beyond June 23, the day when sixty convention delegates would have to attend a session of the state legislature and force the convention to adjourn. Henry took the floor on seventeen days, routinely making three speeches a day. He gave five speeches on two occasions, and eight on two others, sometimes speaking for more than six consecutive hours. Indeed, his speeches accounted for one-fifth of the oratory on the floor of the convention.

Although each had a different thrust, every speech aimed at capturing the emotions of his listeners, and Madison and his team of skilled lawyers took careful notes of each vague assertion before calmly, coldly picking it apart and disproving it with specific facts about the condition of the nation and the remedies provided by the Constitution. Madison opened the counterattack with simple logic. In contrast to Henry's priestlike demeanor and dramatic voice, the elfin Madison was almost invisible—both man and voice—his head bowed, holding his hat in his hand and speaking from notes he kept in it—so softly, however, that he was barely audible. As he spoke, his body rocked in a curious "rapid and forward seesaw motion," according to an onlooker who was writing a history of the convention.[1]

But in a relatively few terse remarks, Madison's logic shattered the credibility of Henry's stunning oratory. He began by attacking

Henry's inconsistencies in objecting to granting Congress the right to raise a federal army:

"Congress ought to have the power," he said simply, "to provide for the execution of the laws, suppress insurrections, and repel invasions. . . . Without a general controuling power to call forth the strength of the Union, to repel invasions, the country might be overrun and conquered by foreign enemies. Without such a power to suppress insurrections, our liberties might be destroyed by domestic faction and domestic tyranny be established."[2]

The next morning, Federalists gambled by sending the young, albeit brilliant barrister Francis Corbin into the fray to lead the assault on Henry. The son of loyalist parents, he had returned to England at the beginning of the Revolution and, while the war raged in America, he had pursued higher education at Cambridge University and studied law at London's Inner Temple. His was not a résumé that exuded patriotism, and his distinctly English accent and aristocratic air offended many Virginians—none more than Patrick Henry. Nonetheless, Corbin entered the lists.

In a scathing attack on virtually every one of Henry's criticisms of the Constitution, Corbin began by questioning Henry's objection to the expression *We the People* in the preamble. "Ought not the people, Sir, to judge of that Government whereby they are to be ruled?" Corbin thundered.

> We are, Sir, deliberating on a question of great consequence to the people of America. . . . He has asked, with an air of triumph, whether the Confederation was not adequate to the purposes of the Federal Government. Permit me to say, No. If, Sir, perfection existed in that system, why was the Federal Convention called? Why did every State except Rhode-Island send deputies to that Convention? Was it not from a persuasion of its inefficacy?
>
> If this be not sufficient to convince him . . . let him go into the interior parts of the country, and enquire into the situation of the farmers. He will be told that tobacco and other produce are miserably low, merchandise dear, and taxes high. Let him go through the United States; he will perceive appearances of ruin and decay every where. Let him visit . . . our ports and inlets . . . he will behold but a few trifling boats—he will every where see com-

merce languish; the disconsolate merchant, with his arms folded, ruminating in despair, on the wretched ruins of his fortune, and deploring the impossibility of retrieving it. The West-Indies are blocked up against us. Not the British only, but other nations exclude us from those islands. Our fur trade gone to Canada, British centinels within our own territories, our posts withheld.

To these distresses, we may add the derangement of our finances. . . . The Honorable Gentleman must be well acquainted with the debts due by the United States, and how much is due to foreign nations. Have not the payment of these been shamefully withheld? . . . No part of the principal is paid to those nations— nor has even the interest been paid as honorably and punctually as it ought. . . . What is to be done? Compel the delinquent States to pay requisitions to Congress? How are they to be compelled?[3]

Henry sat thunderstruck, with no answers to Corbin's humiliating assault. He rose unsteadily and all but whispered that he would delay his response and cede the floor to Governor Randolph, who in turn ceded it to Madison to apply the coup de grâce.

"It is subversive of every principle of sound policy to trust the safety of a community with a Government totally destitute of the means of protecting itself or its members," Madison declared.

The Confederation is so notoriously feeble that foreign nations are unwilling to form any treaties with us. They are apprised that our General Government cannot perform any of its engagements; but that they may be violated at pleasure by any of the States. Our violation of treaties already entered into proves this truth unequivocally. . . .

How have we dealt with that benevolent ally [France]? Have we complied with our most sacred obligations to that nation?

Have we paid the interest punctually from year to year? Is not interest accumulating while not a shilling is discharged of the principal? . . . We have been obliged to borrow money, even to pay the interest of our debts. This a ruinous and most disgraceful expedient.

Madison then played his trump card: George Washington, the Father of His Country. "Can a Government that stands in need of such measures secure the liberty or promote the happiness or glory of any country?" Madison asked.

At the conclusion of the war, that man [Washington] who had the most unequivocal and most brilliant proofs of his attachment to its [the nation's] welfare . . . publicly testified that some alteration was necessary to render it adequate to the security of our happiness. I did not introduce that great name to bias any Gentleman here. Much as I admire and revere the man, I consider these members as not to be actuated by the influence of any man; but I introduced him as a respectable witness to prove that the Articles of Confederation were inadequate, and that we must resort to something else.[4]

Clearly taken aback by the Federalist assault, Henry spent the rest of the weekend closeted with Mason at the Swan Inn to see what cards they had left to play. On Monday morning, they all but skipped arm in arm to the convention hall in high spirits.

"I wish there was a prospect of union in our sentiments," Henry began the debate, then showed his hand and launched a blistering, personal attack on Madison and other Federalist congressmen. "There is a dispute between us and the Spaniards about the right of navigating the Mississippi," Henry all but shouted. Frontiersmen in the gallery joined the crudely clothed delegates from Kentucky in loud applause. The Kentuckians had been growing restive at their ill treatment by Tidewater political leaders who had pointedly excluded them from elegant social gatherings during the convention's off-hours. "I wish to know the origin and progress of the business, as it would probably unfold great dangers. . . . Seven States wished to relinquish this river to them [Spain]. The six southern States opposed it. Seven States not being sufficient to convey it away, it remains now ours. If I am wrong, there is a member on this floor"—Henry paused to glower at Madison—

who can contradict the facts. I will readily retract. This new Government, I conceive, will enable those States who have already discovered their inclination that way to give away this river. Will the Honorable Gentleman advise us to relinquish this inestimable navigation, and place formidable enemies on our backs? . . . I hope this will be explained.

He openly taunted Madison with a grand gesture of his arm, inviting the younger man to stand and answer.

I was not in Congress when these transactions took place. I may not have charged every fact. I may have misrepresented matters. . . . Let us hear how the great and important right of navigating that river has been attended to and whether I am mistaken in my opinion that federal measures will lose it to us forever. If a bare majority of Congress can make laws, the situation of our western citizens is dreadful.

As the frontiersmen in the gallery joined in taunting Madison, Henry then hurled what he thought would be the crushing blow against Federalists, the name of Jefferson: "His opinion is that you reject this Government . . . till it be amended. Let us follow the sage advice of this common friend of our happiness."[5]

Jefferson was furious when he learned that Henry had used his name. "While Henry lives," Jefferson seethed in a letter to Madison, "another bad constitution would be formed and saddled forever on us. What we have to do I think is devoutly pray for his death, in the mean time to keep alive the idea that the present is but an ordinance and to prepare the minds of our young men."[6]

Henry's open taunting of Madison provoked "Light-Horse Harry" Lee to use Henry's opposition to a standing federal army to attack Henry's character and his failure to fight in the Revolutionary War. He began by questioning Henry's "rage for democracy and zeal for the rights of the people. . . .

He tells us that he is a staunch republican, and that he adores lib-erty. I believe him, and when I do so I wonder that he should say . . . that militia alone ought to be depended upon for the de-fence of every free Country. . . .

I have had a different experience of their service from the Honorable Gentleman. It was my fortune to be a soldier of my country. In the discharge of my duty . . . I saw what the Honorable Gentleman did not see—Our men fighting with the troops of the King. . . . I have seen incontrovertible evidence that militia can-not always be relied upon. . . . Let the Gentleman recollect the action of Guilford [North Carolina]. The American regular troops behaved there with the most gallant intrepidity. What did the militia do? The greatest numbers of them fled. . . .

But says the Honorable Gentleman, we are in peace. Does he forget the insurrection in Massachusetts? . . . Had Shays been possessed of abilities . . . nothing was wanting to bring about a revolution.[7]

Henry ignored Lee's attack on his patriotism, but when Randolph resumed the attack, Henry could no longer contain his bitterness at Governor Randolph's desertion of the Antifederalists. "It seems to be very strange and unaccountable that that which was the object of his execration should now receive his encomium," Henry declared. Stopping short of accusing Randolph of accepting a bribe, Henry nonetheless suggested that "something extraordinary must have operated so great a change in his opinions."[8]

Infuriated by Henry's implications, Randolph did his best to remain calm, but after two days, he could not longer contain his anger:

> I find myself attacked, in the most illiberal manner by the Honorable Gentleman [Henry]. I disdain his aspersions and his insinuations. His asperity is warranted by no principle of Parliamentary decency, nor compatible with the least shadow of friendship, and if our friendship must fall, *Let it fall like Lucifer, never to rise again.*
>
> Let him remember that it is not to answer him, but to satisfy this respectable audience that I now get up. He has accused me of inconsistency in this very respectable assembly. Sir, if I do not stand on the bottom of integrity and pure love for Virginia, as much as those who can be most clamorous, I wish to resign my existence. Consistency consists in actions, and not in empty specious words. . . . I understand not him who wishes to give a full scope to licentiousness and dissipation, who would advise me to reject the proposed plan and plunge us into anarchy.[9]

Randolph's reference to *Lucifer* was an oblique method of challenging Henry to a duel for his accusation of apostasy. Randolph went on to read a letter he had sent to his constituents saying that regardless of his objections to the Constitution, he would vote for ratification.

Shaken by the prospects of dueling the thirty-five-year-old governor, the fifty-two-year-old Henry got to his feet and said he had had "no intention of offending anyone"—that he "did not mean to wound the feelings of any Gentleman" and he was "sorry if I offended the Honorable Gentleman without intending it." But Randolph grew only more enraged, saying that he was "relieved" by what Henry had said and that "were it not for the concession of the Gentleman, I would have made some men's hair stand on end by the disclosure of certain facts."

Now it was Henry's turn to grow enraged, telling Randolph that if he had something to say against him to disclose it. Randolph responded calmly, "I beg the Honorable Gentleman to pardon me for reminding him that his historical references and quotations are not accurate. If he errs so much with respect to his facts, as he has done in history, we cannot depend on his information or assertions."[10]

That evening, Henry and his second called on Randolph, and all Richmond buzzed excitedly over prospects of a duel between the two great Virginia governors. Although no record exists of their discussion, Henry did not press his challenge and left without provoking violence.

Henry's strategy continued to aim at capturing the critical votes from Kentucky frontiersmen, who opposed a standing army as much as Henry and whose existence depended far more on obtaining navigation rights on the Mississippi than on amending the Constitution or establishing a new federal government. Henry renewed his accusation that the seven northern states "are determined to give up the Mississippi."[11]

Madison countered by pointing out the contradiction between Henry's advocacy of demanding Mississippi River navigation rights from Spain and his objection to a federal standing army to back up those demands. Henry parried by calling on Monroe to describe northern tactics in Congress to allow Foreign Secretary Jay to cede Mississippi River navigation rights to Spain for twenty-five years. Clearly cornered, Madison had little choice but to admit that the seven northern states had ceded the interests of the western frontier to Spain to further the interests of the eastern carrying trade.

Henry pounced, his voice soaring: "No Constitution under Heaven, founded on the principles of justice, can warrant the relinquishment of the most sacred rights of the society to promote the interest of one part of it. . . . Are not the rivers and waters that wash the shores of the country appendages, inseparable from our right of sovereignty? . . . The people of Kentucky, though weak now, will not let the President and Senate take away this right."[12] It was vintage Patrick Henry; Henry at his best; the Henry who had cried out for liberty or death in 1775. The gallery loved him; Kentuckians loved him; Virginians loved him.

As the convention progressed, the tone of the rhetoric digressed, with Henry and the Antifederalists refusing to limit their arguments to clauses under discussion and invariably expanding their arguments to inflammatory oratory that projected innumerable imagined horrors under the federal government proposed by the Constitution. Henry's evident victory in the debate over the Mississippi navigation question, however, left Madison unnerved and, for the first time, dispirited. "Appearances are at present less favorable than at the date of my last," he wrote to Washington.

> Our progress is slow and every advantage is taken of delay, to work on the local prejudices of particular setts of members. British debts . . . and the Mississippi are the principal topics of private discussion & intrigue, as well as of public declamation. . . . There is reason to believe that the event may depend on the Kentucky members; who seem to lean more agst than in favor of the Constitution. . . . The majority will certainly be very small on whatever side it may finally lie; and I dare not encourage much expectation that it will be on the favorable side.[13]

Madison reported that the publisher of Philadelphia's Antifederalist *Independent Gazetteer* had come to Richmond "with letters for the antifederal leaders from N. York and probably Philada" and had spent time "closeted" with Henry, Mason, and other Antifederalists to coordinate Antifederalist strategy in the two states. Madison tried but was unable to learn details of the strategy, however.

As the convention entered its third week, Henry's rhetoric had worked its magic. The reasoned legal arguments of Madison and his men had been lost on Kentucky frontiersmen. On June 24, Henry stood to deliver what he expected would crush all Federalist chances of victory by declaring that the Constitution would allow the federal government to decree that "every black man must fight . . . [and] that every slave who would go to the army should be free." Staring sternly at Madison, he asked, "May they not pronounce all slaves free?

As much as I deplore slavery, I see that prudence forbids abolition.
I deny that the General Government ought to set them free,
because a decided majority of the States have not the ties of sym-
pathy and fellow-feeling for those whose interest would be affected
by their emancipation. The majority of Congress is in the North,
and the slaves are to the South. In this situation, I see a great deal
of the property of Virginia in jeopardy. . . . I repeat it again, that it
would rejoice my very soul that everyone of my fellow beings was
emancipated . . . but is it practicable by any human means to liber-
ate them, without producing the most dreadful and ruinous consequences? We ought to possess them, in the manner we inherited
them from our ancestors, as their manumission is incompatible
with the felicity of our country. But we ought to soften, as much as
possible the rigor of their unhappy fate. . . . This is a local matter
and I can see no propriety in subjecting it to Congress.[14]

As rage spread across the faces of the gallery, Madison tried to
refute Henry, but Henry would not be silenced. After proposing a
rapid-fire series of amendments, including a bill of rights, his voice
rose to a crescendo as he called on God's wrath to punish the authors
of the Constitution.

"He [Madison] tells you of important blessings, which he imag-
ines will result to us and mankind in general from the adoption of
this system," Henry exclaimed. "I see the awful immensity of the
dangers with which it is pregnant.

"I see it!

"I feel it!"

He all but trembled and looked to the heavens, his arms spread
wide, playing the scene like the veteran actor he was. Outside, the
skies blackened suddenly and turned day into night.

I see *beings* of a higher order—anxious concerning our decision.
When I see beyond the horizon that binds human eyes, and look at
the final consummation of all human things, and see those intelligent beings which inhabit the ethereal mansions, reviewing the
political decisions and revolutions which in the progress of time
will happen in America, and the consequent happiness and misery
of mankind—I am led to believe that much of the account on one
side or the other will depend on what we now decide. Our own happiness alone is not affected by the event. All nations are interested

in the determination. We have it in our power to secure the happiness of one half of the human race. Its adoption may involve the misery of the other hemispheres.[15]

An explosion of thunder interrupted him. Lightning bolts followed, striking the ground outside and shaking the entire hall. More thunder, more lightning. Terrified delegates fell to their knees or raced to the door. "The spirits he had called seemed to come at his bidding," wrote his contemporary biographer William Wirt, "and, rising on the wings of the tempest, [he] seized upon the artillery of heaven, and direct[ed] its fiercest thunders against the heads of his adversaries.' The scene became insupportable; and . . . without the formality of adjournment, the members rush[ed] from their seats with precipitation and confusion."[16]

Although many in the gallery may have fled, the official records do not bear out Wirt's drama of a mass exodus of delegates—or, indeed, the departure of any delegates. At least three delegates, including Madison, spoke on the convention floor for about five minutes each immediately after Henry's speech. Although some members of the gallery returned the next day shaken by what they deemed Henry's summoning of the "black arts," delegates were eager to end the convention and return to their private lives. They rejected his amendments, 88 to 80. Then, in a newfound eagerness to honor Washington, they voted 89 to 79 to become the decisive ninth state to ratify the Constitution. Henry won but three of the fourteen Kentucky votes, which proved not to be decisive after all, and most delegates disregarded Jefferson's letter. Most delegates agreed that Randolph's defection to the Federalists was probably the most decisive factor in the Federalist victory. Federalists wisely acted to heal the wounds of discord as quickly as possible by proposing, as their equivalents had in Massachusetts, forty "conciliatory amendments," including a bill of rights. The amendments, they resolved, "should be recommended to the consideration of the Congress which should first assemble under the Constitution."[17]

Although Washington never set foot in the convention hall, Antifederalists and Federalists agreed that he had dominated the exhausting drama. "Be assured," James Monroe conceded, "his influence carried this Government; for my part I have a boundless confidence in him nor have I any reason to believe he will ever furnish occasion for withdrawing it. More is to be apprehended . . . as he advances in age, from the designs of those around him than from any disposition of his own."[18]

Although they sensed his presence in every utterance, delegates at the convention did not and could not know the extent of his involvement—both public and private. In addition to the influence he exerted as the obvious—indeed, only—choice for first president, he exerted behind-the-scenes political influence by neutralizing two of Virginia's most influential Antifederalists, former governor Thomas Jefferson and the state's sitting governor, Edmund Randolph. It would be no coincidence that Washington would appoint the former as the nation's first secretary of state and the latter as the nation's first attorney general after his election to the presidency.

"I think that, were it not for one great character in America," Antifederalist delegate William Grayson growled at the delegates in his closing argument, "so many men would not be for this Government. . . . We have one ray of hope. We do not fear while he lives, but we can only expect his *fame* to be immortal. We wish to know, who besides him can concentrate the confidence and affections of all America."[19]

Although Henry made a show of publicly accepting the decision of the convention, George Mason and his "Federal Republicans" stormed out of the hall, intent on continuing the fight against ratification by issuing a minority report similar to the Dissent that Pennsylvania Antifederalists had issued. After gathering at a nearby tavern, they sent for Henry. To their astonishment, he spoke to them with an air of contrition, reiterating his closing statement to the convention after his bitter defeat over ratification:

> If I shall be in the minority, I shall have those painful sensations which arise from a conviction of being overpowered in a good cause. Yet I will be a peaceable citizen! My head, my hand, my heart shall be at liberty to retrieve the loss of liberty and remove the defects of that system—in a constitutional way. I wish not to go to violence, but will wait with hopes that the spirit which predominated in the revolution is not yet gone, nor the cause of those who are attached

to the revolution yet lost. I shall therefore patiently wait in expectation of seeing that Government changed so as to be compatible
with the safety, liberty and happiness of the people.[20]

Madison did not believe a word of Henry's declaration and con-
fided his suspicions in a letter to Washington: "Mr. H____y declared
. . . that altho' he should submit as a quiet citizen, he should seize the
first moment that offered for shaking off the yoke in a Constitutional
way. I suspect the plan will be to engage 2/3 of the Legislatures in the
task of undoing the work; or to get a Congress appointed in the first
instance that will commit suicide on their own Authority."[21]

Madison would prove to be correct in his assessment of Henry's
intentions. Indeed, Henry was already working to subvert the North
Carolina ratification convention, and he fully intended to call on
the rest of the states to join Virginia in petitioning Congress to call
a second constitutional convention that would wipe out the work of
the first. If two-thirds of the states agreed, Congress would have to
respond as long as it remained in session—and do so before it ceded
authority to the new government.

After two days of raucous, self-congratulatory celebrations, Virginia Federalists learned that theirs had not been the decisive ninth
state to ratify the Constitution. New Hampshire had reconvened its
ratification convention and ratified the Constitution four days before
Virginia, on June 21.

The North Carolina convention met on July 21 with a large
majority of its 280 delegates opposed to ratification. Patrick Henry
and his emissaries had already wreaked havoc in the state. Like
Henry's own Piedmont area in Virginia, North Carolina was almost
entirely rural, sparsely populated by relatively poor but fiercely independent farmers and frontiersmen who were self-sufficient and
resented any interference in their affairs by government—any government. They suspected the existing state government as well as
the proposed federal government. The former, they knew, was in the
hands of wealthy merchant-bankers; and the latter, they feared,
would be in the hands of the Pope in Rome or perhaps Jews or
Mahometans—or so Henry's men had told them.

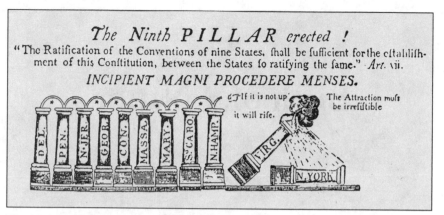

The Ninth Pillar. On June 26, 1788, *The Massachusetts Centinel* published this cartoon symbolizing the ratification of the Constitution by New Hampshire, the ninth state to do so and the last required to form the new government.

Willie Jones, the state's political boss, parroted Clinton's appeal to New York's ratification convention—that North Carolina remain out of the Union until it could negotiate more advantageous terms for joining. Born in North Carolina but educated in England at Eton, Jones read a letter to the North Carolina ratification convention that Patrick Henry had sent him. It was the letter from Thomas Jefferson, declaring, "Were I in America, I would advocate it warmly till nine should have adopted it and then as warmly take the other side to convince the other four that they ought not to come into it till the declaration of rights is annexed to it."[22] On August 2, Jones moved that North Carolina defer ratification. His motion passed by a vote of 184 to 84, with several illiterate frontiersmen voting with the majority.

II

Birth of a Nation

WHEN NEWS OF RATIFICATION REACHED ALEXANDRIA, just north of Washington's home at Mount Vernon, town fathers "illuminated . . . the town . . . in an elegant manner" and "communicated the agreeable intelligence . . . [to] neighbors up and down the river, by a well-timed discharge of cannon."[1] One after another they boomed, down the Potomac to Mount Vernon to deliver the news to Washington. The following day he rode to town triumphantly. A light infantry company saluted him as ten cannons—one for each state—blasted away.

"A party of gentlemen escorted him . . . to Mr. Wise's tavern, where the gentlemen of the town and some from the Country . . . dined together . . . on a sumptuous dinner [with] many genteel strangers."[2] After dinner, Washington and the others drank ten toasts, each followed by a cannon blast. They drank to the Virginia convention and the Constitution, to the ten states, to the "heroes" who died in the Revolution, to the French king, to Lafayette, to the American people, to the Union, to the Potomac, and to anything else they could think of.

"It is with great satisfaction, I have it now in my power to inform you," Washington buzzed with excitement and rum as he wrote, "that on the 25th instant, the Delegates of Virginia adopted the Constitution . . . in consequence of some conciliatory conduct and recommendatory amendments, a happy acquiescence it is said is likely to terminate the business here—in as favorable a manner as could possibly be expected." He was writing to Charles Cotesworth

Pinckney of South Carolina and had just returned from the gala celebration at Alexandria.

> No sooner had the Citizens of Alexandria (who are federal to a
> man) received the intelligence by mail last night, than they deter-
> mined to devote this day to festivity. But their exhilaration was
> greatly encreased and a much keener zest given to their enjoy-
> ment; by the arrival of an Express (two hours before the day) with
> the News that the Convention of New Hampshire had, on the
> 21st instant, acceded to the new Confederacy. . . .
>
> Thus the Citizens of Alexandria . . . had the pleasure of pour-
> ing libation to the prosperity of the ten States that had actually
> adopted the general government. . . . I have Just returned from
> assisting at the entertainment. . . . I think we may rationally in-
> dulge the pleasing hope that the Union will now be established
> upon a durable basis, and that Providence seems still disposed to
> favour the members of it, with unequaled opportunities for politi-
> cal happiness.
>
> From the local situation . . . of North Carolina, I should be
> truly astonished if that State should withdraw itself from the
> Union. . . . At present there is more doubt about how the question
> will be immediately disposed of in New York. For it seems to be
> understood that there is a majority in the Convention opposed to
> the adoption of the New fœderal System.[3]

The following day, Washington wrote to his secretary and aide
Tobias Lear, who had been vacationing at his parents' home in New
Hampshire and had kept Washington informed of events in that
state. Although the second session of the New Hampshire convention had met in the heart of Antifederalist farm country in Concord,
even some of the fiercest Antifederalists realized that without protection of a federal force, many farms in the north lay helpless
against Indian raids and incursions by British troops from Canada.
After four days of relatively bland debate, New Hampshire thus
became the decisive ninth state to ratify.

"No one can rejoice more than I do," Washington wrote to Benjamin Lincoln, "at every step taken by the people of this great country to preserve the Union—establish good order & government—
and to render the Nation happy at home & respected abroad. No

Country upon Earth ever had it more in its power to attain these blessings than United America."[4]

With ten states in the Union, only New York represented a major physical and economic obstacle to unification. Rhode Island was too small to undermine national unity, and North Carolina too weak. On June 17, New York's Antifederalist governor, George Clinton, called his state's ratification convention to order in Poughkeepsie. The New York gathering boasted an overwhelming Antifederalist majority and, as it began its deliberations, Clinton was confident that Patrick Henry's Antifederalists in Virginia would reject the Constitution. The Virginia convention had been under way for two weeks, and Clinton assumed that Virginia governor Randolph had read Clinton's letter to him to the Virginia delegates. Clinton had no way of knowing that Randolph had changed colors and was now riding under the Federalist flag—probably because of assurances from Washington of an appointment in the first administration under the new Constitution.

Even without Virginia, however, Clinton had a grandiose view of the importance of his state, which separated New England from the mid-Atlantic and southern states. All overland commerce between the two sections had to travel through New York and was subject to duties. And without New York harbor, intracoastal commerce would either have to take the excessively long route around Cape Cod to and from Boston or submit to costly duties in either New York harbor or Rhode Island. Clinton saw no reason to rush into union and risk losing control of his mother lode of tariff collections. And when the New York State ratification convention opened, he did not believe he would have to do so. More than two-thirds of the delegates were Antifederalists from his own upstate farm country—most of them his own appointees. He believed that by prolonging debate late enough into summer, the farmers among them would have to return to harvest their crops and force the convention to adjourn without a vote. If New York remained out of the Union until the other states formed the new government, he believed he might be able to negotiate a more favorable arrangement on trade duties with federal authorities.

But that was only one scenario in the scripts that Clinton and the Antifederalists brought to their convention. Despite their majority, even the most ardent among them realized the dangers of stampeding the convention into outright rejection of the Constitution. One danger was the likelihood that New York City and the surrounding counties in the southern part of the state would secede from the state to reap the economic benefits that would accrue to the port of New York if they joined the Union. The second danger in rejecting the Constitution was the difficulty of defending an independent New York against an array of enemies. Hostile British troops and Indian raiders were poised to attack on the northern and western frontiers; Vermont's barbarous "Green Mountain Boys" still harbored ambitions for more New York lands along the eastern border north of Albany; and New York City's port facilities were on islands in waters that could be threatened by New Jersey on the one side and Connecticut on the other. State chancellor (chief justice) Robert R. Livingston warned that both adjoining states "must be considered as independent, and perhaps unfriendly powers . . . in case of a disunion."[5] While the Hudson River was a source of wealth in peacetime, he pointed out, it could prove a grave weakness in war.

Yielding to the logic of such arguments, Clinton retreated from his stance of unbending antifederalism and told the ratification convention that "the dissolution of the Union is, of all events, the remotest from my wishes." Looking at Hamilton, the governor declared, "The object of both of us is a firm energetic government, and we may both have the good of our country in view, though we disagree as to the means of procuring it."[6]

Sensing duplicity in the governor's statement, Hamilton responded with sarcasm, damning the governor with praise for espousing "a strong federal government," but asking why Clinton had not "given us his ideas of the nature of this government, which is the object of his wishes? Why does he not describe it? We have proposed a system, which we supposed would answer the purposes of strength and safety—The gentleman objects to it, without pointing out the grounds, on which his objections are founded, or showing us a better form." Charging Clinton with deception, Hamilton pointed out that Clinton had blocked adoption of an amendment in 1785 that would have given Congress "sole and exclusive right and *power*" to regulate international and interstate trade and commerce and collect "imposts and duties, upon imports and exports."[7] He accused Clinton of having blocked "the only means of supporting the union" and charged that the governor did not "contemplate a fundamental change in government." Like all of Hamilton's speeches to the convention, it was a devastating argument—clear, to the point, with no superfluous rhetoric.

On July 2, Federalists punctuated Hamilton's brilliant arguments with news that produced turmoil in Antifederalist ranks: Virginia had ratified the Constitution. Ten days earlier, they had learned that New Hampshire had ratified, but even then, most believed Governor Clinton's assurances that Virginia would stand firm with New York and demand a bill of rights and other amendments as the price the federal government would have to pay for support from those two states and North Carolina. Without Virginia, however, New York would be unable to form a middle confederacy, and by remaining outside the Union, New York would not only lose revenues from duties on foreign trade, it would itself be the victim of trade barriers by surrounding states and the rest of the new nation. As Federalists poured into the streets to celebrate in Albany, New York, however, an angry mob of Antifederalist farmers attacked them, seriously injuring several dozen celebrants.

Surrounded by a hostile Antifederalist majority at Poughkeepsie, John Jay was nonetheless jubilant when he received news of Virginia's ratification, and he wrote to his friend at Mount Vernon:

> I congratulate you my dear Sir! The adoption of the constitution by Virginia has disappointed the Expectations of opposition here, which nevertheless continues pertinacious. The unanimity of the southern District, and their apparent determination to continue under the wings of the union, operates powerfully on the minds of the opposite Party. The constitution constantly gains advocates among the People, and its Enemies in the Convention seem to be much embarrassed.[8]

Jay wrote again to Washington a few days later to report still better news: "The Ground of Rejection . . . seems to be entirely deserted . . . the Party begins to divide in their opinions—some insist on previous conditional amendments—a greater number will be satisfied with subsequent conditional amendments . . . we learn from Albany that an affray happened there on the 4 inst: between the two parties, in which near thirty were wounded, some few very dangerously."[9]

Virginia's ratification split New York's Antifederalists into several factions. One favored outright ratification with recommendatory amendments similar to those Massachusetts and Virginia planned submitting to the first Congress under the new federal government. Stauncher Clintonites, however, held out for attaching either "explanatory amendments" or "conditional amendments" to the Constitution before ratifying it—in effect, rejecting the Constitution as written. Explanatory amendments requested "explanations" added to articles considered too vague, while conditional amendments imposed conditions and limited federal powers until a new constitutional convention could consider all the amendments proposed by all the states. For Clinton, the most important conditional amendment would have prevented the federal government from collecting taxes in New York without approval of the state legislature.

All sides continued debating for two weeks, with only Clinton himself budging slightly, from espousing outright rejection to recommending adoption with conditional amendments, which was only a different form of rejection. Under Article VII of the Constitution, the Constitutional Convention had given the states only two possible choices, to ratify or to reject—not to amend. Still, Clinton argued, desperately trying to protect his political powers and income stream by insisting that conditional ratification "contains nothing that can give offense or that can prevent its being accepted.

> Its object is barely to prevent the immediate operation of powers the most odious to our Constituents until they can be considered by the people of America to whose decision we declare *our willingness to submit*. There is nothing in the Proposition that can prevent the Government's going into full Operation and having full effect as to all essential National Concerns.

As Federalists reiterated Article VII and emphasized the loss of trade New York would suffer if it remained outside the union, an Antifederalist rose to speak on July 23 and astonished the convention by moving to ratify the Constitution "upon condition."

Aware that those two words represented outright rejection, a second Antifederalist quickly moved to substitute "in full confidence." He pointed out that only by joining the Union and sending its representatives to the First Congress would New York have any chance to participate in amending the Constitution.

Clinton nonetheless kept fighting, convincing the convention to support sending a circular to the states "pressing in the most earnest manner, the necessity of a general convention to take into their consideration the amendments to the Constitution proposed by the several State Conventions."[10] In a behind-the-scenes deal, Federalists agreed to support the motion and allow Clinton to win the battle over the "Circular Letter" by a unanimous vote. In return, however, enough Antifederalists agreed either to abstain from voting or to vote for unconditional ratification to give proponents of ratification a majority. On July 26, 1788, New York's ratification convention voted 30 to 27 for outright ratification of the U.S. Constitution, with recommendatory amendments.

Ironically, the ratification provoked little celebration. New York City had celebrated several days earlier—before the state had ratified. The unlikely celebration was for New Hampshire's entry into the Union as the ninth state. New York City, of course, was Hamilton country, and if the state convention had rejected the Constitution, the city and its surrounding counties had been prepared to secede from the rest of the state and join as a new state rather than sacrifice the economic benefits of union by remaining independent.

Organizers of the ratification procession had planned to celebrate on July 4, but the complexity of the floats forced them to delay it for three weeks, until July 24. By coincidence, therefore, the grand "Federal Procession" got under way three days before New York's ratification. It surpassed any procession ever seen anywhere in the United States, with allegorical ships "sailing" along Broadway, sails and pennants flying, cannons firing explosive puffs of smoke, and thousands upon thousands cheering, chanting, singing, and drinking. It began in the "Fields"—now City Hall Park—and rolled south to the end of Broadway, then east along the docks to Hanover Square and northward along the waterfront on the eastern edge of Manhattan to what is now the South Street Seaport. The outstanding feature was the

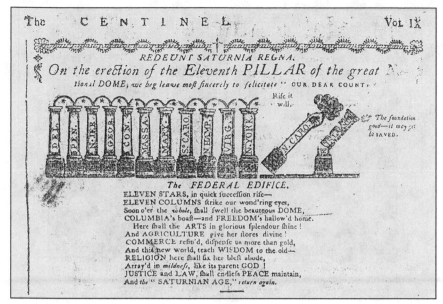

The Federal Edifice. Cartoon in *The Massachusetts Centinel*, August 2, 1788, representing the ratification of the Constitution by New York, the eleventh and last of the states considered vital to the establishment of the new nation.

magnificent *Hamilton*—a real, albeit miniature frigate that had actually been launched into nearby waters. On a float drawn by ten horses and "exhibiting an appearance beyond description splendid and majestic," the ship carried thirty-two guns that fired continual thirteen-gun salutes until it reached its "moorings" at Bowling Green.

Federalist editor Noah Webster described the *Hamilton* in New York's *Daily Advertiser* as a "Frigate . . . with galleries and every thing complete and in proportion, both in hull and rigging; manned with upwards of thirty seamen and marines, in their different uniforms."[11] Led by horsemen with trumpets, the procession included marching bands and almost five thousand "citizens" representing every imaginable trade—foresters, farmers, "taylors," millers, coopers, butchers, tanners, carpenters, hatters, florists, smiths, cutlers, confectioners, stonemasons, cabinetmakers, drummakers, upholsterers, weavers, painters, shipbuilders, engravers, pewterers, potters, candlemakers, Columbia University professors and students, physicians, and even "strangers" who wanted to march, at the end of the line. Webster described the line as extending "upwards of a mile and a half.

Ratification Procession. The "federal ship" *Hamilton* highlighted
a huge parade in New York to celebrate New Hampshire's having
become the ninth state to ratify the Constitution. A real, albeit
miniature, frigate that had been launched into nearby waters, it
carried thirty-two guns that fired continual thirteen-gun salutes as
ten horses pulled its float down Broadway.

The march was slow and majestic, and the general appearance of
the scene as far surpassed every one's expectation. . . . While num-
berless crowds were pressing on every side, the doors and windows
of houses were thronged by the fair daughter of Columbia, whose
animated smiles and satisfaction contributed not a little to complete the general joy.[12]

At the end of the parade route, marchers filed into one of three
specially constructed Federal Banquet Pavilions, with the central
one "majestically rising above . . . with a dome, on the top of which
was a figure of Fame with her trumpet proclaiming a *New Æra* and
holding in her left hand the standard of the United States, and a roll
of parchment, on which was inscribed in large characters, the three
remarkable epochas of the late war: *Independence, Alliance with France,
Peace*. At her side was the American Eagle, with wings extended,
resting on a crown of laurel placed on the top of the pedestal."[13]

Designed by the French architect Major Pierre Charles L'Enfant,
who had fought in the American Revolution, each pavilion featured

ten elaborately decorated colonnades (one for each state) and 440-foot-long banquet tables, each extending from the center of the colonnade like bicycle spokes—but meant to symbolize the rays of the sun. "This noble and beautiful edifice, erected in less than five days, covered a surface of ground 880 feet by 600, and was calculated to accommodate six thousand persons." As dinner ended, the crowd drank thirteen toasts—to the United States, to the states that had ratified the Constitution, to the French king, to the heroes of the Revolution, and so forth—with each followed by blasts from a battery of ten cannons.

Three days later, when New York became the eleventh state to join the Union, Alexander Hamilton, his task complete, wrote to his patron at Mount Vernon:

> I have delivered to Mr Madison to be forwarded to you a sett of the papers under the signature of Publius, neatly enough bound, to be honored with a place in your library. I presume you have understood that the writers of these Papers are chiefly Mr Madison & myself with some aid from Mr Jay.
>
> I take it for granted, Sir, you have concluded to comply with what will no doubt be the general call of your country in relation to the new government. You will permit me to say that it is indispensable you should lend yourself to its first operations—It is to little purpose to have *introduced* a system, if the weightiest influence is not given to its firm *establishment,* in the outset. I remain with the greatest esteem Dr Sir Yr Obed. & hum. servant
>
> A Hamilton[14]

Although Clinton's Antifederalists had ceded the field in their battle against ratification, they renewed their war against the Constitution with new intensity. Deciding to use the Constitution to undermine the government it had created, Clinton convinced the convention to approve his circular letter to the states calling for a second constitutional convention, as provided under Article V for proposing amendments. Although other states had suggested that the First Congress consider amending the Constitution, none had proposed direct action by the states to call another national constitutional convention.

"Governor Clinton's Circular Letter," as it was called, polarized the state and made him the darling of Antifederalists nationwide. In New York City, a Federalist mob retaliated with a midnight march on the governor's house that culminated with destruction of the print shop of Thomas Greenleaf, publisher of New York's fiercely Antifederalist *Journal*. By the end of summer, however, forty newspapers had published Clinton's letter and made it the focus of national attention. A groundswell of Antifederalist sentiment developed for either another constitutional convention, or worse, secession. James Madison called Clinton's letter "a most pestilent tendency. If an Early General Convention cannot be parried," he warned Washington, "it is seriously to be feared that the System which has resisted so many direct attacks may be at last successfully undermined by its enemies."[15]

In addition to the threat of a second constitutional convention, Maryland congressman James McHenry worried that Antifederalists might attempt a violent coup d'état:

> My dear General   Baltimore 27 July 1788.
>   It is whispered here that some leading characters among you have by no means dropped their resentment to the new constitution, but have determined on some secret plan to suspend the proper organization of the government or to defeat it altogether. This is so serious and alarming a circumstance that it is necessary to be apprised of its truth, and extent that we may be on our guard. . . . I am Dr General Yours
>   James McHenry[16]

Madison did not believe Patrick Henry would resort to violence. "Although the leaders, particularly Henry and Mason, will give no countenance to popular violence," he wrote to Jefferson in Paris, "it is not to be inferred that they are reconciled to the event, or will give it positive support. On the contrary, both of them declared they could not go that length, and an attempt was made under their auspices to induce the minority to sign an address to the people, which, if it had not been defeated by the general moderation of the party, probably would have done mischief."[17]

Somewhat nonplussed, and aware that emissaries of George Clinton and Patrick Henry were discussing, if not plotting, destruction of the new government, Washington replied immediately to McHenry:

That some of the leading characters among the Opponents [of] the proposed government have not laid aside their ideas of obtaining great and essential changes, through a constitutional opposition, (as they term it) may be collected from their public speeches. That others will use more secret and, perhaps, insidious means to prevent organization may be presumed from their previous conduct on the subject. In addition to this probability . . . a considerable effort will be made to procure the election of Antifederalists to the first Congress; in order to . . . undo all that has been done. . . . I think there will be great reason . . . that the worthiest Citizens may be appointed to the two houses of the first Congress. . . . I earnestly pray that the Omnipotent Being who hath not deserted the cause of America in the hour of its extremist hazard; will never yield so fair a heritage of freedom a prey to Anarchy or Despotism.[18]

Despite Washington's prayer, Patrick Henry and George Clinton were determined to undermine the new government by either assembling a new constitutional convention or engineering the forthcoming elections to ensure an Antifederalist First Congress that would, as Madison had put it, "commit suicide" with constitutional amendments to return federal powers to the states.

"To be shipwrecked in sight of the Port," Washington fretted to Madison, "would be the severest of all possible aggravations to our misery; and I assure you I am under painful apprehensions from the single circumstance of Mr H____'s having the whole game to play in the Assembly of this State; and the effect it may have in others—It should be counteracted if possible."[19]

Madison was in Congress in New York doing his best to help answer Washington's prayer by resolving a heated debate over whether to install the First Congress in New York or Philadelphia. Madison initially opposed New York because he feared that "people from the interior parts of Georgia, S.C. N.C. Va & Kentucky will never patiently repeat their trips to this remote situation, especially as the legislative sessions will be held in the winter season." After a month of fruitless debate, Federalists hoped that by ceding the new government (and the economic benefits that would accrue from its presence) to New York, the prospects of hosting George Washington and other Revolutionary War leaders in his administration would embarrass, if not shame, Governor Clinton and other Antifederalists

into abandoning efforts to promote a second convention to undermine the new government.

In addition to situating the temporary capital in New York, Congress also fixed dates for electors to vote for president and for federal
elections to be held for the First Congress. Each state legislature
would elect two senators,* and male property owners in each state
would elect members of the House of Representatives, with no more
than one representative for every thirty thousand people. The new
Congress was to convene on the first Wednesday of March 1789,
with the presidential inauguration fixed for April 30.

As Madison and other members of Congress made plans to establish the new government, however, a growing force of Clinton and
Henry Antifederalists were acting to dismantle it by encouraging
states to support Clinton's call for another constitutional convention. On September 3, nearly three dozen Antifederalists met in
Harrisburg, Pennsylvania, and voted unanimously for such a convention. The proceedings at Harrisburg, Madison reported to Washington, "will of course soon be before the public. I find that all the
mischief apprehended from Clinton's circular letter in Virginia will
be verified. The Antifederalists lay hold of it with eagerness as the
harbinger of a second Convention."[20]

On October 15, Edward Carrington, an influential Virginia political leader and member of the Confederation Congress who had been
an officer in the Revolution, arrived at Mount Vernon with confidential papers from Madison. After a two-day visit, Carrington wrote
to Madison saying that "the General . . . is fully persuaded that . . .
great circumspection is necessary to prevent very mischievous effects
from a co-operation in the insidious proposition of New York.

> He is particularly alarmed from a prospect of an election for the
> Senate, entirely anti-Federal. It is said in this part of the State that
> Mr. Henry and Mr. R. H. Lee are to be pushed . . . the General is
> apprehensive . . . that to exclude the former will be impossible;
> and that the latter being supported by his influence, will also get
> in, unless a Federalist very well established in the confidence of

---

*Senators were chosen by the legislatures of their respective states until the adoption of
the Seventeenth Amendment to the Constitution, in 1913.

the people can be opposed. He is decided in his wishes that you may be brought forward upon this occasion.[21]

Though shy and deeply uncomfortable about campaigning, Madison would not deny Washington's request and eventually agreed. Patrick Henry, however, had other plans, and on October 20, Henry's Antifederalists used their fifteen-man majority to crush Madison's bid for the Senate and elect two of Henry's closest Antifederalist allies: Richard Henry Lee and William Grayson. In the North, the New York legislature, under Governor George Clinton's direction, doomed Alexander Hamilton to the same fate. Henry then carried his and Clinton's plans against the Constitution by warning the Virginia Assembly that "rivulets of blood" would flow across Virginia unless assemblymen petitioned the Confederation Congress "to call a Convention of deputies from the several States."

Madison countered by declaring for the House of Representatives, only to have Henry's forces in the Assembly redraw the boundaries of Madison's congressional district to include counties with large enough Antifederalist majorities to offset the Federalist majority in Madison's home county. As Henry's relentless assault against Madison and the Constitution gained momentum, Madison concluded that Henry was seeking "destruction of the whole System" of American government.[22] Federalists in the Virginia Assembly agreed, calling Henry's Antifederalists "a mob majority" and accusing Henry of becoming "the most cruelly oppressive of all possible tyrants."[23]

To cap his assault on federalism, Henry convinced young James Monroe—Madison's friend from a neighboring county—to run against him. In a brilliant political maneuver, however, Madison opened his campaign by pledging that if elected to the First Congress, he would, as his first act, sponsor a bill of rights that would amend the Constitution with guarantees of freedom of religion and other individual liberties. His declaration proved decisive, and on February 2, 1789, James Madison won election to the House of Representatives over James Monroe, 1,308 to 972. Madison would join nine other Virginians to form the largest delegation in the House of Representatives. With no more than one representative for every thirty thousand voters, Delaware had but one representative, Georgia and New Hampshire three each, New Jersey four, Connecticut and South Carolina five each, Maryland and New York six each, Massachusetts and Pennsylvania eight each, and Virginia ten, for a total of fifty-nine representatives. (Rhode Island would have one when it joined the Union, and North Carolina five.) With two senators from each state, the U.S. Senate would have twenty-two members at its opening session.

Although fervent Federalists viewed Madison as a turncoat and even moderates thought him disingenuous, Madison's shift was, in fact, a courageous and patriotic political gesture to reconcile the legitimate differences that threatened to divide Americans and, perhaps, plunge them into civil war. Although Federalists had cast the majority of votes at the various state ratification conventions, Antifederalists made up a large minority of delegates and, indeed, represented a popular majority. Under Patrick Henry's and George Clinton's leadership, Antifederalists had grown strong enough to force the Confederation Congress to call a second constitutional convention to rewrite—or scrap—the existing document and prevent the new government from ever taking office. As one of the three champions of federalism with Washington and Hamilton, Madison recognized his need to take dramatic action to prevent that eventuality. By pledging to satisfy the most important Antifederalist demand and personally sponsor a bill of rights in what would most likely be a Federalist First Congress, Madison effectively divided the Antifederalist camp. In extending a hand of compromise to moderates, he separated them from the Henry-Clinton radicals who had sought amendments to emasculate the new central government. With Washington's hesitant approval, Madison therefore agreed that with the Constitution in place, "amendments . . . may serve the double purpose of satisfying the minds of well meaning opponents, and of providing additional guards in favour of liberty."[24] Four months after his election to Congress, the Federalist Madison presented the Antifederalist amendments to his nation's first House of Representatives, effectively ending the threat of a second constitutional convention and possible dissolution of the nation.

Although scheduled to convene on March 4, 1789, both the House and Senate lacked quorums and would not come to order until the following month. On April 23, Washington arrived in New York to a thirteen-gun salute and a warm welcome from Governor George Clinton, who escorted him on the parade route to the presidential mansion and personally attended him during the subsequent celebrations that led up to the presidential inauguration. They had, after all, been brothers in arms, if not politics. On the morning of April 30, cannons boomed as church bells across New York City called the public to worship and pray to "the Great Ruler of the universe for the preservation of the President." Tobias Lear, George Washington's private secretary and personal aide, described the day's events:

> At twelve the troops of the city paraded before our door, and soon after, the committees of Congress and heads of departments came in their carriages to wait upon the President to the Federal Hall. At half past twelve the procession moved forward, the troops marching in front with all the ensigns of military parade. Next came the committees and heads of departments in their carriages. Next the President in the state coach . . . foreign ministers and a long train of citizens.
>
> About two hundred yards before we reached the hall, we descended from our carriages, and passed through the troops, who were drawn up on each side, into the Hall and Senate-chamber, where we found the Vice-President, the Senate, and House of Representatives assembled. They received the President in the most respectful manner, and the Vice-President conducted him to a spacious and elevated seat at the head of the room. A solemn silence prevailed.[25]

John Adams welcomed Washington before announcing, "Sir, the Senate and House of Representatives are ready to attend you to take the oath required by the Constitution."

"I am ready to proceed," Washington replied. Grim-faced, he stood and followed Adams through a door onto a small portico overlooking the intersection of Wall and Broad streets. New York governor Clinton, effectively ceding victory to Washington's Federalists, waited with Federalist Henry Knox, Washington's close friend who had commanded the Continental Army artillery in the Revolutionary War. Samuel Otis, the secretary of the senate, lifted a red cushion that held a Bible on which Washington placed his huge right hand. New York chancellor (chief justice) Robert R. Livingston administered the oath as thousands looked up from the streets below. It was one in the afternoon:

"Do you solemnly swear that you will faithfully execute the office of President of the United States and will, to the best of your ability, preserve, protect, and defend the Constitution of the United States?"

"I solemnly swear that I will faithfully execute . . ." Washington repeated the oath, then added, "So help me God" and bent over to kiss the Bible.

"It is done," declared Livingston, who turned to the crowd, raised his arms, and shouted, "Long Live George Washington, President of the United States."[26]

According to Lear, "the air was rent by repeated shouts and huzzas,—'God bless our Washington! Long live our beloved President!'" Washington acknowledged the cheers as Otis slipped his hand under Washington's arm to lead him back into the hall to address Congress.[27]

"It was a touching scene," said one congressman. Another described it as "elegant." But a third noted that Washington "trembled. This great man was agitated and embarrassed more than ever he was by the leveled cannon or pointed musket."[28] Never known for his great oratory, he had but one tooth left and pursed his lips to contain his ill-fitting false teeth. During his twelve-minute struggle with oral disabilities, he startled the assembly by tacitly approving amendments to the Constitution. Madison had convinced him that enactment of a bill of rights would persuade the large majority of Antifederalists to abandon Patrick Henry, George Clinton, and the opponents of the new federal government. In the interest of national unity, Washington reached out to Antifederalists and asked Congress "to decide, how far an exercise of the occasional power delegated by the Fifth article of the Constitution is rendered expedient at the present juncture by the nature of the objections which have been urged against the System, or by the degree of inquietude which has given birth to them." He expressed his "entire confidence" that "a reverence for the public harmony, will sufficiently influence your deliberations" on amending the Constitution. He ended his—and the nation's—first presidential inaugural address with a solemn prayer "to the benign Parent of the human race, in humble supplication . . . to favour the American people, with . . . the security of their Union, and the advancement of their happiness."[29]

12

One Nation, Divisible . . .

Washington's tacit support for a bill of rights all but ensured his victory over Patrick Henry and the Antifederalists. On June 8, James Madison stood in Congress to begin the process of amending the Constitution with "a declaration of the rights of the people" to ensure "the tranquility of the public mind, and the stability of the government."[1] He originally offered a preamble and nineteen amendments, attempting to incorporate the principles of some two hundred recommendatory amendments proposed by ratification conventions in Massachusetts, South Carolina, New Hampshire, Virginia, New York, and North Carolina. After eliminating duplicate amendments, he was left with about seventy-five, which he combined into the final nineteen. Although Henry's emissaries in Congress demanded even more—especially abolition of federal taxing powers—Congress was in no mood for any more bitter debates. Virginia senator William Grayson sent his patron the bad news: "I am exceedingly sorry," he wrote to Patrick Henry, "it is out of my power to hold out to you any flattering expectations on the score of amendments; it appears to me that both houses are almost wholly composed of federalists."[2]

In the end, even the dedicated Massachusetts Antifederalist Elbridge Gerry came to Madison's side and, on August 24, after only a week of debate, more than two-thirds of the House approved seventeen amendments, which they forwarded to the Senate. Debating behind closed doors, the Senate proposed twenty amendments, but three weeks later it compressed the number and, on September 25, the U.S. Congress approved the first twelve amendments to the Constitution, which George Washington duly submitted to the eleven states of the Union for ratification. Patrick Henry continued his battle to emasculate the Constitution and the new government by thwarting ratification of the Bill of Rights in the Virginia legislature with demands for "the destruction of direct [federal] taxation."[3]

But Madison's political gamble paid off handsomely outside his home state, as Antifederalists across the nation rejected the call by Henry and Clinton for a second constitutional convention. Even North Carolina, which had pledged not to ratify the Constitution without securing Henry's amendments, now rebuffed him by calling a second ratification convention. On November 12 he admitted defeat, packed up his papers, and abruptly walked out of the Virginia Assembly one month before its adjournment and returned to his mountain mansion.

"Mr. Henry has quitted rather in discontent," wrote the jubilant Federalist Edward Carrington to his friend James Madison. A member of Virginia's House of Delegates, Carrington described Henry's abrupt exit: "Having felt the pulse of the House on several points and finding that it did not beat with certainty in unison with his own, he at length took his departure in the middle of the session without pushing any thing to its issue."[4]

"Virginia has been outwitted," Patrick Henry is said to have admitted to his law clerks after returning home.[5]

On November 19, North Carolina held its second ratification convention and two days later ratified the Constitution and entered the Union as the twelfth state. By the end of the year, six states had ratified some or all of the twelve amendments. In early February, Massachusetts ratified the Bill of Rights amendments after Governor John Hancock gave them his unqualified endorsement. Early in 1790, the U.S. Senate passed a bill severing commercial relations with Rhode Island, and the stubborn little state finally joined the Union after ratifying the Constitution by a mere two votes, 34 to 32, on May 29, 1790.

"Since the bond of Union is now compleat, and we once more consider ourselves as one family," Washington wrote to Rhode Island governor Arthur Fenner, it is much to be hoped that reproaches will cease and prejudice be done away; for we should all remember that we are members of that community upon whose general success depends our particular and individual welfare—and, therefore, if we mean to support the Liberty and Independence which it has cost us so much blood & treasure to establish, we must drive far away the dæmon of party spirit and local reproach.[6]

Patrick Henry continued working behind the scenes to block ratification by Virginia of the twelve amendments that included the Bill of Rights. He succeeded in postponing the inevitable for two years—until December 15, 1791. Two weeks after Virginia had ratified, President Washington notified Congress that the states had ratified ten of the proposed twelve amendments to the Constitution. Among other rights, they guaranteed American citizens freedom of speech, religious choice and peaceable assembly, the right to petition the government for a redress of grievances, the right to a "speedy" trial by jury and the right to counsel, the right to keep and bear arms, and "the right to be secure in their persons, houses, papers, and effects." The Bill of Rights also protected Americans against "unreasonable searches and seizures" by government, against double jeopardy, and against government threats to life, liberty, or property "without due process of law."

And in the most important concession to Antifederalists and neofeudal state political leaders, the tenth and last article of the Bill of Rights stated clearly that "the powers not delegated to the United States by the Constitution, nor prohibited by it to the States, are reserved to the States respectively, or to the people." The article left state leaders with a firm grip on tax revenues and ensured their all but eternal retention of power to rule as they saw fit within their own state borders.

Like Madison, Washington had hoped that his acceptance, if not unqualified endorsement, of the Bill of Rights would encourage near-universal embrace of the new American government. To ensure national unity, Washington went a step further by filling the four most important executive posts in his administration with two Federalists and two Antifederalists—or Democratic-Republicans, as they came to be called. He appointed Federalist champions Alexander Hamilton as secretary of the treasury and Henry Knox as secretary of war, and Antifederalists Thomas Jefferson as secretary of state and Virginia governor Edmund Randolph as attorney general. He appointed Massachusetts Antifederalist Samuel Osgood as postmaster general.

Before their first terms ended, Hamilton and Jefferson were at each other's throats. Hamilton favored a strong, powerful executive to direct national economic growth—regardless of popular sentiment, which he distrusted. Jefferson supported the people's right to govern themselves and distrusted government.

"I believe it will be difficult, if not impracticable," Washington scolded Jefferson, "to manage the Reins of Government or to keep the parts of it together . . . if . . . after measures are decided on, one pulls this way & another that, before the utility of the thing is fairly tried, it must, inevitably, be torn asunder—And, in my opinion, the fairest prospect of happiness & prosperity that ever was presented to man, will be lost—perhaps for ever!

"My earnest wish, and my fondest hope, therefore is, that instead of wounding suspicions, & irritable charges, there may be liberal allowances—mutual forbearance—and temporizing yieldings on *all sides.*"[7]

Hamilton and Jefferson seemed unable to reconcile their differences—the one fearing anarchy or civil war *without* strong government enforcement of the law, the other fearing anarchy or civil war (and a possible monarchy) *because of* strong government enforcement of the law. The irony of their feud—and, indeed, the debate between Federalists and Antifederalists—was that the federal government, regardless of its strength, would, in the end, be unable to deter either anarchy or civil war. Both were inevitable consequences of 150 years of colonial life in America under British and European —not American—rule. Neither Federalists nor Antifederalists could have prevented a violent resolution of many of the deep-seated social, political, economic, and racial divisions between the colonies and the states they became after independence. Nor did they. The Constitution did not prevent the Civil War, the horrors of Reconstruction, the cruelties of segregation, or the many other human indignities that resulted from continuing disunity among the American states and people. Indeed, the more than two hundred years that American leaders have needed since independence to build the nation into the relatively unified political entity we know today exposes the absurdity of recent American government adventures in overseas "nation-building" in regions where self-government is either a relatively recent concept or nonexistent and, indeed, alien to local and regional cultures and religions.

Jefferson resigned at the end of Washington's first term, returned to his home near Charlottesville, Virginia, and temporarily retired from politics, predicting—indeed, almost savoring the prospects—that blood would flow before the end of the Washington administration. As he had asked rhetorically after the Constitutional Convention:

> What country can preserve its liberties if their rulers are not warned from time to time that their people preserve the spirit of resistance? Let them take arms. . . . What signify a few lives lost in a century or two? The tree of liberty must be refreshed from time to time with the blood of patriots & tyrants. It is its natural manure.[8]

Washington appointed Randolph as his new secretary of state and, with Federalist Hamilton becoming the most powerful member of his cabinet, he brought the full weight of the federal government down on settlers and frontiersmen west of the Appalachian Mountains who had refused to pay federal taxes. Hamilton had sought to stave off government bankruptcy with a tax on distilled liquors that western farmers considered legalized government theft—a term they borrowed from Patrick Henry's propaganda against federal taxing powers. Almost every western farmer had a still to convert grain into whiskey, which was easier than grain in bulk to transport over the mountains to eastern markets. After brutalizing Hamilton's tax collectors, they declared "a state of revolution,"[9] and on August 1, 1794, gathered by the thousands outside Pittsburgh. Armed and ready to march, they threatened to burn Pittsburgh and properties of the monied class and secede from their states and the federal union.

A week later, Washington issued a proclamation ordering rebels to return to their homes or face arrest. His words were eerily similar to those of British governors to stamp tax protesters—including

Washington himself—thirty-five years earlier. Washington dismissed comparisons and ordered Pennsylvania, Maryland, Virginia, and New Jersey to draft thirteen thousand troops to march against the rebels.

In mid-September, the "Whiskey Rebels" rejected Washington's ultimatum, and he issued a second proclamation "that the laws be faithfully executed." On November 15, the army approached Pittsburgh, but the rebels had vanished. Although troops captured twenty laggard "Whiskey Boys," all others had either returned to their homes or fled into the wilderness. Without firing a single shot, Washington had crushed the first challenge to constitutional rule by the federal government of the United States. It would not be the last, however.

Ironically, James Madison, of all people, would help provoke the second test, with his friend Thomas Jefferson. Shortly after Washington left office, the two Virginians presented the Kentucky and Virginia resolutions to each of the legislatures of the two states. Arguing that the Constitution was a compact among sovereign states, Madison and Jefferson contended that federal powers were limited to those specifically delegated by the Constitution. They further contended that the Tenth Amendment reserved all other powers to the states and permitted a state to protect its citizens against unconstitutional exercises of power by the federal government. Madison wrote that "in a case of a deliberate, palpable, and dangerous exercise of other powers not granted by the said compact [Constitution], the states, who are parties thereto, have the right and are in duty bound to interpose for arresting the progress of the evil." Although rejected or ignored by legislatures in states other than Kentucky and Virginia, Madison had inadvertently provided an argument that would serve as a basis for the so-called doctrine of "nullification," under which seven southern states would secede from the Union in 1861 and provoke the American Civil War.

A century later, in June 1963, Alabama governor George Wallace invoked the doctrine of nullification to "stand in the schoolhouse door" in Tuscaloosa to prevent enrollment of black students at the all-white University of Alabama, as required under federal civil rights laws. Citing the Tenth Amendment, Wallace argued that the federal government had usurped state authority over public-school education. Neither of the words *education* or *school* appears in the

Constitution. Wallace yielded access to the state university to federal authorities only after the U.S. attorney general ordered federalized National Guard troops to remove him physically.

The irony of Wallace's defeat—and two centuries of similar defeats for Antifederalists like him—was its link to the very Bill of Rights that Antifederalists had insisted on enacting to prevent federal infringements on individual and states' rights. From the beginning of the Constitutional Convention, Federalists had argued that the Constitution clearly *delegated* specific powers to the central government—and nothing more. By specifying what the government *could* do, the Constitution necessarily limited the government from stepping beyond those bounds and doing anything else.

"The great end of the federal government," Connecticut's Roger Sherman stated, "is to protect the several states . . . against foreign invasion, and to preserve peace and a beneficial intercourse among themselves, and to regulate and protect their commerce with foreign nations. . . . The powers vested in the federal government are *particularly defined,* so that each State still retains its sovereignty in what concerns its own internal government, and *a right to exercise every power of a sovereign state not particularly delegated to the government of the United States* [italics added].[10]

The Bill of Rights, on the other hand, actually expanded government powers: by specifying what the federal government *could not do*—that is, the rights it could not abridge—it left the government with some discretion to abridge other, undefined rights. Although the Ninth Amendment* attempted to prevent such an eventuality, its vague language leaves the definition of what other rights were "retained by the people" open to wide interpretation by every branch of government. Among the most discussed examples are so-called individual rights to privacy and whether they fall in the category of Ninth Amendment rights "retained by the people."

The Bill of Rights also enhanced the expansion of federal powers by the use of vague, legally undefinable terms—"freedom," "religion," "speech," "press," and so forth—that allow federal legislators,

---

*"The enumeration in the Constitution, of certain rights, shall not be considered to deny or disparage others retained by the people."

executives, and judges to redefine the Bill of Rights at will and ignore the original intent of its authors. The U.S. Supreme Court, the
U.S. Congress, and the U.S. president have each redefined "freedom
of speech," for example, throughout the nineteenth and twentieth
centuries and continue to do so today. The advent of the Internet
has made earlier definitions of free speech and free press all but
meaningless.

The debate over implied powers—of Congress, the president,
and the Supreme Court—continues today, with each branch of government constantly trying to usurp powers that exceed its constitutional prerogative—intentionally or unintentionally. Until now, one
or both of the other branches has usually succeeded in restraining
the usurper and reining it back within constitutional bounds. There
are endless numbers of examples of executive, judicial, and legislative abuse of constitutional prerogatives, along with equally numerous
examples of federal usurpation of state prerogatives and state usurpation of authority that properly belongs to the federal government.

Perhaps the greatest irony of such efforts lies in the origin of the
federal Constitution itself: its authors clearly and blatantly usurped
power by disregarding the mandate of the legally constituted government—the Confederation Congress. Instead, the Founding Fathers
discarded the Articles of Confederation and replaced the Confederation of American States with a new government. On February 21,
1787, the Congress of the Confederation of American States recommended that states send delegates to a convention "for the sole and
express purpose of *revising the Articles of Confederation* . . . [and] render
the *federal constitution* adequate to the exigencies of government and
the preservation of the union. [italics added]"[11] Once convened, the
nation's most powerful figures, representing but a minority of Americans, ignored the congressional directive and, indeed, "exceeded the
authority given to them," as New York governor George Clinton
charged. In the end, Washington and the other Founding Fathers
engineered a bloodless coup d'état, overthrowing the old government and replacing it with one that Governor Clinton insisted—
correctly—was "founded in usurpation."

It is hardly surprising that each branch of government, and
the states, have continued trying—sometimes subtly, sometimes fla-

grantly—to usurp powers not delegated under the Constitution, and they will almost certainly continue. As Elbridge Gerry warned the Constitutional Convention more than two centuries ago, "some of the powers of the Legislature are ambiguous, and others indefinite and dangerous . . . the Executive is blended with and will have an undue influence over the Legislature . . . the judicial department will be oppressive."[12] Benjamin Franklin was convinced that the nation would never be "without sufficient number of wise and good men to undertake and execute well the office in question,"[13] but Gerry may yet have the last word: "The evils we experience," he insisted, "flow from the excess of democracy. The people . . . are the dupes of pretended patriots . . . daily misled into the most baneful measures and opinions by false reports circulated by designing men."[14]

Benjamin Franklin was the first of the signers of the Constitution to die—on April 19, 1790—at age eighty-four, just short of a year after Washington took the oath as America's first president. Washington served two four-year terms in office and retired to his home in Mount Vernon, where he died on December 14, 1799, at age sixty-seven.

Although Patrick Henry constantly proclaimed his loyalty to the United States and fealty to the president, Henry refused, to his dying day, to have anything to do with the new federal government, whose course he had ample opportunities to influence. From its origins, however, Henry rejected everything that smacked of federalism. After refusing to participate in the Constitutional Convention, he subsequently refused appointment to the first U.S. Senate, to the U.S. Supreme Court, and to the cabinet as secretary of state. He also rejected nomination as U.S. vice president.

Bitter over his failure to preserve state sovereignty, Henry retired from public life at the end of 1788 and returned home to practice law and speculate in land—an occupation then fraught with danger and adventure. By 1789 he had already accumulated more than 22,000 acres in Virginia, the Carolinas, Georgia, and Kentucky, along with more than five dozen slaves. In November 1789 he embarked on the most ambitious venture of his life, joining six other Virginians in forming the Virginia Yazoo Company to buy 11.4 million acres of state-owned land in northwestern Georgia at less than one cent an acre—even then, an outright steal. After laying plans to form a new, independent territory and secede from the United States, Henry and his cronies lured other speculators into buying or claiming millions of acres of public and tribal lands stretching across present-day Alabama and Mississippi to the Mississippi River. Using armed bands of ruthless frontiersmen, they seized lands from reluctant squatters and Indians and spread an atmosphere of savagery throughout the Deep South. Their activities provoked a surge of resentment and often fierce warfare with Indians, who charged Henry and his associates with violating their treaty rights. After a tumultuous public inquiry, the federal government agreed—and, despite Henry's bitter protests, invalidated most of the purchases. Although some Yazoo investors suffered huge losses, Henry and his cronies emerged with handsome profits by converting Yazoo shares into state debt certificates that they redeemed in specie at par.

Although the Yazoo land deal ranked among the worst territorial land scandals of the early national era—and there were many—the authoritarian federal invalidation of Yazoo investments, without trial or public hearings, left many in the South with a deep hatred of the federal government and an equally deep yearning for secession from the United States.

Infuriated by federal government interference in his private business, Henry returned to public life and ran for election to the Virginia Assembly against Federalist candidate John Marshall—once a close boyhood friend. Although Henry won the election, he died on June 6, 1799, before he could take office. George Washington died six months later.

In contrast to the federal establishment that was Washington's legacy, Patrick Henry's legacy was a powerful rural political machine that would ultimately help lead to Virginia's secession from the federal government that Henry despised so deeply.

Like Henry, George Mason refused appointment as one of Virginia's first two U.S. senators, preferring retirement to further involvement in public affairs. He died in October 1792, less than three and one-half years after his neighbor George Washington assumed the presidency. Richard Henry Lee, who did accept appointment to the Senate, resigned because of ill health in 1792 and died two years later. Governor Edmund Randolph served the Washington administration as the nation's first attorney general and second secretary of state before resigning in the face of accusations that he had accepted bribes from the French government. In 1795 he returned to private law practice in Virginia, climaxing his career by defending former vice president Aaron Burr against treason charges. Burr, of course, had abruptly ended Alexander Hamilton's career as a New York attorney and political leader in a duel in 1804. Randolph spent his last years writing his brilliant *History of Virginia*. He died in September 1813, at sixty.

After serving in Congress until 1797, James Madison retired until 1801, when Thomas Jefferson won the presidential election and appointed Madison secretary of state. He served in that office for eight years, before winning election to two consecutive terms as president, defeating New York governor George Clinton in 1808. As runner-up in the presidential race, Clinton served as vice president during the second term of the Jefferson administration and the first term of the Madison administration. Clinton died in 1812, leaving behind him, as his legacy, one of the most corrupt state governments in the nation—one that continues to this day to be based on arbitrary gubernatorial rule and sustained by thousands of powerful sinecures disguised as justices of the peace. Elbridge Gerry served as Madison's vice president during the first two years of Madison's second term. It was as governor of Massachusetts, from 1810 to 1812, that Gerry pushed a law through the state legislature redrawing state congressional districts to ensure his party's domination. One new district was shaped like a salamander, which his political opponents and the press immediately derided as a "gerrymander." Gerry died in 1814.

James Madison outlived all the other major figures of America's Second Revolution, succeeding Thomas Jefferson not only as president of the United States, but as rector (president) of the University of Virginia, which Jefferson had founded in 1819. Madison died in 1836, at age eighty-five.

The United States remains the oldest popularly governed republic on Earth, with its government having functioned uninterruptedly under the same constitution since its ratification more than two centuries ago.

Appendix A

Proceedings of the Constitutional Convention

The Constitution of the United States

We the People of the United States, in Order to form a more perfect Union, establish Justice, insure domestic Tranquility, provide for the common defence, promote the general Welfare, and secure the Blessings of Liberty to ourselves and our Posterity, do ordain and establish this Constitution for the United States of America.

ARTICLE I

Section 1. All legislative Powers herein granted shall be vested in a Congress of the United States, which shall consist of a Senate and House of Representatives.

Section 2. The House of Representatives shall be composed of Members chosen every second Year by the People of the several States, and the Electors in each State shall have the Qualifications requisite for Electors of the most numerous Branch of the State Legislature.

No Person shall be a Representative who shall not have attained to the Age of twenty five Years, and been seven Years a Citizen of the United States, and who shall not, when elected, be an Inhabitant of that State in which he shall be chosen.

Representatives and direct Taxes shall be apportioned among the several States which may be included within this Union, according to their respective Numbers, which shall be determined by adding to the whole Number of free Persons, including those bound to Service for a Term of

---

The Constitution was engrossed on four sheets of parchment ($23^1/2' \times 27^1/2'$). This reprint uses the original words and spellings, which differ somewhat from those in current U.S. Government Printing Office reprints.

Years, and excluding Indians not taxed, three fifths of all other Persons. The actual Enumeration shall be made within three Years after the first Meeting of the Congress of the United States, and within every subsequent Term of ten Years, in such Manner as they shall by Law direct. The Number of Representatives shall not exceed one for every thirty Thousand, but each State shall have at Least one Representative; and until such enumeration shall be made, the State of New Hampshire shall be entitled to chuse three, Massachusetts eight, Rhode-Island and Providence Plantations one, Connecticut five, New-York six, New Jersey four, Pennsylvania eight, Delaware one, Maryland six, Virginia ten, North Carolina five, South Carolina five, and Georgia three.

When vacancies happen in the Representation from any State, the Executive Authority thereof shall issue Writs of Election to fill such Vacancies.

The House of Representatives shall chuse their Speaker and other Officers; and shall have the sole Power of Impeachment.

Section 3. The Senate of the United States shall be composed of two Senators from each State, chosen by the Legislature thereof, for six Years; and each Senator shall have one Vote.

Immediately after they shall be assembled in Consequence of the first Election, they shall be divided as equally as may be into three Classes. The Seats of the Senators of the first Class shall be vacated at the Expiration of the second Year, of the second Class at the Expiration of the fourth Year, and of the third Class at the Expiration of the sixth Year, so that one third may be chosen every second Year; and if Vacancies happen by Resignation, or otherwise, during the Recess of the Legislature of any State, the Executive thereof may make temporary Appointments until the next Meeting of the Legislature, which shall then fill such Vacancies.

No Person shall be a Senator who shall not have attained to the Age of thirty Years, and been nine Years a Citizen of the United States, and who shall not, when elected, be an inhabitant of that State for which he shall be chosen.

The Vice President of the United States shall be President of the Senate, but shall have no Vote, unless they be equally divided.

The Senate shall chuse their other Officers, and also a President pro tempore, in the Absence of the Vice President, or when he shall exercise the Office of President of the United States.

The Senate shall have the sole Power to try all Impeachments. When sitting for that Purpose, they shall be on Oath or Affirmation. When the President of the United States is tried, the Chief Justice shall preside: And no Person shall be convicted without the Concurrence of two thirds of the Members present.

Judgment in Cases of Impeachment shall not extend further than to removal from Office, and disqualification to hold and enjoy any Office of honor, Trust or Profit under the United States: but the Party convicted shall nevertheless be liable and subject to Indictment, Trial, Judgment and Punishment, according to Law.

Section 4. The Times, Places and Manner of holding Elections for Senators and Representatives, shall be prescribed in each State by the Legislature thereof; but the Congress may at any time by Law make or alter such Regulations, except as to the Places of chusing Senators.

The Congress shall assemble at least once in every Year, and such Meeting shall be on the first Monday in December, unless they shall by Law appoint a different Day.

Section 5. Each House shall be the Judge of the Elections, Returns and Qualifications of its own Members, and a Majority of each shall constitute a Quorum to do Business; but a smaller Number may adjourn from day to day, and may be authorized to compel the Attendance of absent Members, in such Manner, and under such Penalties as each House may provide.

Each House may determine the Rules of its Proceedings, punish its Members for disorderly Behaviour, and, with the Concurrence of two thirds, expel a Member.

Each House shall keep a Journal of its Proceedings, and from time to time publish the same, excepting such Parts as may in their Judgment require Secrecy; and the Yeas and Nays of the Members of either House on any question shall, at the desire of one fifth of those Present, be entered on the Journal.

Neither House, during the Session of Congress, shall, without the Consent of the other, adjourn for more than three days, nor to any other Place than that in which the two Houses shall be sitting.

Section 6. The Senators and Representatives shall receive a Compensation for their Services, to be ascertained by Law, and paid out of the Treasury of the United States. They shall in all Cases, except Treason, Felony and Breach of the Peace, be privileged from Arrest during their Attendance at the Session of their respective Houses, and in going to and returning from the same; and for any Speech or Debate in either House, they shall not be questioned in any other Place.

No Senator or Representative shall, during the Time for which he was elected, be appointed to any civil Office under the Authority of the United States, which shall have been created, or the Emoluments whereof shall have been encreased during such time; and no Person holding any Office under the United States, shall be a Member of either House during his Continuance in Office.

Section 7. All Bills for raising Revenue shall originate in the House of Representatives; but the Senate may propose or concur with Amendments as on other Bills.

Every Bill which shall have passed the House of Representatives and the Senate, shall, before it become a Law, be presented to the President of the United States; If he approve he shall sign it, but if not he shall return it, with his Objections to that House in which it shall have originated, who shall enter the Objections at large on their Journal, and proceed to reconsider it. If after such Reconsideration two thirds of that House shall agree to pass the Bill, it shall be sent, together with the Objections, to the other House, by which it shall likewise be reconsidered, and if approved by two thirds of that House, it shall become a Law. But in all such Cases the Votes of both Houses shall be determined by yeas and Nays, and the Names of the Persons voting for and against the Bill shall be entered on the Journal of each House respectively. If any Bill shall not be returned by the President within ten days (Sundays excepted) after it shall have been presented to him, the Same shall be a Law, in like Manner as if he had signed it, unless the Congress by their Adjournment prevent its Return, in which Case it shall not be a Law.

Every Order, Resolution, or Vote to which the Concurrence of the Senate and House of Representatives may be necessary (except on a question of Adjournment) shall be presented to the President of the United States; and before the Same shall take Effect, shall be approved by him, or being disapproved by him, shall be repassed by two thirds of the Senate and House of Representatives, according to the Rules and Limitations prescribed in the Case of a Bill.

Section 8. The Congress shall have Power To lay and collect Taxes, Duties, Imposts and Excises, to pay the Debts and Provide for the common Defence and general Welfare of the United States; but all Duties, Imposts and Excises shall be uniform throughout the United States;

To borrow Money on the credit of the United States;

To regulate Commerce with foreign Nations, and among the several States, and with the Indian Tribes;

To establish an uniform Rule of Naturalization, and uniform Laws on the subject of Bankruptcies throughout the United States;

To coin Money, regulate the Value thereof, and of foreign Coin, and fix the Standard of Weights and Measures;

To provide for the Punishment of counterfeiting the Securities and current Coin of the United States;

To establish Post Offices and post Roads;

To promote the Progress of Science and useful Arts, by securing for limited Time to Authors and Inventors the exclusive Right to their respective Writings and Discoveries;

To constitute Tribunals inferior to the supreme Court;

To define and punish Piracies and Felonies committed on the high Seas, and Offences against the Law of Nations;

To declare War, grant Letters of Marque and Reprisal, and make Rules concerning Captures on Land and Water;

To raise and support Armies, but no Appropriation of Money to that Use shall be for a longer Term than two Years;

To provide and maintain a Navy;

To make Rules for the Government and Regulation of the land and naval Forces;

To provide for calling forth the Militia to execute the Laws of the Union, suppress Insurrections and repel Invasions;

To provide for organizing, arming, and disciplining, the Militia, and for governing such Part of them as may be employed in the Service of the United States, reserving to the States respectively, the Appointment of the Officers, and the Authority of training the Militia according to the discipline prescribed by Congress;

To exercise exclusive Legislation in all Cases whatsoever, over such District (not exceeding ten Miles square) as may, by Cession of Particular States, and the Acceptance of Congress, become the Seat of the Government of the United States, and to exercise like Authority over all Places purchased by the Consent of the Legislature of the State in which the Same shall be, for the Erection of Forts, Magazines, Arsenals, dock-Yards, and other needful Buildings;—And

To make all Laws which shall be necessary and proper for carrying into Execution the foregoing Powers, and all other Powers vested by this Constitution in the Government of the United States, or in any Department or Officer thereof.

Section 9. The Migration or Importation of such Persons as any of the States now existing shall think proper to admit, shall not be prohibited by the Congress prior to the Year one thousand eight hundred and eight, but a Tax or duty may be imposed on such Importation, not exceeding ten dollars for each Person.

The Privilege of the Writ of Habeas Corpus shall not be suspended, unless when in Cases of Rebellion or Invasion the public Safety may require it.

No Bill of Attainder or ex post facto Law shall be passed.

No Capitation, or other direct, Tax shall be laid, unless in Proportion to the Census or Enumeration herein before directed to be taken.

No Tax or Duty shall be laid on Articles exported from any State.

No Preference shall be given by any Regulation of Commerce or Revenue to the Ports of one State over those of another: nor shall Vessels bound to, or from, one State, be obliged to enter, clear, or pay Duties in another.

No Money shall be drawn from the Treasury, but in Consequence of Appropriations made by Law; and a regular Statement and Account of the Receipts and Expenditures of all public Money shall be published from time to time.

No Title of Nobility shall be granted by the United States: And no Person holding any Office of Profit or Trust under them, shall, without the Consent of the Congress, accept of any present, Emolument, Office, or Title, of any kind whatever, from any King, Prince, or foreign State.

Section 10. No State shall enter into any Treaty, Alliance, or Confederation; grant Letters of Marque and Reprisal; coin Money; emit Bills of Credit; make any Thing but gold and silver Coin a Tender in Payment of Debts; pass any Bill of Attainder, ex post facto Law, or Law impairing the Obligation of Contracts, or grant any Title of Nobility.

No State shall, without the Consent of the Congress, lay any Imposts or Duties on Imports or Exports, except what may be absolutely necessary for executing its inspection Laws: and the net Produce of all Duties and Imposts, laid by any State on Imports or Exports, shall be for the Use of the Treasury of the United States; and all such Laws shall be subject to the Revision and Controul of (the) Congress.

No State shall, without the Consent of Congress, lay any Duty of Tonnage, keep Troops, or Ships of War in time of Peace, enter into any Agreement or Compact with another State, or with a foreign Power, or engage in War, unless actually invaded, or in such imminent Danger as will not admit of delay.

ARTICLE II

Section 1. The executive Power shall be vested in a President of the United States of America. He shall hold his Office during the Term of four Years, and, together with the Vice President, chosen for the same Term, be elected, as follows

Each State shall appoint, in such Manner as the Legislature thereof may direct, a Number of Electors, equal to the whole Number of Senators and Representatives to which the State may be entitled in the Congress: but no Senator or Representative, or Person holding an Office of Trust or Profit under the United States, shall be appointed an Elector.

The Electors shall meet in their respective States, and vote by Ballot for two Persons, of whom one at least shall not be an Inhabitant of the same State with themselves. And they shall make a List of all the Persons voted for, and of the Number of Votes for each; which List they shall sign and certify, and transmit sealed to the Seat of the Government of the United States, directed to the President of the Senate. The President of the Senate shall, in the Presence of the Senate and House of Representatives, open all the Certificates, and the Votes shall then be counted. The Person having the greatest Number of Votes shall be the President, if such Number be a Majority of the whole Number of Electors appointed; and if there be more than one who have such Majority, and have an equal Number of Votes, then the House of Representatives shall immediately chuse by Ballot one of them for President; and if no Person have a Majority, then from the five highest on the List the said House shall in like Manner chuse the President. But in chusing the President, the Votes shall be taken by States, the Representation from each State having one Vote; A quorum for this Purpose shall consist of a Member or Members from two thirds of the States, and a Majority of all the States shall be necessary to a Choice. In every Case, after the Choice of the President, the Person having the greatest Number of Votes of the Electors shall be the Vice President. But if there should remain two or more who have equal Votes, the Senate shall chuse from them by Ballot the Vice President.

The Congress may determine the Time of chusing the Electors, and the Day on which they shall give their Votes; which Day shall be the same throughout the United States.

No Person except a natural born Citizen, or a Citizen of the United States, at the time of the Adoption of this Constitution, shall be eligible to the Office of President; neither shall any Person be eligible to that Office who shall not have attained to the Age of thirty five Years, and been fourteen Years a Resident within the United States.

In Case of the Removal of the President from Office, or of his Death, Resignation, or Inability to discharge the Powers and Duties of the said Office, the Same shall devolve on the Vice President, and the Congress may by Law provide for the Case of Removal, Death, Resignation or Inability, both of the President and Vice President, declaring what Officer shall then act as President, and such Officer shall act accordingly, until the Disability be removed, or a President shall be elected.

The President shall, at stated Times, receive for his Services, a Compensation, which shall neither be encreased nor diminished during the Period for which he shall have been elected, and he shall not receive within that Period any other Emolument from the United States, or any of them.

Before he enter on the Execution of his Office, he shall take the following Oath or Affirmation:—"I do solemnly swear (or affirm) that I will faithfully execute the Office of President of the United States, and will to the best of my Ability, preserve, protect and defend the Constitution of the United States."

Section 2. The President shall be Commander in Chief of the Army and Navy of the United States, and of the Militia of the several States, when called into the actual Service of the United States; he may require the Opinion, in writing, of the principal Officer in each of the executive Departments, upon any Subject relating to the Duties of their respective Offices, and he shall have Power to grant Reprieves and Pardons for Offences against the United States, except in Cases of Impeachment.

He shall have Power, by and with the Advice and Consent of the Senate, to make Treaties, provided two thirds of the Senators present concur; and he shall nominate, and by and with the Advice and Consent of the Senate, shall appoint Ambassadors, other public Ministers and Consuls, Judges of the supreme Court, and all other Officers of the United States, whose Appointments are not herein otherwise provided for, and which shall be established by Law: but the Congress may by Law vest the Appointment of such inferior Officers, as they think proper, in the President alone, in the Courts of Law, or in the Heads of Departments.

The President shall have Power to fill up all Vacancies that may happen during the Recess of the Senate, by granting Commissions which shall expire at the End of their next Session.

Section 3. He shall from time to time give to the Congress Information of the State of the Union, and recommend to their Consideration such

Measures as he shall judge necessary and expedient; he may, on extraordinary Occasions, convene both Houses, or either of them, and in Case of Disagreement between them, with Respect to the Time of Adjournment, he may adjourn them to such Time as he shall think proper; he shall receive Ambassadors and other public Ministers; he shall take Care that the Laws be faithfully executed, and shall Commission all the Officers of the United States.

Section 4. The President, Vice President and all civil Officers of the United States, shall be removed from Office on Impeachment for, and conviction of, Treason, Bribery, or other high Crimes and Misdemeanors.

ARTICLE III

Section 1. The judicial Power of the United States, shall be vested in one supreme Court, and in such inferior Courts as the Congress may from time to time ordain and establish. The Judges, both of the supreme and inferior Courts, shall hold their Offices during good Behaviour, and shall, at stated Times, receive for their Services, a Compensation, which shall not be diminished during their Continuance in Office.

Section 2. The judicial Power shall extend to all Cases, in Law and Equity, arising under this Constitution, the Laws of the United States, and Treaties made, or which shall be made, under their Authority;—to all Cases affecting Ambassadors, other public Ministers and Consuls;—to all Cases of admiralty and maritime Jurisdiction;—to Controversies to which the United States shall be a Party;—to Controversies between two or more States;—between a State and Citizens of another State;—between Citizens of different States,—between Citizens of the same State claiming Lands under Grants of different States, and between a State, or the Citizens thereof, and foreign States, Citizens or Subjects.

In all Cases affecting Ambassadors, other public Ministers and Consuls, and those in which a State shall be Party, the supreme Court shall have original Jurisdiction. In all the other Cases before mentioned, the supreme Court shall have appellate Jurisdiction, both as to Law and Fact, with such Exceptions, and under such Regulations as the Congress shall make.

The Trial of all Crimes, except in Cases of Impeachment, shall be by Jury; and such Trial shall be held in the State where the said Crimes shall have been committed; but when not committed within any State, the Trial shall be at such Place or Places as the Congress may by Law have directed.

Section 3. Treason against the United States, shall consist only in levy-ing War against them, or in adhering to their Enemies, giving them Aid and Comfort. No Person shall be convicted of Treason unless on the Testimony of two Witnesses to the same overt Act, or on Confession in open Court.

The Congress shall have Power to declare the Punishment of Treason, but no Attainder of Treason shall work Corruption of Blood, or Forfeiture except during the Life of the Person attainted.

ARTICLE IV

Section 1. Full Faith and Credit shall be given in each State to the public Acts, Records, and judicial Proceedings of every other State. And the Congress may by general Laws prescribe the Manner in which such Acts, Records and Proceedings shall be proved, and the Effect thereof.

Section 2. The Citizens of each State shall be entitled to all Privileges and Immunities of Citizens in the several States.

A Person charged in any State with Treason, Felony, or other Crime, who shall flee from Justice, and be found in another State, shall on Demand of the executive Authority of the State from which he fled, be delivered up, to be removed to the State having Jurisdiction of the Crime.

No Person held to Service or Labour in one State, under the Laws thereof, escaping into another, shall, in Consequence of any Law or Regu-lation therein, be discharged from such Service or Labour, but shall be delivered up on Claim of the Party to whom such Service or Labour may be due.

Section 3. New States may be admitted by the Congress into this Union; but no new State shall be formed or erected within the Jurisdiction of any other State; nor any State be formed by the Junction of two or more States, or Parts of States, without the Consent of the Legislatures of the States concerned as well as of the Congress.

The Congress shall have Power to dispose of and make all needful Rules and Regulations respecting the Territory or other Property belonging to the United States; and nothing in this Constitution shall be so con-strued as to Prejudice any Claims of the United States, or of any particular State.

Section 4. The United States shall guarantee to every State in this Union a Republican Form of Government, and shall protect each of them against Invasion; and on Application of the Legislature, or of the Executive (when the Legislature cannot be convened) against domestic Violence.

ARTICLE V

The Congress, whenever two thirds of both Houses shall deem it necessary, shall propose Amendments to this Constitution, or, on the Application of the Legislatures of two thirds of the several States, shall call a Convention for proposing Amendments, which, in either Case, shall be valid to all Intents and Purposes, as Part of this Constitution, when ratified by the Legislatures of three fourths of the several States, or by Conventions in three fourths thereof, as the one or the other Mode of Ratification may be proposed by the Congress; Provided that no Amendment which may be made prior to the Year One thousand eight hundred and eight shall in any Manner affect the first and fourth Clauses in the Ninth Section of the first Article; and that no State, without its Consent, shall be deprived of its equal Suffrage in the Senate.

ARTICLE VI

All Debts contracted and Engagements entered into, before the Adoption of this Constitution, shall be as valid against the United States under this Constitution, as under the Confederation.

This Constitution, and the Laws of the United States which shall be made in Pursuance thereof; and all Treaties made, or which shall be made, under the Authority of the United States, shall be the supreme Law of the Land; and the Judges in every State shall be bound thereby, any Thing in the Constitution or Laws of any State to the Contrary notwithstanding.

The Senators and Representatives before mentioned, and the Members of the several State Legislatures, and all executive and judicial Officers, both of the United States and of the several States, shall be bound by Oath or Affirmation, to support this Constitution; but no religious Test shall ever be required as a Qualification to any Office or public Trust under the United States.

ARTICLE VII

The Ratification of the Conventions of nine States, shall be sufficient for the Establishment of this Constitution between the States so ratifying the Same.

The Word, "the," being interlined between the seventh and eighth Lines of the first Page, the Word "Thirty" being partly written on an Erazure in the fifteenth Line of the first Page, The Words "is tried" being interlined between the thirty second and thirty third Lines of the first Page and the Word "the" being interlined between the forty third and forty fourth Lines of the second Page.

Attest William Jackson Secretary

Done in Convention by the Unanimous Consent of the States present the Seventeenth Day of September in the Year of our Lord one thousand seven hundred and Eighty seven and of the Independence of the United States of America the Twelfth *In witness* whereof We have hereunto subscribed our Names,

G°. Washington
Presidt. and deputy from Virginia

Delaware
Geo: Read
Gunning Bedford jun
John Dickinson
Richard Bassett
Jaco: Broom

North Carolina
Wm. Blount
Richd. Dobbs Spaight.
Hu Williamson

Maryland
James McHenry
Dan of St. Thos. Jenifer
Danl. Carroll

South Carolina
J. Rutledge
Charles Cotesworth Pinckney
Charles Pinckney
Pierce Butler

Virginia
John Blair
James Madison Jr.

Georgia
William Few
Abr Baldwin

New Hampshire
John Langdon
Nicholas Gilman

Connecticut
Wm: Saml. Johnson
Roger Sherman

Massachusetts
Nathaniel Gorham
Rufus King

New York
Alexander Hamilton

New Jersey
Wil: Livingston
David Brearley.
Wm. Paterson.
Jona: Dayton

Pennsylvania
B. Franklin
Thomas Mifflin
Robt. Morris
Geo. Clymer
Thos. FitzSimons
Jared Ingersoll
James Wilson
Gouv Morris

Resolution of the Convention

September 17, 1787

In Convention Monday September 17th. 1787

PRESENT, *The States of New-Hampshire, Massachusetts, Connecticut, Mr. Hamilton from New-York, New Jersey, Pennsylvania, Delaware, Maryland, Virginia, North Carolina, South Carolina, and Georgia.*

Resolved, That the preceding Constitution be laid before the United States in Congress assembled, and that it is the Opinion of this Convention, that it should afterwards be submitted to a Convention of Delegates, chosen in each State by the People thereof, under the Recommendation of its Legislature, for their Assent and Ratification; and that each Convention assenting to, and ratifying the Same, should give Notice thereof to the United States in Congress assembled.

Resolved, That it is the Opinion of this Convention, that as soon as the Conventions of nine States shall have ratified this Constitution, the United States in Congress assembled should fix a Day on which Electors should be appointed by the States which shall have ratified the same, and a Day on which the Electors should assemble to vote for the President, and the Time and Place for commencing Proceedings under this Constitution. That after such Publication the Electors should be appointed, and the Senators and Representatives elected: That the Electors should meet on the Day fixed for the Election of the President, and should transmit their votes certified signed, sealed and directed, as the Constitution requires, to the Secretary of the United States in Congress assembled, that the Senators and Representatives should convene at the Time and Place assigned; that the Senators should appoint a President of the Senate, for the sole Purpose of receiving, opening and counting the Votes for President; and, that after he shall be chosen, the Congress, together with the President, should, without Delay, proceed to execute this Constitution.

By the Unanimous Order of the Convention.
Go: Washington, *President.*
William Jackson, *Secretary*

Letter of the Convention to Congress

In Convention, September 17, 1787

Sir,

    We have now the honor to submit to the consideration of the United States in Congress assembled, that Constitution which has appeared to us the most adviseable.

    The friends of our country have long seen and desired, that the power of making war, peace and treaties, that of levying money and regulating commerce, and the correspondent executive and judicial authorities should be fully and effectually vested in the general government of the Union: but the impropriety of delegating such extensive trust to one body of men is evident—Hence results the necessity of a different organization.

    It is obviously impracticable in the fœderal government of these States, to secure all rights of independent sovereignty to each, and yet provide for the interest and safety of all—Individuals entering into society, must give up a share of liberty to preserve the rest. The magnitude of the sacrifice must depend as well on situation and circumstance, as on the object to be obtained. It is at all times difficult to draw with precision the line between those rights which must be surrendered, and those which may be reserved; and on the present occasion this difficulty was increased by a difference among the several States as to their situation, extent, habits, and particular interests.

    In all our deliberations on this subject we kept steadily in our view, that which appears to us the greatest interest of every true American, the consolidation of our Union, in which is involved our prosperity, felicity, safety, perhaps our national existence. This important consideration, seriously and deeply impressed on our minds, led each State in the Convention to be less rigid on points of inferior magnitude, than might have been otherwise expected; and thus the Constitution, which we now present, is the result of a spirit of amity, and of that mutual deference and concession which the peculiarity of our political situation rendered indispensable.

    That it will meet the full and entire approbation of every State is not perhaps to be expected; but each will doubtless consider, that had her interest alone been consulted, the consequences might have been particularly disagreeable or injurious to others; that it is liable to as few exceptions as could reasonably have been expected, we hope and believe; that it may promote the lasting welfare of that country so dear to us all, and secure her freedom and happiness, is our most ardent wish.

> With great respect,
> We have the honor to be.
> SIR,
> Your EXCELLENCY'S most
> Obedient and humble Servants,
> *George Washington*, President

By unanimous Order of the Convention

> His Excellency
> The President of Congress

Appendix B

Signers of the Constitution

Who they were before they signed, and || what they became in the new nation they created.

Connecticut

William Samuel Johnson (1727–1819). Yale B.A., clergyman, professor at King's College (later Columbia), Connecticut state legislator || president of Columbia College, U.S. senator.

Roger Sherman (1721–1793). Shoemaker, lawyer, state legislator, judge, member of Continental Congress, signs Declaration of Independence, mayor of New Haven || U.S. congressman, U.S. senator.

Delaware

Richard Bassett (1745–1815). Lawyer, militia officer || U.S. senator, state jurist, Delaware governor.

Gunning Bedford Jr. (1747–1821). Princeton B.A., lawyer, Confederation Congress member, state attorney general || U.S. district judge for Delaware.

Jacob Broom (1752–1810). Surveyor, businessman || postmaster of Wilmington, director of Bank of Delaware.

John Dickinson (1732–1808). Maryland-born, law degree from London's Middle Temple, admitted to Philadelphia bar, Continental Congress member, author of *Letters from a Farmer in Pennsylvania*, earns epithet as "Penman of the Revolution," walks out of Congress, refuses to sign Declaration, chairman of committee to draft Articles of Confederation, Pennsylvania militia colonel, president [governor] of Delaware, president of Pennsylvania Supreme Executive Council, president of Annapolis Convention || attorney, political essayist.

George Read (1733–1798). Lawyer, member of Continental Congress, signs Declaration of Independence || U.S. senator, chief justice Delaware Supreme Court, law practice.

Georgia

Abraham Baldwin (1754–1807). Connecticut-born, Yale B.A., clergyman, Continental Army chaplain, member Confederation Congress || U.S. congressman, U.S. senator, founder of University of Georgia.

William Few (1748–1828). Maryland-born, militia officer, member of Continental Congress || U.S. senator; Georgia jurist; moves to New York City and becomes, successively, inspector of prisons, U.S. commissioner of loans, director of Manhattan Bank, president of City Bank.

Maryland

Daniel Carroll (1730–1796). Planter-merchant, state legislator, member Confederation Congress || member of first U.S. House of Representatives, planner of new Federal City (later Washington, D.C.).

Daniel of Saint Thomas Jenifer (1723–1790). Planter, merchant, partner in ironworks, state senator, member of Confederation Congress || returns to private life.

James McHenry (1753–1816). Irish-born, studies medicine in Philadelphia under Benjamin Rush, Continental Army surgeon, secretary and personal aide to Washington and Lafayette, Confederation Congress member || U.S. secretary of war.

Massachusetts

Nathaniel Gorham (1738–1796). Merchant, state legislator, Confederation Congress president || copurchaser of six million acres in western New York, bankruptcy, Massachusetts supervisor of revenue.

Rufus King (1755–1827). Harvard B.A., lawyer, state legislator || U.S. senator, minister to Great Britain, unsuccessful Federalist vice-presidential candidate in 1804 and 1808 and presidential candidate in 1816.

New Hampshire

Nicholas Gilman (1755–1814). Storekeeper, militia and Continental Army officer, Confederation Congress member || U.S. House of Representatives, U.S. Senate.

John Langdon (1741–1819). Anti-British activist, Continental Congress member, naval agent, helps organize and serves in campaign against Burgoyne, president [governor] of New Hampshire || governor of New Hampshire, U.S. senator.

New Jersey

David Brearley (1745–1790). Lawyer, Continental Army officer, chief justice New Jersey Supreme Court || U.S. District judge for New Jersey, leader of New Jersey Masons and Episcopal Church.

Jonathan Dayton (1760–1824). Princeton B.A., lawyer, Continental Army officer || U.S. congressman, Speaker of the House of Representatives (1795–1799), U.S. Army brigadier general (1798), U.S. senator, indicted for treason in Aaron Burr affair, but government entered a nolle prosequi in 1807.

William Livingston (1723–1790). New York-born, Yale B.A., lawyer, militia brigadier general, governor of New Jersey, prolific essayist || deceased.

William Paterson (1745–1806). Irish-born, Princeton B.A., lawyer, minuteman, state attorney general, Confederation Congress member || U.S. senator, New Jersey governor, associate justice U.S. Supreme Court (1793–1806).

New York

Alexander Hamilton (1755–1804). Born in Nevis, King's College (Columbia) B.A., Continental Army lieutenant colonel, secretary and aide-de-camp to Washington, lawyer, coauthor of "Publius" in *The Federalist* || first U.S. secretary of the treasury, U.S. Army inspector general with rank of major general, leader of Federalist political party, mortally wounded in duel with Vice President Aaron Burr.

North Carolina

William Blount (1749–1800). State militiaman, Confederation Congress member || governor of transallegheny Southwest Territory, leads Tennessee to statehood, first U.S. senator from Tennessee, expelled from Senate for plotting British takeover of Spanish Florida and Louisiana.

Richard Dobbs Spaight (1758–1802). North Carolina–born, nephew of royal governor, educated at University of Glasgow, state legislator, member Confederation Congress || state legislator, governor of North Carolina, member U.S. House of Representatives, killed in duel with Federalist rival for state senate.

Hugh Williamson (1735–1819). College of Philadelphia (now University of Pennsylvania) B.A.; professor of mathematics; Presbyterian minister; physician; studies medicine in Edinburgh, London; earns M.D. in Utrecht; prolific science researcher while practicing medicine in Philadelphia;

enters mercantile trade in North Carolina while still practicing medicine; elected to state legislature; Confederation Congress || member of first U.S. House of Representatives; moves to New York in 1793 to assume private pursuits as scholar, teacher, minister, scientist, physician, historian, and humanitarian.

Pennsylvania

George Clymer (1739–1813). Merchant, Continental Congress member, signs Declaration of Independence, helps establish Bank of North America || U.S. House of Representatives, federal tax collector for Pennsylvania.

Thomas FitzSimons (1741–1811). Irish-born, militiaman, founder and director Bank of North America, Confederation Congress member || U.S. House of Representatives, founder-director-president of Insurance Company of North America.

Benjamin Franklin (1706–1790). Statesman, scientist, philosopher, educator, prolific author, diplomat, political leader, signs of Declaration of Independence || deceased.

Jared Ingersoll (1749–1822). Yale B.A., lawyer, king's attorney, Connecticut agent (envoy) in London, vice-admiralty court judge in Philadelphia || private law practice.

Thomas Mifflin (1744–1800). Princeton B.A., merchant, Continental Congress member, Continental Army major general, part of cabal to oust Washington as commander in chief, Pennsylvania Assembly Speaker || Pennsylvania president, then governor.

Gouverneur Morris (1752–1816). King's College (Columbia) B.A., helps write New York State constitution, Continental Congress member, becomes Pennsylvania citizen and lawyer, assistant director in Confederation Office of Finance || business agent in Europe for Robert Morris banking interests, American minister to France, U.S. senator.

Robert Morris (1734–1806). Merchant-banker, Continental Congress member, votes against independence but signs Declaration of Independence, U.S. superintendent of finance, establishes Bank of North America || U.S. senator, land speculator, bankruptcy, and debtors' prison.

James Wilson (1742–1798). Scottish-born, educated at Glasgow and Edinburgh universities, studies law in Philadelphia, Continental Congress member, signs Declaration of Independence || associate justice of U.S. Supreme

Court (1789–1798), fails in land speculations, flees to New Jersey and then to North Carolina to avoid imprisonment, dies in North Carolina.

South Carolina

Pierce Butler (1744–1822). Born in Ireland; son of Irish baronet; fights with British troops at Louisbourg, Nova Scotia; sells commission to buy lands in Georgia, Pennsylvania, Tennessee, and South Carolina; state legislator in South Carolina II in first U.S. Senate; champions slavery; resigns in 1796, reelected in 1802, resigns a second time in 1804 after hiding the fugitive Aaron Burr, who had killed Alexander Hamilton, bitter retirement to private life.

Charles Pinckney (1757–1824). Lawyer, state legislator, militiaman, captured when Charleston surrendered, practices law II governor of South Carolina, U.S. senator, minister to Spain, reelected governor in 1806, state legislator, U.S. House of Representatives.

Charles Cotesworth Pinckney (1746–1825). South Carolina–born, Oxford-educated, law degree from London's Middle Temple, officer in South Carolina regiment II refuses Washington nominations as army commander in chief, supreme court justice, and secretaryships of war and state; minister to France; major general in charge of American forces south of Maryland; unsuccessful Federalist candidate for president in 1804 and 1808; practices law in South Carolina; a founder of South Carolina College (later University of South Carolina); first president of Charleston Bible Society.

John Rutledge (1739–1800). South Carolina–born heir to important plantation, trains for law in England, colonial legislator, Continental Congress member, serves gallantly in war, Confederation Congress member, helps write South Carolina constitution, elected state's first "president" [governor], then governor II associate justice of U.S. Supreme Court (1789–1791); resigns to become chief justice of South Carolina; named by Washington as second chief justice of U.S. Supreme Court and serves in 1795 while Senate was not in session, Senate reconvenes and refuses to confirm appointment; he slips into insanity.

Virginia

John Blair (1732–1800). College of William and Mary B.A., London's Middle Temple law degree, jurist and state legislator II associate justice of U.S. Supreme Court (1789–1796).

James Madison Jr. (1751–1836). Princeton B.A., state legislator, Confederation Congress member, coauthor of "Publius" in *The Federalist*, note taker at Constitutional Convention || U.S. House of Representatives, coauthor of and key figure in adding Bill of Rights to Constitution, secretary of state under Jefferson (1801–1809), fourth president of the United States (1809–1817), succeeds founder Jefferson as rector (president) of University of Virginia.

George Washington (1732–1799). Surveyor, wilderness explorer, Virginia militia commander, planter, state legislator, Continental Congress member, commander in chief of Continental Army, president of Constitutional Convention || first president of the United States, commander in chief of the U.S. Army, frees slaves in his will.

The Delegates Who Refused to Sign

Elbridge Gerry (1744–1814). Harvard B.A., merchant, Continental Congress member, signs Declaration of Independence || U.S. House of Representatives, envoy to France in "XYZ Affair," elected Massachusetts governor in 1810, elected U.S. vice president in 1812.

George Mason (1725–1792). Self-educated planter, drafter of Virginia Declaration of Rights and first Virginia constitution, state legislator || retires to plantation, refusing appointment as one of Virginia's first two senators.

Edmund Randolph (1753–1813). College of William and Mary B.A., lawyer, aide to Washington in 1775, Virginia attorney general for ten years, member of Continental Congress, Virginia governor (1786–1789) || first U.S. attorney general, second secretary of state, resigns over bribery accusations, resumes law practice, defends Aaron Burr in 1807 treason trial.

The Delegates Who Withdrew from the Constitutional Convention before the Signing

Connecticut

Oliver Ellsworth (1745–1807). Yale and Princeton degrees, lawyer, jurist, Confederation Congress || U.S. senator, chief justice U.S. Supreme Court (1796–1800).

Georgia

William Houston (c. 1757–1812). Born in Savannah, studies law at London's Inner Temple, lawyer and Assembly delegate, member of Continental Congress || moves to New York, admitted to bar of U.S. Supreme Court.

William Pierce (c.1740–1789). Continental Army officer, aide to Generals Sullivan and Greene, member of Georgia Assembly, member of Confederation Congress || deceased.

Maryland

Luther Martin (1748?–1826). Lawyer, member of Continental Congress || defends Aaron Burr, Maryland attorney general.

John Francis Mercer (1759–1821). Virginia-born, B.A. College of William and Mary, major in Continental Army, lieutenant colonel in Virginia militia, reads law with Governor Thomas Jefferson and at William and Mary, elected to Confederation Congress, marries in and moves to Maryland || member of Maryland General Assembly, elected to Third U.S. Congress, elected to Maryland House of Delegates, governor for two terms, House of Delegates.

Massachusetts

Caleb Strong (1745–1819). Harvard, lawyer, state legislator || U.S. senator, Massachusetts governor (1800–1807, 1812–1816).

New Jersey

William Churchill Houston (1746–1788). B.A. College of New Jersey (Princeton); successively professor of mathematics and philosophy, librarian, treasurer of college; militia captain; delegate to Confederation Congress; admitted to bar; member of federal court || deceased.

New York

John Lansing Jr. (1754–1829). Lawyer, mayor of Albany, state legislator, state Supreme Court justice, chief justice, state chancellor || remains on bench.

Robert Yates (1738–1801). Lawyer, mayor of Albany, state legislator, state Supreme Court justice || resumes career on bench.

North Carolina

William Richardson Davie (1756–1820). English-born, patriot cavalry commander, North Carolina legislator || founds University of North Carolina, North Carolina governor.

Alexander Martin (1740–1807). New Jersey–born, Princeton B.A. and M.A., buys property in North Carolina, studies and practices law, colonial Assembly member, militia colonel, state senator, three-term North Carolina governor,

Confederation Congress member || reelected governor, U.S. senator, state senator.

Virginia

James McClurg (1746–1843). Virginia-born, B.A. College of William and Mary, M.D. University of Edinburgh, world-renowned scientific pioneer in functions of human digestive tract, Williamsburg physician, American Navy surgeon, Virginia physician-general and director of hospitals during Revolutionary War, chair of anatomy and medicine at College of William and Mary, Virginia Council of State || resumes private practice in Richmond, mayor of Richmond, president of Medical Society.

George Wythe (1726–1806). Lawyer, colonial legislature, Continental Congress, signs Declaration of Independence, judge, professor of law || returns to Richmond, founds private law school, frees slaves in his will.

Other Major Figures

George Clinton (1739–1812). Farmer, lawyer, New York legislator, member Continental Congress, militia and Continental Army general, New York governor (1777–1795) || New York governor (1801–1804), U.S. vice president (1805–1812).

John Hancock (1737–1793). Harvard B.A., merchant, president of Massachusetts Provincial Congress [in effect, governor], president of U.S. Continental Congress, first to sign Declaration of Independence, first governor of Massachusetts || regularly reelected governor of Massachusetts, died serving ninth term in office.

Patrick Henry (1736–1799). Farmer, self-educated lawyer, member of Continental Congress, member of Virginia House of Burgesses, calls for revolution with famed "liberty or death" speech, named militia commander but resigns without seeing action, first governor of Virginia || retires to practice law, rejecting all offers of appointment to high federal office.

John Jay (1745–1829). King's College [now Columbia] B.A., M.A., and law degree, prosperous lawyer, member Continental Congress, writes New York State's first constitution, chief justice state Supreme Court, American envoy to Spain, with John Adams and Franklin negotiates peace treaty with England, U.S. secretary of foreign affairs, coauthors *The Federalist* with Hamilton and Madison || first chief justice U.S. Supreme Court (1789–1795), governor of New York (1795–1801), remaining years in retirement.

<u>Richard Henry Lee</u> (1732–1794). Virginia-born, educated in England, member of Virginia House of Burgesses, delegate to First Continental Congress, introduces resolution for independence, state legislator, president of Continental Congress || U.S. senator; with Madison, coauthor of amendments for Bill of Rights.

Appendix C

The Bill of Rights

The first ten amendments of the Constitution—collectively called the "Bill of Rights"—did not carry any official numbers in the original document. Although twelve amendments were proposed to the several legislatures, only the ten shown here were adopted, and each acquired a new number, but the appropriate changes were never entered.

[ARTICLE I]

Article the [first]

Congress shall make no law respecting an establishment of religion, or prohibiting the free exercise thereof; or abridging the freedom of speech, or of the press; or the right of the people peaceably to assemble, and to petition the Government for a redress of grievances.

[ARTICLE II]

Article the [second]

A well regulated Militia, being necessary to the security of a free State, the right of the people to keep and bear Arms, shall not be infringed.

[ARTICLE III]

Article the [third]

No Soldier shall, in time of peace be quartered in any house, without the consent of the Owner, nor in time of war, but in a manner to be prescribed by law.

[ARTICLE IV]

Article the [fourth]

The right of the people to be secure in their persons, houses, papers, and effects, against unreasonable searches and seizures, shall not be violated, and no Warrants shall issue, but upon probable cause, supported by Oath or affirmation, and particularly describing the place to be searched, and the persons or things to be seized.

[ARTICLE V]

Article the [fifth]

No person shall be held to answer for a capital, or otherwise infamous crime, unless on a presentment or indictment of a Grand Jury, except in cases arising in the land or naval forces, or in the Militia, when in actual service in time of War or public danger; nor shall any person be subject for the same offence to be twice put in jeopardy of life or limb; nor shall be compelled in any criminal case to be a witness against himself, nor be deprived of life, liberty, or property, without due process of law; nor shall private property be taken for public use, without just compensation.

[ARTICLE VI]

Article the [sixth]

In all criminal prosecutions, the accused shall enjoy the right to a speedy and public trial, by an impartial jury of the State and district wherein the crime shall have been committed, which district shall have been previously ascertained by law, and to be informed of the nature and cause of the accusation; to be confronted with the witnesses against him; to have compulsory process for obtaining witnesses in his favor, and to have the Assistance of Counsel for his defence.

[ARTICLE VII]

Article the [seventh]

In suits at common law, where the value in controversy shall exceed twenty dollars, the right of trial by jury shall be preserved, and no fact tried by a jury, shall be otherwise reexamined in any Court of the United States, than according to the rules of the common law.

[ARTICLE VIII]

Article the [eighth]

Excessive bail shall not be required, nor excessive fines imposed, nor cruel and unusual punishments inflicted.

[ARTICLE IX]

Article the [ninth]

The enumeration in the Constitution, of certain rights, shall not be construed to deny or disparage others retained by the people.

[ARTICLE X]

Article the [tenth]

The powers not delegated to the United States by the Constitution, nor prohibited by it to the States, are reserved to the States respectively, or to the people.

Notes

Chapter 1. Victory's Bitter Fruits

1. George Washington (hereinafter GW), Circular to the States, October 18, 1780; GW to George Mason, October 22, 1780, in John C. Fitzpatrick, ed., *The Writings of George Washington* (Washington, D.C.: U.S. Government Printing Office, 39 vols.), 20:211, 242.

2. GW to the Magistrates of New Jersey, January 8, 1780, in Fitzpatrick, *Writings*, 17:363.

3. GW to the Officers of the Army, March 15, 1783, in Fitzpatrick, *Writings*, 26:222–227.

4. Ibid.

5. Douglas Southall Freeman, *George Washington: A Biography* (New York: Charles Scribner's Sons, 1948–1957, 7 vols., completed by John Alexander Carroll and Mary Wells Ashworth), 5:435.

6. "The Journals of Major Samuel Shaw . . . with a Life of the Author by Josiah Quincy," ibid.

7. GW Circular to the States, June 8, 1783, Fitzpatrick, *Writings*, 26:483–496.

8. GW to Rev. William Gordon, July 8, 1783, Fitzpatrick, *Writings*, 27:48–52.

9. John Adams to Robert R. Livingston, July 14 and 18, 1783, in Charles Francis Adams, ed., *The Works of John Adams* (Boston: Little, Brown, 1856, 10 vols.), 98, 108.

10. Merrill Jensen, John P. Kaminski, Gaspare Saladino, Richard Leffler, and Charles H. Schoenleber, eds., *The Documentary History of the Ratification of the Constitution* (hereinafter DHRC) (Madison, Wis.: State Historical Society of Wisconsin, 1976–[in progress],19 vols. to date), XIII:25.

11. GW to Jonathan Trumbull Jr., January 5, 1784, Fitzpatrick, *Writings*, 27:293–295.

12. John J. McCusker, *How Much Is That In Real Money? A Historical Commodity Price Index for Use as a Deflator of Money Values in the Economy of the United States* (Worcester, Mass.: American Antiquarian Society, 2001), 34.

13. James Madison, *Notes of Debates in the Federal Convention of 1787 Reported by James Madison* (New York: W. W. Norton, 1987), 7.

14. Benjamin Franklin to James Parker, March 20, 1750, in Leonard W. Labaree et al., *Papers of Benjamin Franklin* (New Haven, Conn.: Yale University Press, 1959–[in progress], 38 vols. to date), IV:117–121.

15. John Steele Gordon, *An Empire of Wealth: The Epic History of American Economic Power* (New York: HarperCollins, 2004), 61–63.

16. Henry Knox to GW, January 31, 1785, in W. W. Abbot and Dorothy Twohig, eds., *The Papers of George Washington, Confederation Series January 1784–September 1788*. 6 vols. (Charlottesville: University Press of Virginia, 1992–1997), 2:301–306.

17. *DHRC* XIII:154–155.

18. Ibid., 57.

19. Ibid., 32.

20. Henry Knox to GW, New York, October 23, 1786, *PGWC* 4:299–302.

21. GW to Benjamin Harrison, October 10, 1784, *PGWC* 2:86–99.

22. GW to James Madison, November 30, 1785, *PGWC* 3:419–421.

23. *DHRC* I:184.

24. Richard B. Morris, *Witnesses at the Creation: Hamilton, Madison, Jay, and the Constitution* (New York: Holt, Rinehart, & Winston, 1985), 171.

25. Lee to GW, October 1, 1786, *PGWC* 4:281–282.

26. Lee to GW, October 17, 1786, ibid., 4:295–296.

27. GW to Lee, October 31, 1786, ibid., 4:318–320.

28. *DHRC* XIII: 71.

29. Madison, *Notes*, 15–16.

30. Ibid., 35.

31. Ibid., 42.

32. GW Address to Congress on Resigning His Commission, December 23, 1783, Fitzpatrick, *Writings*, 27:284–285.

33. GW to Lafayette, February 1, 1784, *PGWC* 1:87–90.

34. John Jay to GW, March 16, 1786, ibid., 3:601–602.

35. GW to John Jay, May 18, 1786, ibid., 4:55–56.

36. GW to John Jay, August 15, 1786, ibid., 212–213.

37. Ibid.

38. Knox to GW, April 9, 1787, ibid., 5:133–135.

39. GW to Knox, April 27, 1787, ibid., 157–159.

40. Edmund Randolph to Patrick Henry, December 6, 1786, in William Wirt Henry, *Patrick Henry: Life, Correspondence, and Speeches* (New York: Charles Scribner's Sons, 1891, 3 vols.), II:310–311.

41. Madison to GW, March 18, 1787, *PGWC* 5:92–95.

42. Madison to Thomas Jefferson, March 19, 1787, Henry II:313.

43. Edward Carrington to Henry Knox, February 10, 1788, in *DHRC* XVI: 101–103.

Chapter 2. The Great Debate

1. GW to George Augustine Washington, May 17, 1787, *PGWC* 5:189.

2. GW to Henry Knox, February 3, 1787, ibid., 7–9.

3. Freeman VI:44.

4. Madison, *Notes*, 23–24.

5. Ibid., 19.

6. Ron Chernow, *Alexander Hamilton* (New York: Penguin, 2004), 229.

7. James Madison to Thomas Ritchie, September 15, 1821, in Max Farrand, ed., *The Records of the Federal Convention of 1787* (New Haven, Conn.: Yale University Press, 1911, 3 vols.), III:447–448.

8. Madison, *Notes*, 17–18.

9. Chernow, *Alexander Hamilton*, 174.

10. "William Pierce: Character Sketches of Delegates to the Federal Convention," Farrand III:94.

11. Ibid.

12. Madison, *Notes*, 25.

13. Ibid., 26.

14. Donald Jackson and Dorothy Twohig, eds., *The Diaries of George Washington* (Charlottesville: University Press of Virginia, 1976–1979, 6 vols.), V:164.

15. *Pennsylvania Herald*, June 2, 1787, in DHRC XIII:122.

16. Carl Van Doren, *The Great Rehearsal: The Story of the Making and Ratifying of the Constitution of the United States* (New York: The Viking Press, 1948), 181.

17. DHRC XIII:144.

18. "Pierce: Character Sketches," in Farrand III:95.

19. Madison, *Notes*, 28.

20. Ibid., 30.

21. Madison, *Notes*, 34.

22. Ibid., 31.

23. PGWC 5:239–241.

24. Madison, *Notes*, 33.

25. PGWC 5:203–208.

26. Madison, *Notes*, 42–43.

27. Ibid., 39.

28. Ibid., 39–40.

29. Van Doren, *Great Rehearsal*, 189–190.

30. Farrand I:501.

31. Ibid., I:529–531.

32. Madison, *Notes*, 67–68.

Chapter 3. The Great Compromise

1. "Pierce: Character Sketches," in Farrand III:89.

2. Madison, *Notes*, 98.

3. Ibid., 103.

4. DHRC I:241.

5. Madison, *Notes*, 502.

6. Ibid., 45–47.

7. Ibid., 46.

8. Ibid., 49.

9. Ibid., 51–55.

10. Ibid., 59ff.

11. Ibid., 45.

12. Van Doren, *Great Rehearsal*, 40.

13. GW to George Augustine Washington, June 10, 1787, PGWC 5:224.

14. Chernow, *Alexander Hamilton*, 84.

15. Ibid., 91.

16. Madison, *Notes*, 129–139.

17. Van Doren, *Great Rehearsal*, 39.

18. Farrand, *Records* III:92.

19. John Dos Passos, *The Men Who Made the Nation* (Garden City, N.Y.: Doubleday, Inc., 1957), 65.

20. Chernow, *Alexander Hamilton*, 233.

21. *DHRC* XIII:136.

22. Ibid., 135–136.

23. Ibid., 135.

24. GW to Alexander Hamilton, July 10, 1787, PGWC 5:257.

25. GW *Diaries* V:179.

26. Ibid., V:180.

27. Madison, *Notes*, 385.

28. Ibid., 503.

29. Ibid., 613.

30. GW to the marquis de Lafayette, August 17, 1787, Freeman 6:105.

31. Madison, *Notes*, 651, 656.

32. Ibid., 566.

33. Ibid., 651.

34. Ibid., 652.

35. *DHRC* XV:280–283.

36. Madison, *Notes*, 657.

37. Ibid., 288.

38. Ibid.

39. Ibid.

40. Ibid., 652–654.

41. Ibid., 659.

42. *DHRC* XIV:454.

43. *New-Jersey Journal*, November 7, 1787, p. 2; also *Pennsylvania Journal*, *New-Hampshire Spy*, *Massachusetts Gazette*, *Connecticut Gazette*, and other newspapers.

44. GW *Diaries* V:185.

45. Ibid., 185–186.

46. *Pennsylvania Packet*, August 17, 1787.

Chapter 4. "The Seeds of Civil Discord"

1. GW to James Madison, October 10, 1787, *PGWC* 5:366–368.

2. Richard B. Morris, ed., *Encyclopedia of American History* (New York: Harper & Brothers, 1953), 91.

3. Henry II:320–321.

4. Benjamin Harrison to GW, October 4, 1787, *PGWC* 5:353–354.

5. George Mason to GW, October 7, 1787, ibid., 355–358.

6. James Madison to Thomas Jefferson, New York, October 24, 1787, *DHRC* I:347.

7. Ibid., I:337–339.

8. Richard Henry Lee to Elbridge Gerry, New York, September 29, 1787, ibid., 342.

9. Ibid., VIII:65–67.

10. Richard Henry Lee to GW, October 11, 1787, *PGWC* 5:370–371.

11. GW to David Humphreys, October 19, 1787, ibid., 5:365–366.

12. Van Doren, *Great Rehearsal*, 178.

13. GW to Thomas Jefferson, January 1, 1788, *PGWC* 6:2–5.

14. Thomas Jefferson to W. S. Smith, February 2, 1788, in Dumas Malone, *Jefferson and the Rights of Man* (Boston: Little, Brown, 1951), 171.

15. Thomas Jefferson to John Adams, November 13, 1787, in Lester J. Cappon, ed., *The Adams-Jefferson Letters: The Complete Correspondence between Thomas Jefferson and Abigail and John Adams* (Chapel Hill: University of North Carolina Press, 1959), 211–212. Poland's new constitution had just proclaimed the nation a hereditary monarchy.

16. Thomas Jefferson to William S. Smith, November 13, 1787, Malone 165–166.

17. Thomas Jefferson to GW, Paris, May 2, 1788, *PGWC* 6:251–257.

18. Richard R. Beeman, *Patrick Henry: A Biography* (New York: McGraw-Hill, 1974), xii.

19. Farrand, *Records* III:123–127.

20. Patrick Henry to GW, October 19, 1797, *PGWC* 5:384.

21. Henry II:323.

22. *DHRC* VIII:69–70.

23. Ibid., 70–76.

24. Henry II:324.

25. Ibid., 322.

26. Madison to Jefferson, December 9, 1787, Henry II:324.

27. Ibid., 6:17–18.

Chapter 5. The Road to Ratification

1. GW to Henry Knox, October 15, 1787, *PGWC* 5:288–290.

2. Ibid.

3. *Massachusetts Centinel*, November 17, 1787, *DHRC* IV:259–262.

4. Centinel I, Philadelphia *Independent Gazetteer*, October 5, 1787, ibid., XIII:326–337.

5. Philadelphia *Freeman's Journal*, September 26, 1787, ibid., XIII:243–245.

6. Elbridge Gerry to James Warren, New York, October 18, 1787, ibid., XIII:407–408.

7. Ibid., XVI:272–291.

8. Ibid., 274.

9. *Pennsylvania Gazette*, September 26, 1787, ibid., XIII:252–254.

10. GW to Bushrod Washington, November 9, 1787, *PGWC* 5:420–425.

11. *DHRC* XIII:399–403.

12. Ibid., 221–222.

13. Matthew M'Connell to William Irvine, Philadelphia, September 20, 1787, ibid., 220.

14. Farrand, *Records* III:91.

15. *DHRC* II:104.

16. Ibid., 105.

17. Ibid., 103–110.

18. *New York Morning Post*, October 9, 1787, ibid., XIII:294.

19. *Pennsylvania Herald*, September 29, 1787, ibid., II:123.

20. *Pennsylvania Gazette*, October 3, 1787, ibid., 124.

21. Ibid., VIII:86–87.

22. Louis Guillaume Otto to French minister of foreign affairs, comte de Montmorin, New York, October 10, 1787, Correspondence politique, États-Unis 32, 368ff, Archives du Ministre des Affaires Étrangères, Paris.

23. Farrand, *Records* III:91.

24. *DHRC* XIII:337–344.

25. Ibid., 337n.

26. Benjamin Franklin to Mr. Grand, October 22, 1787, Farrand, *Records* III:131.

Chapter 6. "Unite or Die"

1. David Humphreys to GW, New Haven, Conn., September 28, 1787, *PGWC* 5:342–344.

2. *DHRC* IV:98–100.

3. GW to Samuel Powel, Mount Vernon, January 18, 1788, *PGWC* 6:45–46.

4. *DHRC* XIV:455.

5. *Philadelphia Gazette*, November 22, 1787, *DHRC* XIV:164.

6. Governeur Morris to GW, Philadelphia, October 30, 1787, *PGWC* 5:398–401.

7. *DHRC* XIX:9–10.

8. *New York Journal*, September 27, 1787, ibid., 58–61.

9. *DHRC* XIV:170.

10. Ibid., 171.

11. Chernow, *Alexander Hamilton*, 248.

12. Hamilton to GW, October 30, 1787, *PGWC* 5:396–397.

13. *DHRC* XIII:487n.

14. Ibid., XIV:117.

15. *Albany Gazette*, December 20, 1787, *DHRC* XV:557.

16. James Madison to GW, New York, November 18, 1787, *PGWC* 5:444–445.

17. GW to David Stuart, Mount Vernon, November 30, 1787, ibid., 466–468.

18. Alexander Hamilton, James Madison, John Jay, *The Federalist Papers* (New York: New American Library, 1961), no. 1: Hamilton, 33–37.

19. GW to James Madison, Mount Vernon, December 7, 1787, *PGWC* 5:477–481.

20. *DHRC* II:346.

21. Ibid., 447–448.

22. Ibid., 448.

23. Ibid., 458.

24. Ibid., 459.

25. Ibid., 547.

26. Ibid., 547–548.

27. Ibid., 553.

28. Van Doren, *Great Rehearsal*, 186.

29. GW to Sir Edward Newenham, Mount Vernon, December 25, 1787, *PGWC* 5:508–509.

30. *DHRC* XV:18–19.

31. *DHRC* II:709.

32. *Carlisle Gazette*, January 2, 1788, ibid., 670–673.

33. Philadelphia *Independent Gazetteer*, January 12, 1788, *DHRC* V:817.

34. Ibid., II:709.

35. Ibid., 710.

Chapter 7. "Words to My Brother Ploughjoggers"

1. GW to Henry Knox, Mount Vernon, January 10, 1788, ibid., 28–29.

2. Van Doren, 195.

3. *Connecticut Journal*, New Haven, ibid., 195.

4. Jonathan Trumbull Jr. to GW, Hartford, Conn., January 9, 1788, *PGWC* 6:25–26.

5. Boston *American Herald*, *DHRC* IV:161.

6. Benjamin Lincoln to GW, Boston, January 9, 1788, *PGWC* 6:22–24.

7. *DHRC* IV:264.

8. "Pierce: Character Sketches," in Farrand III:88.

9. Ibid., IV:291.

10. Northampton *Hampshire Gazette*, November 21, 1787, ibid., 293–294.

11. Ibid., 303–304.

12. *DHRC* V:761.

13. Ibid., 765.

14. *DHRC* VI:1175.

15. Rufus King to George Thatcher, January 20, 1788, in Harlow Giles Unger, *John Hancock: Merchant King and American Patriot* (New York: John Wiley & Sons, 2000), 313.

16. James Madison to GW, New York, January 20, 1788, *PGWC* 6:51–52.

17. *DHRC* XIV:487.

18. Lafayette to GW, January 1, 1788, *PGWC* 6:5–7.

19. James Madison to GW, New York, December 20, 1787, *PGWC* 5:499–501.

20. *DHRC* V:788–790.

21. *DHRC* VI:1117.

22. Van Doren, *Great Rehearsal*, 197–198.

23. Ibid., 198–200.

24. Ibid., 201.

25. Unger, *Hancock*, 314–315.

26. *DHRC* VI:1477.

27. Ibid., VII:1618–1623.

28. Benjamin Lincoln to GW, Boston, February 9, 1788, *PGWC* 6:104–105.

29. *DHRC* VII: 1618–1623.

Chapter 8. "A Fig and a Fiddle-stick's End"

1. *DHRC* XIX:71.

2. Ibid., 82.

3. *New York Journal*, October 18, 1787, ibid., 118–119.

4. Matthew Prior, *An English Padlock* (1705), cited in *DHRC* XIX:119n.

5. Ibid., 85.

6. Ibid., 125–130.

7. Ibid., 144–147.

8. Hamilton et al., *The Federalist Papers*, no. 10; Madison, *Notes*, 77–84.

9. Ibid., 154–160.

10. Ibid., 340.

11. Philadelphia *Independent Gazetteer*, November 24, 1787, ibid., 307–308.

12. James Madison to GW, New York, December 20, 1787, *PGWC* 5:499–501.

13. Philadelphia *Independent Gazetteer*, December 7, 1787, and *New York Morning Post*, December 13, 1787, *DHRC* XIX, 308.

14. Louis Guillaume Otto to Comte de Montmorin, New York, November 26, 1787, ibid., 309.

15. *Independent Journal*, December 1, 1787, ibid., 345.

16. *New York Daily Advertiser*, December 4, 1787, ibid., 353.

17. *New York Daily Advertiser*, December 11, 1787, ibid., 386.

18. *New York Journal*, December 11, 1787, ibid., 390.

19. *New York Journal*, December 14, 1787, ibid., 421.

20. Ibid., 423.

21. *New York Journal*, December 12, 1787, ibid., 404–405.

22. *DHRC* XX:693.

23. James Madison to George Washington, New York, January 20, 1788, *PGWC* 6:52.

24. *DHRC* XX: 687–688.

25. Alexander Hamilton to Gouverneur Morris, May 19, 1788, Kaminski, 149.

26. Henry II:342–343.

27. *New Hampshire Spy,* December 11, 1787, *DHRC* XIV:409.

28. *New Hampshire Spy,* August 7, 1787, *DHRC* XIII:187.

29. *DHRC* XIV: 409–410.

30. Henry Knox to GW, New York, February 14, 1788, *PGWC* 6:113–114.

31. James Madison to GW, New York, February 15, 1788, ibid.,115.

32. Van Doren, *Great Rehearsal,* 294.

33. Jeremiah Libbey to Jeremy Belknap, February 19, 1788, *DHRC* XVI:179.

34. John Langdon to GW, Portsmouth, New Hampshire, February 28, 1788, *PGWC* 6:132–133.

35. *DHRC* XVI:180.

36. *Massachusetts Gazette,* February 26, 1788, *DHRC* XVI:180.

37. GW to Henry Knox, March 30, 1788, *PGWC* 6:182–183.

38. *DHRC* XIV:164.

39. Ibid., 455.

40. Ibid.

41. Farrand III:85.

42. GW to James Madison, May 2, 1788, *PGWC* 6:258–259.

43. GW to Gouverneur Morris, May 2, 1788, ibid., 259.

44. Van Doren, *Great Rehearsal,* 209.

45. Charleston *Columbian Herald,* February 4, 1788, *DHRC* XVI:22.

46. GW to Lafayette, May 28, 1788, *PGWC* 6:297–299.

47. Henry Knox to GW, May 25, 1788, ibid., 290–291.

48. John Jay to GW, May 29, 1788, ibid., 303–304.

49. GW to James Madison, Mount Vernon, June 8, 1788, ibid., 320–321.

Chapter 9. The Language of Secession

1. Moses Coit Tyler, *Patrick Henry* (Boston: Houghton Mifflin, 1887), 317.

2. Henry II:344.

3. *DHRC* IX:898–899.

4. Robert Douthat Meade, *Patrick Henry: Patriot in the Making* (Philadelphia: J. B. Lippincott, 1957), 31.

5. Beeman, *Patrick Henry,* 41.

6. Ibid., 132.

7. Ibid.

8. *DHRC* IX: 929–931.

9. Ibid., 931.

10. Ibid., 931–936.

11. Morris, *Witnesses at the Creation,* 197.

12. James Madison to GW, Richmond, June 4, 1788, *PGWC* 6:313–314.

13. Bushrod Washington to GW, June 7, 1788, ibid., 315–316.

14. GW to John Jay, Mount Vernon, June 8, 1788, ibid., 318–319.

15. *DHRC* IX: 944–949.

16. Ibid., 949–951.

17. Ibid.

18. Ibid., 951–968.

19. Henry II:359.

20. *DHRC* IX: 951–968.

21. Ibid., 968.

Chapter 10. On the Wings of the Tempest

1. Robert Douthat Meade, *Patrick Henry: Practical Revolutionary* (Philadelphia and New York: J. B. Lippincott Company, 1966), 360–361.

2. *DHRC* IX:992.

3. Ibid., 1007–1015.

4. Ibid., 1028–1035.

5. Ibid., 1050–1052.

6. Beeman, *Patrick Henry*, 133.

7. *DHRC* IX:1072–1080.

8. Ibid., 1036.

9. Ibid., 1082.

10. Ibid., 1082–1083.

11. Ibid., X:1220–1221.

12. Ibid., 1246.

13. James Madison to GW, June 13, 1788, *PGWC* 6:329.

14. *DHRC* X, 1476–1477.

15. Henry III:586; George Morgan, *The True Patrick Henry* (Philadelphia: J. B. Lippincott, 1907), 354.

16. Henry II:371.

17. Ibid., 364.

18. James Monroe to Thomas Jefferson, July 12, 1788, Malone, *Jefferson and the Rights of Man*, 175.

19. *DHRC* X:1498.

20. Ibid., 1537.

21. James Madison to GW, Richmond, June 27, 1788, *PGWC* 6:356–357.

22. Thomas Jefferson to William S. Smith, Feb. 2, 1788, Malone, *Jefferson and the Rights of Man*, 171.

Chapter 11. Birth of a Nation

1. *Virginia Journal*, July 3, 1788, *PGWC* 6:362.

2. Ibid.

3. GW to Charles Cotesworth Pinckney, June 28, 1788, ibid., 360–362.

4. GW to Benjamin Lincoln, Mount Vernon, June 29, 1788, ibid., 365–366.

5. Van Doren, *Great Rehearsal*, 232.

6. John P. Kaminski, *George Clinton: Yeoman Politician of the New Republic* (Madison, Wis.: Madison House Publishers, Inc., 1993), 151–152.

7. *DHRC* I:153–156.

8. John Jay to GW, Poughkeepsie, New York, July 4, 1788, *PGWC* 6:371.

9. Ibid., July 8, 1788.

10. Kaminski, *George Clinton*, 161.

11. *DHRC* XXI:1630–1661.

12. Ibid.

13. Ibid.

14. Alexander Hamilton to GW, New York, August 13, 1788, *PGWC* 6:443–444.

15. James Madison to GW, New York, August 11, 1788, ibid., 437–439.

16. James McHenry to GW, Baltimore, July 27, 1788, ibid., 403.

17. James Madison to Thomas Jefferson, New York, July 24, 1788, Henry II:414.

18. GW to James McHenry, Mount Vernon, July 31, 1788, *PGWC* 6:409–410.

19. GW to James Madison, Mount Vernon, September 23, 1788, ibid., 533–534.

20. Ibid., September 14, 1788, 513–514.

21. Henry, II:415.

22. Richard Labunski, *James Madison and the Struggle for the Bill of Rights* (New York: Oxford University Press, 2006), 64.

23. Ibid., 143.

24. Ibid.

25. W. W. Abbot, ed., *The Papers of George Washington, Presidential Series* (hereinafter *PGWP*) (Charlottesville: University Press of Virginia, 1987–in progress), 2:154–155, Tobias Lear's diary entry for April 30, 1789, cited in editor's introductory *Notes*, "First Inaugural Address," and presumably drawn from Stephen Decatur Jr., *Private Affairs of George Washington, from the Records and Accounts of Tobias Lear, Esquire, His Secretary* (Boston: Houghton, Mifflin, 1933).

26. Ibid.

27. Ibid.

28. Ibid., 2:155–157, introductory notes to "First Inaugural Address," citing Fisher Ames to George Richard Minot, May 3, 1789, in Seth Ames, ed., *Works of Fisher Ames* (Boston, 1854, 2 vols.), I:34–36.

29. Ibid., 2:152–177, "First Inaugural Address."

Chapter 12. One Nation, Divisible . . .

1. Robert R. Rutland, ed., *The Papers of James Madison* (Charlottesville: University Press of Virginia, 1984–1989, 16 vols.), 12:203.

2. William Grayson to Patrick Henry, June 12, 1789, in Charlene Bangs Bickford et al., eds., *Documentary History of the First Federal Congress* (Baltimore: Johns Hopkins University Press, 1992), 16:759.

3. Patrick Henry to Richard Henry Lee, August 28, 1789, in Labunski, *James Madison*, 242.

4. Edward Carrington to James Madison, December 20, 1789, Papers of James Madison 12:463.

5. Labunski, *James Madison*, 251.

6. GW to Arthur Fenner, Mount Vernon, June 4, 1790, *PGWP* 5:470.

7. GW to Thomas Jefferson, August 23, 1792, *PGWP* 11:28–32.

8. Thomas Jefferson to W. S. Smith, November 13, 1787, Malone, 165–166.

9. *Kentucky Gazette* (Lexington), April 5, 1794.

10. *DHRC* XV:280–283.

11. *DHRC* I:187.

12. *DHRC* XIII:548.

13. Madison, *Notes*, 51–55.

14. Ibid., 39.

Bibliography

Abbot, W. W., and Dorothy Twohig, eds. *The Papers of George Washington, Confederation Series*, January 1784–September 1788. 6 vols. Charlottesville: University Press of Virginia, 1992–1997.

———. *The Papers of George Washington, Presidential Series*, September 1788–May 1793. 12 vols. [in progress]. Charlottesville: University Press of Virginia—University of Virginia Press, 1987–2007.

Abbott, W. W., Dorothy Twohig, Philander D. Chase, and Theodore J. Crackel, eds. *The Papers of George Washington, Revolutionary War Series*, June 1775–April 1778. 14 vols. [in progress]. Charlottesville: University of Virginia Press, 1984–2007.

Adams, Charles Francis, ed. *The Works of John Adams*. 10 vols. Boston: Little, Brown, 1856.

Beeman, Richard R. *Patrick Henry: A Biography*. New York: McGraw-Hill, 1974.

Bickford, Charlene Bangs, et al., eds. *Documentary History of the First Federal Congress*. Baltimore: Johns Hopkins University Press, 1992.

Boyd, Julian P. et al., eds. *The Papers of Thomas Jefferson*. 34 vols. [in progress]. Princeton, N.J.: Princeton University Press, 1950–2007.

Cappon, Lester J., ed. *The Adams-Jefferson Letters: The Complete Correspondence between Thomas Jefferson and Abigail and John Adams*. Chapel Hill: University of North Carolina Press, 1959.

Chernow, Ron. *Alexander Hamilton*. New York: Penguin, 2004.

Dorf, Philip. *Visualized American Government: Constitutional Government and Problems of Democracy*. New York: Oxford Book Company, 1947.

Dos Passos, John. *The Men Who Shaped the Nation*. Garden City, N.Y.: Doubleday, 1957.

Farrand, Max. *The Fathers of the Constitution: A Chronicle of the Establishment of the Union*. New Haven, Conn.: Yale University Press, 1921.

———, ed. *The Records of the Federal Convention of 1787*. 4 vols. New Haven, Conn.: Yale University Press, 1911.

Fitzpatrick, John C., ed. *The Writings of George Washington*. 39 vols. Washington, D.C.: U.S. Government Printing Office, 1931–1944.

Freeman, Douglas Southall. *George Washington: A Biography.* 7 vols., completed by John Alexander Carroll and Mary Wells Ashworth. New York: Charles Scribner's Sons, 1948–1957.

Gordon, John Steele. *An Empire of Wealth: The Epic History of American Economic Power.* New York: HarperCollins, 2004.

Hamilton, Alexander. *The Papers of Alexander Hamilton.* Edited by Harold C. Syrett and Jacob E. Cooke. 27 vols. New York: Columbia University Press, 1961–1987.

————. *Writings.* Edited by Joanne B. Freeman. New York: Library of America, 2001.

Hendrick, Burton J. *The Lees of Virginia: Biography of a Family.* Boston: Little Brown, 1935.

Henry, William Wirt. *Patrick Henry: Life, Correspondence and Speeches.* 3 vols. New York: Charles Scribner's Sons, 1891.

Isaacson, Walter. *Benjamin Franklin: An American Life.* New York: Simon & Schuster, 2003.

Jackson, Donald, and Dorothy Twohig, eds. *The Diaries of George Washington.* 6 vols. Charlottesville: University Press of Virginia, 1976–1979.

Jensen, Merrill. *The New Nation: A History of the United States during the Confederation, 1781–1789.* New York: Alfred A. Knopf, 1950.

Jensen, Merrill, John P. Kaminski, Gaspare Saladino, Richard Leffler, and Charles H. Schoenleber, eds. *The Documentary History of the Ratification of the Constitution.* 19 vols. [in progress]. Madison, Wis.: State Historical Society of Wisconsin, 1976–2007.

Kaminski, John P. *George Clinton: Yeoman Politician of the New Republic.* Madison, Wis.: Madison House Publishers, 1993.

Kaminski, John P., and Richard Leffler, eds. *Federalists and Antifederalists: The Debate over the Ratification of the Constitution.* Madison, Wis.: Madison House Publishers, 1998.

Kennedy, Roger G. *Burr, Hamilton, and Jefferson: A Study in Character.* New York: Oxford University Press, 2000.

Labaree, Leonard W., et al. *Papers of Benjamin Franklin.* 39 vols. [in progress]. New Haven, Conn.: Yale University Press, 1959–2007.

Labunski, Richard. *James Madison and the Struggle for the Bill of Rights.* New York: Oxford University Press, 2006.

Madison, James. *Notes of Debates in the Federal Convention of 1787 Reported by James Madison.* New York: W. W. Norton, 1987.

————. *The Papers of James Madison.* Edited by Robert R. Rutland. 16 vols. Charlottesville: University Press of Virginia, 1984–1989.

Malone, Dumas. *Jefferson and the Rights of Man.* Boston: Little, Brown, 1951.

McCusker, John J. *How Much Is That in Real Money? A Historical Commodity Price Index for Use as a Deflator of Money Values in the Economy of the United States*. Worcester, Mass.: American Antiquarian Society, 2001.

―――. *Money & Exchange in Europe & America, 1600–1775: A Handbook*. Chapel Hill: University of North Carolina Press, 1978.

Meade, Robert Douthat. *Patrick Henry: Patriot in the Making*. Philadelphia: J. B. Lippincott, 1957.

―――. *Patrick Henry: Practical Revolutionary*. Philadelphia: J. B. Lippincott, 1969.

Monroe, James. *The Writings of James Monroe: Including a Collection of His Public and Private Papers and Correspondence Now for the First Time Printed*. Edited by Stanislaus Murray Hamilton. 7 vols. Washington, D.C.: Government Printing Branch, U.S. Department of State, 1898.

Morgan, Edmund S. *Benjamin Franklin*. New Haven, Conn.: Yale University Press, 2002.

Morgan, George. *The True Patrick Henry*. Philadelphia: J. B. Lippincott, 1907.

Morris, Richard B. *Encyclopedia of American History*. New York: Harper & Brothers, 1953.

―――. *Witnesses at the Creation: Hamilton, Madison, Jay, and the Constitution*. New York: Holt, Rinehart, & Winston, 1985.

Randolph, Edmund, *History of Virginia*. Edited by Arthur H. Shaffer. Charlottesville: Virginia Historical Society, 1970.

Stewart, Donald H. *The Opposition Press of the Federalist Period*. Albany, N.Y.: State University of New York Press, 1969.

Tagg, James. *Benjamin Franklin Bache and the Philadelphia Aurora*. Philadelphia: University of Pennsylvania Press, 1991.

Tyler, Moses Coit. *Patrick Henry*. Boston: Houghton Mifflin, 1887.

Unger, Harlow Giles. *John Hancock: Merchant King and American Patriot*. New York: John Wiley & Sons, 2000.

―――. *The Unexpected George Washington: His Private Life*. Hoboken, NJ: John Wiley & Sons, 2006.

Van Doren, Carl. *The Great Rehearsal: The Story of the Making and Ratifying of the Constitution of the United States*. New York: The Viking Press, 1948.

Credits

Pages vii, 11, 13, 39, 44, 51, 53, 59, 61, 75, 78, 81, 107, 117, 125, 129, 135, 143, 183, 191, 192: Library of Congress; page 17: adapted from *America: Its History and People* by Harold Underwood Faulkner and Tyler Kepner, NY: Harper & Brothers, 1934; page 33: Independence National Historic Park; page 84: Dunston Hall; page 114: from the first edition, 1788, in a private collection.

Index

Alabama, 206–207
Adams, John, 12, 13, 84, 199
Adams, Samuel, 80, 125, 131
"Agrippa," 126
Albany, N.Y., riots, 188
Allen, Ethan, 1
Allen, Ira, 1
amendments to the Constitution
  Bill of Rights as, 202, 203, 207–208,
    239–241
  as subject of debate before
    ratification, 67, 76, 121, 137,
    193, 198, 201–202
American Revolution
  Continental Army troop mutiny, 6
  Patrick Henry's failure to fight in,
    74, 76, 160–161, 175
anarchy, dangers of, 26, 72, 99, 127,
    133, 204
  Clinton's arguments against, 139
  Federalist concerns about, 94
  "Light-Horse Harry" Lee's warnings
    about, 23
  Randolph's warnings about, 176
  Washington's warnings about, 1,
    10, 46, 77, 82–83, 84–85, 115,
    131, 195
Antifederalists, 76
  efforts of to undermine the new
    government, 193–197, 198
  as opponents of the Constitution,
    80, 83, 92–94, 100–101, 106,

108, 109–110, 116, 119, 121,
  126, 127, 130, 141, 147–148
  at the New York ratification
    convention, 186–190
  renewed efforts of, following
    ratification, 193–198
  at the Virginia ratification
    convention, 158–159, 164
  See also Clinton, George; Henry,
    Patrick; Lee, Richard Henry
Articles of Confederation
  amending of, 1, 10–11, 26, 56
  Constitution as substitute for, 1–2,
    26–27, 33–34, 42–43, 47, 208
  Patrick Henry as advocate of, 28
  inherent limitations of, 8–9, 95, 130
  state sovereignty under, 13–14,
    20–21
Atherton, John, 149

Baldwin, Abraham, 36, 230
Bassett, Richard, 229
Bedford, Gunning, Jr., 49, 229
Belknap, Jeremy, 128
Bill of Rights, 202, 203, 207–208,
  239–241
  Tenth Amendment, 206–207
  See also Constitution: and advocates
    for the bill of rights
Blair, John, 28, 72, 233
Blount, William, 231
Bowdoin, James, 24, 127

261